GOLDEN DAWN MAGIC

About the Authors

Chic Cicero

Charles "Chic" Cicero was born in Buffalo, New York. An early love of music, particularly of the saxophone, resulted in Chic's many years of experience as a lead musician in several jazz, blues and rock ensembles, working with many famous performers in the music industry. Chic's interest in Freemasonry and the Western Esoteric Tradition resulted in research articles on Rosicrucianism and the Knights Templar, printed in such publications as "Ars Quatuor Coronatorum" and the "1996-2000 Transactions of the Metropolitan College of the SRIA." Chic is a member of several Masonic, Martinist, and Rosicrucian organizations. He is a Past Grand Commander of the Grand Commandery of Knights Templar in Florida (2010–2011) and is the current Chief Adept of the Florida College of the Societas Rosicruciana in Civitatibus Foederatis. He was also a close personal friend and confidant of Dr. Israel Regardie. Having established a Golden Dawn temple in 1977, Chic was one of the key people who helped Regardie to resurrect a legitimate, initiatory branch of the Hermetic Order of the Golden Dawn in the United States in the early 1980s. He met his wife and co-author, Sandra Tabatha Cicero, shortly thereafter.

Chic is an author and a skilled craftsman who has constructed all of the ritual implements of the Golden Dawn. He is particularly fond of ritual, skrying, and the tarot.

Sandra Tabatha Cicero

Sandra "Tabatha" Cicero was born in rural Wisconsin. Her areas of interest include drawing, painting, poetry, theater, dance, and printmaking. A lifelong fascination with the creative arts has served to inspire her work in the magical world. After graduating from the University of Wisconsin-Milwaukee with a Bachelor's Degree in Fine Arts in 1982, Tabatha worked as an entertainer, typesetter, editor, commercial artist, and computer graphics illustrator. In 2009 she obtained an Associate in Science degree in Paralegal Studies. Tabatha is a member of several Martinist and Rosicrucian organizations. She met her husband and co-author Charles "Chic" Cicero in the early 1980s and the Golden Dawn system of magic has been her primary spiritual focus ever since. Tabatha spent five years working on the paintings for the Golden Dawn Magical Tarot, which she began at the encouragement of Israel Regardie.

———

Both Chic and Tabatha are Chief Adepts of the Hermetic Order of the Golden Dawn as reestablished by Israel Regardie (www.hermeticgoldendawn.org). The Hermetic Order of the Golden Dawn, of which Chic is the G.H. Imperator and Tabatha is the G.H. Cancellaria, is an international Order with temples in several countries. Tabatha is also the Imperatrix of the Societas Rosicruciana in America (www.sria.org).

GOLDEN DAWN MAGIC

A Complete Guide to the High Magical Arts

CHIC CICERO &
SANDRA TABATHA CICERO

Llewellyn Publications
Woodbury, Minnesota

FIRST EDITION
Third Printing, 2021

Cover design by Shira Atakpu
Interior art by James Clark on pages 112, 118, 128, 141–144, 150, 155, 157, 179, 181, 187, 188, 191, 192, 196, 197, 205, 207, 208, 263, 287, 328, 336 and 364; interior art by Mary Ann Zapalac on page 104; all other art by the Llewellyn Art Department
Project management by Samantha Lu Sherratt
Tarot card on page 160 is from the *Golden Dawn Magical Tarot* (created by Chic Cicero and Sandra Tabatha Cicero, © 1997) is used with permission.

Llewellyn Publications is a registered trademark of Llewellyn Worldwide Ltd.

Library of Congress Cataloging-in-Publication Data
Names: Cicero, Chic, author.
Title: Golden dawn magic : a complete guide to the high magical arts / Chic Cicero, Sandra Tabatha Cicero.
Description: First Edition. | Woodbury : Llewellyn Worldwide, Ltd., 2019. | Includes index.
Identifiers: LCCN 2018060956 (print) | LCCN 2019010944 (ebook) | ISBN 9780738757988 (ebook) | ISBN 9780738757889 (alk. paper)
Subjects: LCSH: Hermetic Order of the Golden Dawn. | Magic.
Classification: LCC BF1623.R7 (ebook) | LCC BF1623.R7 C4725 2019 (print) | DDC 135/.4--dc23
LC record available at https://lccn.loc.gov/2018060956

Llewellyn Publications
A Division of Llewellyn Worldwide Ltd.
2143 Wooddale Drive
Woodbury, MN 55125-2989
www.llewellyn.com

Printed in the United States of America

Other Books by Chic Cicero & Sandra Tabatha Cicero

The Babylonian Tarot

Tarot Talismans

The Essential Golden Dawn: An Introduction to High Magic

Self-Initiation into the Golden Dawn Tradition

The Enochian Skrying Tarot (co-authored with Bill and Judi Genaw)

The Golden Dawn Magical Tarot (tarot kit)

Creating Magical Tools: The Magician's Craft

Ritual Use of Magical Tools

Experiencing the Kabbalah

Secrets of a Golden Dawn Temple: The Alchemy and Crafting of Magical Implements

The Golden Dawn Journal series:

- *Book I: Divination*
- *Book II: Qabalah: Theory and Magic*
- *Book III: The Art of Hermes*
- *The Magical Pantheons: A Golden Dawn Journal*

Secrets of a Golden Dawn Temple: Book I: Creating Magical Tools
(Thoth Publications)

Basics of Magic: The Best of the Golden Dawn Journal: Book I: Divination
(HOGD Books)

The Book of Concourse of the Watchtowers (HOGD Books)

Regardie Books Edited and Annotated by Chic Cicero & Sandra Tabatha Cicero

The Middle Pillar: The Balance Between Mind and Magic
By Israel Regardie (3rd edition, edited and annotated with new material by the Ciceros)

A Garden of Pomegranates: Skrying on the Tree of Life
By Israel Regardie (3rd edition, edited and annotated with new material by the Ciceros)

The Tree of Life: An Illustrated Study in Magic
By Israel Regardie (3rd edition, edited and annotated with new material by the Ciceros)

The Philosopher's Stone: Spiritual Alchemy, Psychology, and Ritual Magic
By Israel Regardie (3rd edition, edited and annotated with new material by the Ciceros)

Gold: Israel Regardie's Lost Book of Alchemy
By Israel Regardie (1st edition, edited and annotated by the Ciceros)

Dedication

To all true seekers of the Light
May what they find herein sustain them in their search for
the Quintessence; the Stone of the Philosophers, true Wisdom
and perfect Happiness, the Summum Bonum.

CONTENTS

CHAPTER 2: LEARNING THE LANGUAGE OF MAGIC . . . 47

Chapter 5: The Tarot: Interpreting Magical Images . . . 159

CHAPTER 9: THE FAR-WANDERING SOUL . . . 283

Chapter 10: The Magic of Light . . . 333

FIGURES

TABLES

INTRODUCTION

The Golden Dawn, often abbreviated as simply "GD," has been called the most famous and influential magical group of the modern era, and it continues to be one of the primary vehicles for teaching new generations of ceremonial magicians. Over the decades many have pronounced the Golden Dawn dead and gone, its teachings antiquated, and its practitioners out of step with the times. In spite of this, large sections of Golden Dawn rituals and techniques have been plucked wholesale and placed squarely within the practices of New Agers, Wiccans, Neopagans, and others, often without any knowledge or acknowledgment of their GD roots. This material is so prevalent within the greater magical and Neopagan community that many practitioners of the various spiritual paths simply assume that it was always a part of their own respective traditions.

There is certainly nothing wrong with various spiritual paths borrowing liberally from the Golden Dawn. If imitation is the sincerest form of flattery, then the adoption of these methods points out just how useful and contemporary the Golden Dawn teachings are. Many magical groups and individual seekers are able to take what they need from the tradition and adapt it to their own needs. More power to them! The sheer volume of material, the comprehensive scope and effectiveness of the Golden Dawn system, makes it ripe for cherry-picking. And this is not a bad thing—when presented with the origins of such practices as the Lesser Ritual of the Pentagram and the Middle Pillar exercise, some readers will want to know more about *our* tradition.

Nevertheless, the best way to understand the Golden Dawn is to experience it in the manner in which the system was created. This involves more than a piecemeal attitude: there is simply no substitute for a holistic approach. The various parts of the system are intimately interconnected, even if this is not immediately apparent to beginners. There are built-in safeguards that were designed with the student's psychic well-being in mind. Rather than rushing headlong into advanced practices before one is ready for them,

Golden Dawn magicians learn their art at a reasoned, steady pace meant to promote discipline, good judgment, gradual skill, spiritual integrity, and reverence for the Divine.

This emphasis on psychic safeguards is exactly why the Golden Dawn system of magic has remained vibrant for 130 years. Far from being some outdated relic of Victorian times, the Golden Dawn is a living, breathing, growing tradition. Various Golden Dawn groups currently exist all over the globe. Today there are more practicing Golden Dawn magicians than at any other time since 1888. Many of them can fully attest to the beauty, efficacy, and transformative power of this spiritual path. Several quality books on the system, penned by accomplished magicians who wish to share their knowledge and experience, have been published in recent years. In short, it is a great time to begin to explore the teachings and magic of the Golden Dawn.

The heart of the Golden Dawn system of magic is often referred to as *theurgy*, or "God-working." It is summed up in the Obligation of the Adeptus Minor: "I further promise and swear that with the Divine Permission I will, from this day forward, apply myself to the Great Work—which is, to purify and exalt my spiritual nature so that with the Divine Aid I may at length attain to be more than human, and thus gradually raise and unite myself to my higher and Divine Genius…" This is the light that guides the path of the Golden Dawn magician.

Borrowed from the lexicon of alchemy, the Great Work refers to the esoteric journey for illumined awareness of Divinity, which is the ultimate goal of theurgy. It indicates the spiritual seeker's quest for union with the Divine. Although the practice of magic often involves consecrating talismans, performing invocations, carrying out divinations, and similar magical techniques for purposes both spiritual and worldly, it should never be forgotten that the single overriding objective of the Golden Dawn system is the aspirant's constant quest for inner communion with the Sacred Source. Everything else is a distant second.

Anyone who has ever paged through Israel Regardie's classic text *The Golden Dawn* immediately realizes just how complicated and comprehensive the Golden Dawn system is. The sheer size of the book is enough to scare many away. You will often hear the Golden Dawn curriculum described as "the equivalent of a PhD in magic." Some of us have fallen in love with this system right off the start; we relish the rich complexity and the endless insights gained through working with it. It is a boundless, living fountain of inspiration, and the depths of the system have yet to be plumbed.

But complexity can be a poor tutor. How much easier our own journey would have been with a simple introductory text on the subject! The two of us often look at each other and say, "If only *we* had a book like this when we were first starting out! That would have been so helpful!"

This book was written for beginners as well as more seasoned magicians. Some students may already have considerable esoteric knowledge, while others do not. Many readers may want to explore the Golden Dawn system before deciding if it is something they wish to pursue. We take nothing for granted here. We do not assume that readers have any prior knowledge of astrology, tarot, or Qabalah. Therefore, we present many aspects of the Golden Dawn system as succinctly as possible. This gives beginners the material they need without becoming overwhelmed, and provides more advanced students with concise information for resource and review.

By necessity, we occasionally use the words *beginner*, *novice*, and *newcomer*. More often, however, we employ the terms "student," "seeker," and "aspirant." These terms are more inclusive and they cover all of us, not just some of us. As Israel Regardie stated, "We are all students and should be for life."

Golden Dawn Magic is not structured in a series of lessons, nor does it align with the ordering of grade work given to initiates in a fully functioning Golden Dawn Temple. Many of the exercises presented here are our own, designed to supplement the more traditional ritual work of the later chapters. The book is organized into chapters that contain information, meditations, and exercises or rituals, along with review questions as aids to learning. It is not our purpose to fully explain all the topics presented here. No introductory book can do that. We do, however, supply you with the tools needed to understand the basics of Golden Dawn ritual magic and the principles of our tradition. If you decide to seek out more information, a list of helpful texts is provided at the end of this book.

One point that we cannot stress strongly enough is that the process of spiritual growth is not a race. Take your time with the exercises. Meditate frequently on the topics provided. Don't get discouraged if you think you are not getting anywhere at first. Take a step back when you feel you need to. There is no merit badge given to the fastest learner.

We can personally affirm that the Golden Dawn has changed our lives and continues to enrich our spiritual and magical practices every day. This tradition is a labor of love for us, as well as a calling to teach what we have learned. It is a reminder to help other aspiring magicians in the same manner that we ourselves were helped years ago. If only a small number of readers consider this book to be a useful stretch of road on their journey in quest of the Great Work, it will have been well worth the effort.

chapter 1

GETTING STARTED

WHY PRACTICE GOLDEN DAWN MAGIC?

When someone picks up a book on magic for the first time, it is usually because they have questions. More often than not their initial question is "What is magic?" Other questions soon follow: "Is magic real?" "How can I perform magic?" "What can magic do for me?" and so on.

We propose to turn the tables here and ask questions of the reader. What do *you* think magic is? How do you think it works? What do you think magic will do for you? Why do you want to practice magic? And, most importantly with regard to the book you now hold, why do you want to learn about Golden Dawn magic? What is it that draws you to this tradition?

Many newcomers are attracted to magic's age-old reputation as a secret practice of mysterious ceremonies and forbidden knowledge. Fear of the unknown brings its own fascination factor. Anyone who has ever read a fantasy novel about dragons, ghosts, curses, or sorcerers can certainly understand how magic came to be perceived this way by the masses.

The Golden Dawn is frequently mentioned in occult circles. Due to the system's fame and longevity, the GD is often lauded as a "most powerful system of magic." Such praise tends to incite dabblers with the promise of irresistible magical power. Yet the true nature of Golden Dawn magic and the work required in accomplishing it doesn't fit the scary tabloid model of magic in general.

If you think that this book will teach you magic for winning millions of dollars in the lottery, casting a love spell on someone who ignores you, cursing your noisy neighbor, or binding a demon to do your bidding, well, then this book is not the one you are looking for.

One of the truths of magic is this: people sometimes take up the practice of magic for purely mundane reasons—they hope to "invoke" riches, love, or power. Yet if they persevere in their training, students often come to a realization concerning the true purpose of magic, and their motivation for performing magic changes completely.

First and foremost, Golden Dawn magicians are healers. We seek to heal ourselves, body, soul, and Spirit, from every form of imbalance from without as well as from within. Through our magical work in the higher realms, we also seek to heal others by the diffusion of the "Light Divine" throughout the Sacred Universe.

Golden Dawn magicians are truth seekers and explorers. We are also questioners. We are inherently curious about things that we cannot see or touch with our physical senses. We want to know about the origins and mechanics of the Universe and our place within that Universe. We seek to understand the transcendent and ineffable nature of God. We wish to commune with Gods, Goddesses, angels, and all aspects of Deity. We pursue a relationship with the highest aspects of the soul. We desire to expand our awareness beyond our five senses. We strive to cleanse our souls and balance our psyches. We investigate higher planes of existence. We dedicate ourselves to esoteric studies. We seek union with the Divine.

We also have a healthy dose of skepticism, meaning we don't simply accept everything—every vision or inner communication—at face value with blind faith. We test our interactions on the invisible planes. We question our spiritual guides. We question our own motives and biases. Basically, we question the nature of everything. If you think that the Golden Dawn, or *any* spiritual path for that matter, will answer all of your questions, be prepared to be disappointed. The moment you have no further questions to ask is the moment that you cease the act of learning. In affinity with Regardie's sentiment cited earlier, "You are always a student, never a master. You have to keep moving forward."

In truth, magic is a spiritual science. At its core, Golden Dawn magic explores the fundamental working relationship between humanity and divinity. It expresses fundamental knowledge of the true human self that lies beneath the illusion of the outer, secular human; that inner self that is inextricably linked with the Sacred Source of Ultimate Unity.

Golden Dawn magic incorporates a process of memorization, creation, ritual work, and internal work that results in the direct stimulation of the magician's will and imagination. Memorization means learning the language of magic—its primary symbol-systems, mythic patterns, alphabets, philosophies, and correspondences. Aspirants must commit the rudimentary knowledge of the GD system to memory, just as if they were entering a school of medicine or engineering. Creation is the process by which the magician builds his or her Sacred Space and everything in it to represent the hidden mechanics of the Mystic Cosmos. Ritual work is the bread and butter of the magician—enacting a ceremonial approach to working with spiritual energies and entities. Finally, internal work, assisted by meditation and other exercises, sets the groundwork for psychic cleansing, higher awareness, and active linkage with Deity.

There are many steps along the way involving balancing, cleansing, and training the magician's psychic faculties and abilities. To the outsider, some of these steps might not appear to further the magician's quest for the "Light Divine." For example, magicians create talismans for a whole host of reasons. Jupiter talismans are a perennial favorite for any magician who might feel the need for resources. And Libra talismans have surely been created to help resolve legal disputes. Similarly, some may wonder how performing a tarot reading for another person could possibly promote one's desire for union with the Divine. To critics of magic, these objectives seem self-centered.

The key to these workings is ethical motivation. Western magicians view magic as an *active* rather than a passive procedure for spiritual growth. This is what differentiates the magician from the mystic (although all true magicians must *also* be mystics). So long as we live in the physical world, we try to influence our circumstances and environment through our actions, both magical and mundane. And we reinforce our magic with ethical action in the physical world to help support our objectives. When will and imagination are strengthened through persistence and practice, the fruits of magic are able to manifest. Skilled magicians are able to build an image of their goal in the subtle layers of the astral plane, just as skilled engineers are able to craft a blueprint of a building or a new piece of technology. What is first imagined can then be created. Bringing the astral image of something into manifestation, be it an object, event, circumstance, or spiritual state of mind, has always been one of the stated goals of magic. At the same time, we hold that the most important part of our practice is the Great Work of Divine Union. So long as the magician's motivations and objectives are ethical and not harmful to anyone, there is no conflict. And if the primary motivation for an act of magic includes healing or helping another person who asks for help, then there is no question that one is truly "on the side of the angels."

Additionally, all of these techniques help to hone the magician's skills and inner perceptions, which all serve the ultimate objective: the purification of the lower personality and the realization of an elevated state of consciousness, wherein the magician's ego enters into a union with the Higher Self and ultimately with the Divine. Each and every detail of a Golden Dawn ritual serves to remind us of this supreme goal. Every impression, by means of a Hermetic and Qabalistic system of associated ideas, is made the beginning of a sequence of related thoughts that culminate in the ultimate aim of the ceremony. When emblem after emblem has infiltrated the mind of the magician, and the ritual act has stimulated the emotions to a fever pitch, then a profound state of awareness can be attained. A clear and open path is created between mind, soul, and Spirit. To travel this passageway freely and regularly, we must be open to the Divine Spirit and Source of All.

The following is a brief list of some of the ways students benefit by the teachings, exercises, and ritual work of the system. It is by no means a complete list. The Golden Dawn system of magic:

- Teaches students about the Western Esoteric Tradition and its various component sources: Hermeticism, Khemetism, Qabalah, Greco-Egyptian Mystery Traditions, Neoplatonic Philosophy, and Rosicrucianism.

- Provides instruction on the fundamentals (the ABCs) of magic: the basic alphabet, symbol-systems, principles, and language (tool kit) of magical practice.

- Gives students an introduction to the principles and ethics of Golden Dawn magic.

- Teaches basic steps in ceremonial magic.

- Provides exercises and meditations for different magical techniques.

- Works with deities, archangels, angels, and other spiritual entities as companions on the Path of Light.

- Promotes elemental balance that is a prerequisite to more advanced magical work.

- Supplies students with a solid curriculum of gradual step-by-step instruction.

- Provides an introduction to the principles and methods involved in more advanced magical workings.

- Imparts a course of training for the psychic faculties: increased awareness, and attention to patterns and synchronicities that also aid in magic, divination, Spirit vision work, etc.

- Offers an introduction to the link between magic, psychology, and spiritual alchemy.

- Teaches ritual structure in a Temple setting exemplified by the structure of the GD system: the grades, the officers, and their correspondences.

- Works to cleanse and clarify the connection between the magician and the Higher Self in a system of spiritual unfoldment and growth.

- Emphasizes the supreme importance of the Sacred in the Great Work of Divine Union.

Golden Dawn magic is ultimately a Path of Light, knowledge, and healing as typified in one of its most quoted lines from the initiation ceremony of the Neophyte: "Long hast thou dwelt in Darkness, Quit the Night and Seek the Day."

That's not how we did it in Kalamazoo! Avoiding "one True way-ism"

One of the things that students sometimes get hung up on is the impossible search for "The One True Way." This would appear to be a by-product of the same kind of <u>unfortunate tribalism</u> that causes strife between various religious sects, cultures, and political groups. Some will always be convinced that there is "One True Way" to practice the Golden Dawn, and everyone who practices the magic differently must be wrong. The fact of the matter is that the Golden Dawn tradition has always been growing and evolving over time and continues to do so. Today Golden Dawn Temples exist in nearly every continent on Earth; they have naturally adapted and developed their own unique ways. Rather than arguing with someone whose ritual minutiae is designated (by them!) to be "The One True Way," magicians should be open to new interpretations and insights, whether they agree with them or not. Knowledge is not static, and the depth and breadth of our system is

[handwritten margin note: this very tribalistic attitude that sets even Christians against each other at times.]

nearly endless. Spiritual growth is unique, and our experiences with it are personal. Although we can agree on most of the standard precepts of our system, we cannot insist everyone agree with us on everything. And that is perfectly alright!

WHAT IS A MAGICAL ORDER?

The term "order" comes from the Latin word *ordo*, which means a condition, rank, or degree, referring to the original threefold division of Roman society. Today the term is used to indicate a group, fraternity, fellowship, or association of individuals "united by laws and statutes peculiar to the society, engaged in a common object or design, and distinguished by particular habits, ensigns, badges, or symbols." It is often used to describe certain Masonic organizations or ecclesiastic societies.

A magical order is just such a group of individuals joined together in a common purpose: to study and practice the magical arts in a certain manner, espousing specific principles and using methods and techniques that are unique to the order. Members are usually admitted to the society by way of ritual initiation that is infused with magic.

Like a Masonic order, a magical order such as the Golden Dawn is not a religion, although religious imagery and spiritual concepts play an important role in its work. Today members from many spiritual paths consider themselves practicing Golden Dawn magicians, including Neopagans, Jews, Christians, Sufis, and Buddhists.

The Golden Dawn is called a Hermetic Order because it emphasizes the magical and occult sciences deriving from Western Esoteric Tradition, also known as Hermeticism. This is in reference to Hermes Trismegistus or "Hermes the Thrice-Great"—the Greek God Hermes and the Egyptian God Thoth merged into one figure said to be the first and greatest of all magicians.

At certain points in this text, we reference the "order system" or the "order setting," meaning group work within a fully functioning and initiating Golden Dawn Temple. More often than not, however, we cite the magical work of the solo practitioner, which is more in keeping with the objective of this book.

A BRIEF HISTORY OF THE GOLDEN DAWN

The Hermetic Order of the Golden Dawn was founded in London in 1888 by a group of Qabalists, Rosicrucians, Freemasons, and Theosophists. It was the brainchild of Dr.

William Wynn Westcott, a London coroner and prominent Freemason. Westcott envisioned the concept of an esoteric order open to both men and women, after coming across an intriguing manuscript, written in cipher, containing the outlines of a series of quasi-Masonic initiation rites. With the aid of two other Masonic Rosicrucians, Dr. William Robert Woodman and Samuel Liddell "MacGregor" Mathers, who helped develop Westcott's translations of the rituals, the Order materialized in February of 1888 with the inauguration of the Isis-Urania Temple in London. The Golden Dawn was born.

The exact origins of the Order have long been a point of contention—the dispute centers on the set of papers called the Cipher Manuscript. In 1886, Westcott acquired the set of documents written in cipher. They turned out to be coded outlines for the rituals and teachings of a magical order. A letter accompanying the manuscript claimed to have been written by a "Fraulein Sprengel," a mysterious German adept of an occult order called *Die Goldene Dammerung,* or the Golden Dawn. But where did the Cipher Manuscript actually come from? Westcott claimed that he got the papers from Rev. A. F. A. Woodford, but this version of events has become highly suspect in recent years. It now seems fairly certain that the Cipher Manuscript was written by Kenneth Mackenzie, the author of *The Royal Masonic Cyclopaedia* and a leading member of the Societas Rosicruciana in Anglia, a Rosicrucian fraternity composed of Master Masons. The Cipher Manuscript was probably intended to be the blueprint for the Society of Eight, a Golden Dawn prototype group founded in 1883, which never fully got off the ground. Westcott received the documents after Mackenzie's death in 1886 and a couple years later the Golden Dawn came into being.

Never designed to be a religion or to take the place of religion, the Golden Dawn was created be a Hermetic Society of like-minded men and women who were dedicated to the philosophical, spiritual, and psychic evolution of humanity. The Order was designed to be a school and a repository of arcane knowledge where students learned the fundamentals of occult science and the various elements of Western philosophy before proceeding to the next fundamental step envisioned by Westcott—practical magic. It was this aspect of the Golden Dawn, its stated goal of teaching members the basics of high magic, along with the fact that the members of higher grades were expected to perform works of ritual magic (divinations, invocations, skrying, talisman consecrations, etc.), that set the Golden Dawn apart from other esoteric organizations of the period such as the Societas Rosicruciana in Anglia, from which the Golden Dawn borrowed much of its structure.

But as with any organization involving human beings and their egos, problems eventually developed. By 1903 the original Order of the Golden Dawn was no more, having split into different factions. The work of the Golden Dawn continued in the form of offshoot orders that sprang up from the ashes of the original. The two main offshoots were the Order of the Alpha et Omega and the Order of the Stella Matutina. The AO survived until the outbreak of World War II, and the SM survived until 1978 when it was officially closed down.

Survival of the Golden Dawn System of Magic

The Golden Dawn tradition has largely survived because of the writings of three magicians who were members of the Golden Dawn or its immediate offshoots: Aleister Crowley, who went off to found his own order and published parts of the rituals and knowledge lectures in his magazine *The Equinox*; Dion Fortune, who published much of the Order's Qabalistic teachings in her magnum opus *The Mystical Qabalah*; and lastly Israel Regardie, our mentor and the man most credited with fostering the current Golden Dawn revival, beginning with his publication of *The Golden Dawn: The Original Account of the Teachings, Rites and Ceremonies of the Hermetic Order*. Regardie's book is often cited as the twentieth century's most influential text on occultism.

whence comest thou?

Having men and women on a completely equal footing in the late Victorian era of the 1880s made the Golden Dawn exceptionally progressive for its time. Then as well as now, women can attain the highest offices and grades that the order system has to offer. Nevertheless, the language of some of the rituals, including gender pronouns, tends to sound archaic to modern ears. Many of us regard this traditional language as the poetic melody of ceremonial magic that sets it above our everyday mundane speech: it connects us linguistically to magicians from centuries past. But not all magicians feel this way. Our system is certainly strong enough to allow for both time-honored and contemporary manners of speaking.

WHAT IS MAGIC?

Magic is an art, a science, and, for those of us who are drawn to the mysteries, it is a passionate pursuit. Like many of the creative arts, its power comes from deep within the human soul. Herein lies a subconscious wellspring of inspiration, knowledge, and possibility. Each and every time we tap into this source, we awaken a divine spark that may have been dormant, invigorate that which was static, and make the possible probable. We create and recreate the Cosmos around us, and make our very soul a magic mirror of the Universe, reflecting divine truths. While the origins of magic are ancient, its influence continues to evolve with the times.

Yet magic gets little respect from the public at large. According to one online dictionary, magic signifies "the mysterious power that some people believe can make impossible things happen if you do special actions or say special words called spells." Another dictionary derisively calls magic "imaginary power."

The word "magic" is derived from the Greek *mageia*, the science and religion of the Zoroastrian priests. According to some, it is derived from the Greek *megas,* meaning "great," indicating the "great" science. As long as humans have walked the earth, the practice of magic has existed in one form or another.

Regarding the question "What is magic?" opinions on the subject generally fall into two camps: those who think that belief in magic is the sign of an uneducated and superstitious mind, and those who believe that magic and its effects are very real. Nonpractitioners commonly hold the first opinion. But magicians who actually practice the art have little doubt that magic works and is a fruitful undertaking. According to famed Renaissance magician Henry Cornelius Agrippa: "Magick is a faculty of wonderful virtue, full of most high mysteries, containing the most profound contemplation of most secret things, together with the nature, power, quality, substance, and virtues thereof, as also the knowledge of whole nature. ... This is the most perfect, the chief science ... the most absolute perfection of all most excellent philosophy."[1]

Part of the problem lies within the very nature of magic itself. Magic is mysterious and enigmatic. Its mechanics are not easily explained. And the entertainment industry continues to misrepresent what magic is, how it works, and why magicians practice it.

Magic is a spiritual science as well as a technical system of training. It requires work and discipline. It is often described in terms that are both scientific and religious, to the

---

1. Cornelius Agrippa, *Three Books of Occult Philosophy*, edited and annotated by Donald Tyson (St. Paul, MN: Llewellyn Publications, 1993), 5.

dismay of both scientists and clergy. Magic has been defined as "the method of science, the aim of religion." It is precisely because magic encroaches upon the territories of both, that this spiritual science often receives the ire of scientists and clerics alike.

Ritual magicians have long tried to adequately describe their art. Aleister Crowley stated that "Magic is the Science and Art of causing change to occur in conformity with Will."[2] While certainly true, this definition is too narrow since it implies that every intentional act is a magical act so long as the magician wills it. Although magicians believe that the Universe we live in is completely divine and magical in all its aspects, it doesn't follow that every single willed action, such as moving your foot, is a magical act. Dion Fortune expanded the definition: "Magic is the art of causing changes to take place in consciousness in accordance with will."[3] This points to the power of the human mind to effect an inner spiritual change that will influence the outer, physical world. One of the best definitions came from our friend and fellow Golden Dawn magician Donald Michael Kraig: "Magic is the science and art of causing change (in consciousness) to occur in conformity with will, using means not currently understood by traditional Western science."[4]

Our definition of magic comes down to this:

> *Magic is an art and a science the goal of which is to produce changes in both internal and external reality (subjective and objective reality) through the knowledge of divine powers and the manipulation of unseen forces inherent to both realities.*

The change caused through magic can occur in the outer world, in the magician's consciousness, and most often in both, for changing one often changes the other.

In ancient times, magic and religion were considered one and the same, but not today. Modern magicians can belong to any number of different faiths. While religion often embraces a specific set of beliefs, values, creeds, and official doctrines, magic is a method or mechanism for causing change in accordance with divine and cosmic laws. The practice of magic is not restricted to any one faith or dogma, and it works according

---

2. Aleister Crowley, *Magic in Theory and Practice* (New York: Dover Publications, 1976), xii.

3. Dion Fortune, quoted by Charles Seymour in "Magic in the Ancient Mystery Religions," published in Dolores Ashcroft-Nowicki, *The Forgotten Mage* (Wellingborough, UK: Aquarian Press, 1986), 24.

4. Donald Michael Kraig, *Modern Magic* (Woodbury, MN: Llewellyn Publications, 2010), 15–16.

to the same set of natural principles. However, magical methods and rites may be used to supplement one's religious practice.

Magic in and of itself is neither black nor white, good nor bad, beneficial nor harmful. At its most basic level magic is simply a process. It is the intent of the magician that makes it positive or negative. We should not have to remind our readers that ethical magicians who seek spiritual wisdom do not engage in harmful acts of magic. Therefore, it is wise to remember that whatever magic you send out into the Universe is exactly what the Universe will send back to you.

We've defined what magic is but many questions still remain. How does magic work? What are the mechanics involved? Why practice magic? What are its benefits? And finally, what is Golden Dawn magic and does one practice it?

How Magic Works

Magic does *not* work by simply uttering a few special words or making some strange gestures in the air. If only it were that easy!

The Universe is both divine and natural. Magic is entirely natural—it functions in accordance with natural law even if we do not always perceive it that way. Magical change occurs in a way that is not understood by science because it works through the Unmanifest—through subtle manipulations of the nonphysical realms that are populated by divine forces and spiritual entities.

What other characteristics describe magic? We can briefly list them as follows:

- Magic is creativity in action: all creative acts are magical acts.

- The effects of magic are sometimes clearly visible in the physical world and other times they are only apparent on a personal, spiritual level.

- The workings of magic are not limited by the constraints of time and space. These terms have no meaning or existence in the unseen realms.

- Magic in action always seeks the path of least resistance.

- Successful magic often resembles luck and coincidence. Swiss psychologist Carl Jung referred to this as *synchronicity*.

The techniques of magic are many, but all are concerned with awakening psychic abilities or faculties of perception within the mind of the magician.

THE LAWS OF MAGIC

Nineteenth-century French occultist Eliphas Levi, widely acknowledged as the father of the modern occult revival, gave an explanation of how magic worked in his books on *Dogma and Ritual of High Magic* and *The Mysteries of Magic*. Three basic "laws," or theories, of magic can be gleaned from his writings:

1. **The law of human willpower.** Human willpower is not some abstract idea, but a real force that is capable of being trained. A trained human will is capable of causing change and producing physical effects.

2. **The law of the astral light.** Alchemists sometimes refer to it as the great Universal Agent, the Magical Agent, or the Soul of the World. Others have called it *mana, chi,* or *prana*. The astral light is an invisible spiritual substance that penetrates and mirrors everything in the Universe. The astral plane is a higher, more subtle level of existence than that of the physical realm. It contains an ethereal "image" of everything—whether it be living or nonliving, organic or inorganic. Magic works through the manipulation of the astral light, which is fluid, plastic, and malleable.

   The astral plane is a region where the magical process begins. This is an invisible plane of initial formation where everything in the physical Universe first comes into being as an incorporeal idea or prototypal design. When something is created in the astral light, it will eventually filter down and become a reality in the physical realm.

3. **The law of correspondence.** This law is centered on medieval theories concerning the "magical virtues" of different substances, which state that everything in the Greater Universe has a corresponding part in the Lesser Universe (the human soul), and that the Greater and Lesser are connected. As the famous Hermetic Axiom states: "As above, so below." To effect a change in one is to effect a change in the other. Certain objects, symbols, or substances are linked to different energies—through vibration, color, or character. These associations are usually planetary, zodiacal, or elemental, but they can also include the characteristics of plants, stones, metals, deities, etc. By choosing certain substances over others, the magician selects things that are in magical alignment with specific forces. Such choices will also help the magician focus his or her attention and willpower on a specific goal.

The Golden Dawn added what might be called a fourth magical law:

4. **The law of imagination (or visualization).** Human willpower must be combined with the faculty of imagination because that is what directs and guides willpower. Levi referred to the cognitive power of imagination as the *Diaphane* or the *Translucent* and stated that it "exalts the will and gives it power over the universal agent."

Using these laws as a guide, we may summarize the mechanics of magic as follows: The magician sets a specific magical goal in mind—that is, what he or she wills to accomplish. The goal of a specific magical working may vary—it may be to build an astral Temple, to heal a sick friend, or to communicate with angelic beings. The image created by the magician in the astral light would reflect the desired end—the image of a great Temple, a friend healed with no sign of illness, the figure of an angel speaking, a cherished project completed, or the light of the Divine descending on the magician. Working with the faculty of the imagination combined with the skill of visualization, the magician creates a form in the astral light. He or she chooses objects and substances that correspond to the nature of the working, such as solar-related items for a healing or lunar items for an astral Temple. But this image-form will remain inert unless vitalized by the force of the current of willpower.

The steps of the magical process can be more easily understood if we order them as follows:

1. *Intent.* The magician must have a clear, precise goal in mind.

2. *Correspondence.* The magician must choose which symbols, tools, and correspondences will best suit his or her needs.

3. *Image.* An image of the goal of the working is created and visualized in the astral light and built up through the faculty of imagination.

4. *Willpower.* The magician directs and focuses the force of will, like a laser, upon the desired end. This energizes the astral image so that its effects are felt on a personal, psychic, or physical level.

The magician's willpower is a crucial factor in magic because every magical action has a magical reaction. Some of our mundane actions might trigger a magical response as well. Every cause has an effect, and the effort you put into your magic will determine its ultimate success. For example, if you do a Jupiter talisman ritual to get money, but never once go out of the house to actually apply for a job, your action, or inaction in this case, on the material plane shows a lack of willpower as well as sheer laziness and will defeat your purpose. If you perform a twenty-minute ritual invoking peace and harmony in your household and then spend six hours fighting with your spouse, you will defeat your magic. Negativity will also counteract your magic because magic requires positive thinking, and if you think your magic is going to fail, it will fail.

There could be other reasons for your magic failing as well. There can be factors that you have not accounted for: planetary energies could be retrograde or otherwise in flux, some part of your ritual may have gotten lost in translation, you might be coming down with something and your energy level is not what it should be, or you may not have done the necessary inner work required for a successful outcome.

The practice of magic usually involves just that—*practice*. Magic is a discipline that requires focus, balance, determination, perseverance, and above all, patience.

Working with the Divine

Do not make the mistake of assuming that magic is simply a cold, mechanical formula—just an unusual method for building a better widget. This is definitely not the case! Golden Dawn magic is inherently spiritual. It involves the active invocation of deities, angels, archangels, and other spiritual entities. Every aspect of Golden Dawn practice is intricately associated with the idea of a transcendent, ineffable Deity or the highest concept of Divinity.

The Divine World of Spirit and the physical world of matter are two halves of a symbiotic whole; therefore, everything that exists out in the Greater Universe also exists within the soul and psyche of humanity. They are connected and what affects one will affect the other. This divine symbiosis is easily recognized by those who have a religious or mystical inclination. Simply put, there exists a *nous*, or universal consciousness, that permeates everything. It gives purpose and meaning to all things in creation. Whether one calls this consciousness God, Goddess, Deity, the Divine, Ain Soph, the Oversoul, the Eternal Source, or the Absolute Unity—the name is basically irrelevant so long as the term used is understood to be one's highest idea of pure, transcendent Divinity.

The Divine enlivens the Universe and ultimately grants the human mind those creative, psychic faculties needed to perform acts of magic. In ritual, magicians usually invoke this highest aspect of the Divine before all else.

The magician's ability to tap into this universal consciousness will determine the accuracy of his or her divinations, as well as the success of ritual magic.

Golden Dawn magicians often profess what might be described as ultimate monotheism—the idea that the Divine manifests in diverse forms, including Gods, archangels, angels, intelligences, and Spirits. But ultimately all of these beings may be traced back to the One Divine Source of All. *This monotheism makes more sense than the tribalism of many organized religions.*

the Absolute
↓
triad
or
Trinity

THE GODS

Some believe that the Gods and Goddesses are real and very powerful beings who dwell in another plane of existence and have been around since the beginning of the known Universe. Others hold the opinion that the Gods are thought-forms—anthropomorphic images created in the mind of humanity that have been empowered and brought to life by centuries of continuous prayer and veneration. This latter view holds that the divine realities behind the images of the Gods and Goddesses are enormous reservoirs of energy that are fed by the strong, passionate devotion and focused thoughts of human worshippers. These ancient reservoirs are still in existence, and although centuries of neglect have depleted them, they can yet be reenergized through the ceremonies and invocations of modern-day priests and priestesses. These deific energies may be asleep, but they never cease to be.

Magicians are able to access the various power reservoirs represented by the Gods and utilize them in ritual work. Through willpower and the imaginative faculties of the psyche, magicians are able to tap into these vessels of god-energy and invoke them to effect magic.

ANGELS

Between the world of humans and the Absolute Unity of God exist myriad spiritual beings. The entities that magicians work with most often are angels.

The word "angel" comes from the Greek *angelos,* which is itself a translation of the Hebrew *melakh,* meaning "messenger." Angels have been described as "messengers of the soul." A more precise definition states that an angel is "an intermediate Intelligence between the human and the One in the Great Chain of Being."

The magician, too, is a part of this uninterrupted chain of Being. This hierarchy includes various aspects of divinity or "essences" of God that can be identified as the many "divine names of God" in the Qabalistic tradition, or as the many Celestial deities known in the pantheons of different religions. After the highest aspects of divinity, archangels, angels, and intelligences are next in the hierarchy. In the Qabalah, archangels and angels are considered specific aspects of God, each with a particular purpose and jurisdiction. Nearly all of the Hebraic angels have the suffixes "el" or "yah" at the end of their names, indicating that they are "of God." Human beings are ranked in the middle of this divine hierarchy, connected to it by virtue of the human soul and the Higher Self, sometimes called the Holy Guardian Angel—one's personal angelic contact with the higher realms. Next in line after humans come the lower Spirits and elementals.

Golden Dawn magicians adhere to this chain of command whenever they perform magical ceremonies. Regardless of how well a magician can perform the mechanics of magic, the work of art can only take place when the magician's will is in alignment with the Higher and Divine Will of the Universe. This can only come about through purification of soul and psyche, purity of intent, and spiritual discipline. And in a Divine Universe, the Powers that Be must be petitioned through the proper channels, from the highest to lowest spiritual ranks. Therefore, in any ritual the magician first invokes the highest divine names of God before invoking any lesser aspects of divinity, angels, or Spirits to carry out the goal of the magical working.

Archangels and angels lack physical form, although representations of them in art come from the inventions of the human mind, which often turns to anthropomorphic images to enhance our understanding. The true form of an archangel would be similar to a great pillar of energy or a geometric shape.

Ritual work involving Gods, archangels, and angels will be presented in later chapters of this book.

THAUMATURGY VERSUS THEURGY

The manner in which magicians work with spiritual beings can be generally classified under the terms "thaumaturgy" and "theurgy."

Thaumaturgy

The term "thaumaturgy" is derived from the Greek word *thaumaturgia*, meaning "wonder working" or "miracle working." Sometimes referred to as simply "practical magic" or "low magic," thaumaturgy often involves practical magical work done in the service of others rather than for one's own spiritual progress.

For centuries magicians and clerics were employed to lift curses; heal illnesses; provide divinations, blessings, and invocations; and create amulets. However, this also led to abuse—in ancient Greece, thaumaturgy gained a bad reputation as magical "miracle workers" sometimes defrauded clients out of their money and valuables.

In this regard it might be useful to differentiate *high thaumaturgy*, which sincerely seeks to use the magical arts to help others through practical magic, from more mundane thaumaturgic goals.

Some groups today use the term "thaumaturgy" to indicate magic that does not involve invoking the Divine, angels, or Spirits, but is dependent on the natural powers of certain substances or the natural abilities and magical intentions of the magician.

Theurgy

Golden Dawn magic falls under the heading of high magic, also called "ceremonial magic" or "theurgy," meaning "divine action" or "god-working." A ceremonial magician is often referred to as a theurgist.

Theosis is the goal not a large bank account.

The Greek term *theurgia* was first used by second-century Platonists to explain the transformative power of sacred rites. It indicated a process of ritual purification designed to cleanse the lower aspects of the self in order to prepare for union with the Divine. During the fourth century, Neoplatonic philosopher Iamblichus provided a coherent rationale for performing ritual acts of theurgy. He taught that each individual human soul was immersed within the body of matter, and that the soul required divine aid to free itself and return to the One Source of All. This divine assistance was given in the form of theurgic rites and ceremonies made potent by the Gods. Iamblichus insisted that union with the transcendent God was only possible through the practice of these holy rituals.

Theurgy is not simply a discussion or contemplation about "things divine"—but rather a total involvement on the part of the theurgist who works to invoke and embody the divine principles of the Cosmos, with the aid of divine entities, archangels, angels, and Spirits.

Today the term "theurgy" is used to describe any form of magic having the primary goal of advancing the magician's spiritual transformation while also embracing practical ethical goals in service to others.

WILL VERSUS WILLPOWER

In our discussion on the mechanics of magic, we stated that human willpower is a real magical force. However, we need to distinguish between *will* and *willpower*.

The term "will" is often used to indicate a person's inclination, drive, or motivation. We often speak of the necessity of bringing the magician's will into alignment with the Higher or Divine Will as a prerequisite for successful Golden Dawn magic. When we speak of Divine Will, we are not referring to strict adherence to some dogmatic vision of obedience and insubordination, or reward and punishment, but rather to the inclination of Deity toward the natural cosmic order of involution and evolution, or the experiential inhaling and exhaling of Spirit into the material world and back again. As we all contain sparks of that Divine Light and exist within the Great Chain of Being, our magic should inevitably reflect this; when it doesn't, we risk failure or worse.

Therefore, a good deal of the part of the magician's continuing practice is to create the conditions that help us orient ourselves to the Higher Will. We do this by purifying the auric sphere through meditation, exercises such as the Middle Pillar, and cleansing rituals such as the Lesser Ritual of the Pentagram. Magical Hygéne

Closely aligned with the idea of will, *willpower* goes a step beyond inclination. Willpower denotes self-control and the disciplined ability to choose one's actions. Willpower is considered by many to be a virtue, but it is much more in line with a learned skill or a muscle. Like all muscles, it can be strengthened with practice. A dictionary definition of willpower would be "energetic determination." In magic, we understand that this is *willed force,* consciously summoned, shaped, and cultivated by the discipline of our art for a specific purpose.

But what purpose? This brings us to the subject of intention.

MAGICAL INTENTION

This has to be said: In magic, intention is *not* everything. While it is an important factor in any successful magical operation, it is not the only factor. Too often, magicians use the mantra of "intention is all that matters" as an excuse to evade the daily discipline and exercises involved in effective magical practice. If magic was simply intention, we would all have everything we ever wanted. This is the stuff of fairy tales.

Nevertheless, when you activate the force of willpower, it must have an intended goal, purpose, or point of focus. This intention must be clearly envisioned and precisely worded. Donald Michael Kraig once said: "If someone has an unclear intention and (poorly) reads a ritual out of some book while waving a wand, it is highly unlikely that he or she will achieve the goal of their intention. All they're doing is mumbling and wand waving. Magick is more than intention, more than just repeating some poorly-understood or pronounced words."[5]

Your intention should also be realistic or within the realm of possibility. For example: I might state my intention of being a concert pianist. But I can't read music and I've never touched a piano. So, unless I decide to devote most of my waking hours studying music, practicing scales, and hitting the ivory keys, chances are high that my intention alone will never get me to my stated goal. As my hypothetical piano teacher might tell me, "practice, practice, practice!"

This is also where the alignment with the Higher Will comes in. Your magical intention should be in alignment with the Will of the Divine, or *at the very least*, not conflict with it in any way. Fighting against the universal stream is like swimming against a rip-tide: the only way to safety is to go with the flow of the current.

Instead of viewing it as a kind of wish-fulfillment cure-all, a clear and aligned intention is a good starting point in magic; the combined forces of willpower and imagination need a goal to focus on.

Magical Ethics

Upon entry into a Golden Dawn Temple, every new Neophyte swears an oath: "I will not debase my mystical knowledge in the labor of Evil Magic at any time tried or under any temptation."

One would think that all magicians would have an intuitive understanding that any magic that is harmful to another person runs completely contrary to the holistic nature of the Great Work. Sadly, this is not always the case. There will always be those who cherry-pick portions of magical texts in order to "curse someone," or cast a black magic spell, or some equally idiotic endeavor. And unfortunately, there are some otherwise intelligent magicians who ought to know better, yet continue to perform negative magic against others. Israel Regardie advised his students to "shun those who practice black magic as you would shun a foul disease."

Worrying about someone casting evil spells against you is very much overrated and rather pointless. Because black magic runs contrary to the Divine Will, it tends

---

5. Donald Michael Kraig, "The Superficiality of Intentionality," *Llewellyn Unbound,* http://www.llewellyn .com/blog/2013/08/the-superficiality-of-intentionality/ (accessed June 26, 2018).

to "boomerang" back on the person who performs it. Author Carroll "Poke" Runyon has a wonderful analogy on the subject: Someone casting a black magic spell is like a person in a phone booth with a hand grenade. He dials the phone number of a person he wants to "curse" and when that person answers the phone, the magician pulls the pin out of his hand grenade. His intended victim may hear the explosion on the other end of the receiver, but it is the magician in the phone booth who takes the full force of the blast. Just remember that whatever you send out into the Universe is what the Universe will send back to you.

Always keep magical ethics in mind and consider how your magic may affect others. This is a prerequisite for anyone who wishes to call themselves a Golden Dawn magician.

PITFALLS TO WATCH FOR

The practice of magic paves the way to encounters with higher levels of reality. Therefore, it is important that the would-be magician be free from neuroses and other forms of mental illness that tend to cloud one's perceptions and can in fact worsen when magic is undertaken.

Ego-Inflation

Magical practice works to release latent energy from the subconscious and expand the mind's horizons. As the magician becomes proficient in the theurgical arts, he or she undergoes an increase in psychic awareness, knowledge, and self-confidence. This is often accompanied by feelings of new life-purpose and direction. But magic can also sometimes reawaken the mechanism of the infantile mega-ego, causing delusions of grandeur and self-importance.

One of the things that Israel Regardie was adamant about was that the occult student should seek out a course of psychotherapy as a safeguard against inflation of the ego and other problems that might crop up as a result of the increased activation of the psyche through magical training. We also hold this view but have found that it is not always possible for students to find a good therapist who is sympathetic to the magical arts. The solitary student in particular is at a disadvantage here, not having a group of Temple-mates to consult if problems arise.

Delusion

People who are natural clairvoyants and mediums are especially susceptible, as are those with chemical imbalances or other psychological problems. As ironic as it sounds, a healthy dose of skepticism is required to safely traverse the astral planes where magic is worked. Magicians must be scientists of the mind—testing every visionary experience for kernels of truth and husks of delusion. Without taking the proper precautions, it becomes far too easy for some to lose their way in the ethereal realms. They run the risk of becoming unable to distinguish divine revelation from flights of fantasy—spiritual breakthrough from psychic breakdown.

The would-be magician must be mentally fit, balanced, and well-grounded because the practice of magic tends to bring out one's personal demons or shadow aspects of the self that most people would prefer remain buried deep within the psyche. He or she must take to heart the ancient Greek aphorism *Gnothi Seauton*, "know thyself." Balance and common sense must be maintained in order to keep self-deception and egomania at bay. This is absolutely crucial to the magician's spiritual well-being.

The Paper Chase and the Lineage Leap

Too often you will hear of magicians whose major claim to fame is that they own more rare magical documents than the next person or that they have unbroken Golden Dawn lineage that dates back to … however far back in time they can convince others of. Unfortunately, there is no line of apostolic succession that leads directly from Christian Rosenkreutz to MacGregor Mathers. Since the Order of the Golden Dawn ceased to exist in 1903, splitting apart into three separate splinter groups, no one in this day and age can claim institutional lineage to the original Order—much less back to the mythological character of Christian Rosenkreutz. Those who do so are often simply looking to impress people, gain power over others, or claim to be something more than what they are. These are usually symptoms of insecurity and its doppelganger, ego-inflation. They are not things to be pursued but rather obstacles to be overcome. Forget about them and carry on with the only thing that really matters: the work itself.

GOLDEN DAWN PRINCIPLES

The Golden Dawn is a child of the *Western Esoteric Tradition*, a venerable heritage that includes alternative spirituality, astrology, ancient Greek philosophy and mystery religions, Qabalah, spiritual alchemy, and ceremonial magic. This great river of spiritual thought has continually fed several smaller streams of which the Golden Dawn is one form.

Ours is a living tradition of philosophical principles, spiritual illumination, and magical practice. And while magicians of our ilk have long used the teachings of the GD in personal magic designed to better their immediate circumstances, conditions, or environments (or that of others), we cannot stress strongly enough that the main goal of the Golden Dawn system is identical with that of any genuine spiritual path: the renewal of the human Spirit, the healing of our world and soul, and the return of Sacredness to human life and living. In order to accomplish these lofty goals, we must be willing to aid the expansion of Divinity into our ailing world. One proverb sums this up beautifully: "Physician, heal thyself." In order to take our right place as companions to the angels on the Path of Light, we must heal ourselves so that we may serve and heal others. This should be our primary motivation for studying the many components of the GD's teachings and performing its various meditations, exercises, and rituals.

The essential principles of the Golden Dawn include the following.

Macrocosm and Microcosm

There is a connection between a higher divine reality called the *Macrocosm,* or the "Greater Universe," and the earthly realm of the *Microcosm*, the "Small Universe" of human beings. Creator and Creation. Divinity and humanity. All is linked. As above, so below.

Ultimate Divinity

The Golden Dawn is ultimately monotheistic although it conceives of the Divine Unity or Ultimate Divinity as emanating itself through a multitude of forms, aspects, characteristics, and manifestations. In other words, the transcendent God who is the ineffable Source of All presents itself to humanity in the forms of various Gods and Goddesses for our better understanding and development. Although the system may appear to be outwardly polytheistic, all deities are thought to be the various faces and rich expressions of the ultimate Divine Unity. While the Cosmos appears to be diverse, at its most fundamental level, All is One.

the point in the circle

- Divine Masks
- Much more useful than the harsh tribalism of orthodox religion.

Immanence and Transcendence

Ultimate Divinity is both immanent (within everything) and transcendent (beyond everything). The Universe is completely divine, living, and animated.

The Way of Return

Humanity has become separated from the Divine through *involution*, the process by which the Spirit manifested into matter. We seek "the Way of Return" back to unity with the Divine, through *evolution*, the process by which Spirit reconnects with Divinity. Involution and evolution are both natural and necessary processes of creation. They function as the exhalation and inhalation of Spirit. However, the Way of Return requires aspiration and discipline. It cannot be attained without hard work and dedication. And although many ancient and Sacred texts hold valuable, profound, precious keys that provide guidance toward the Way of Return, no text is thought to be infallible or free of error. Although spiritual teachers can provide guidance, each individual aspirant must ultimately tread the way back to the Divine alone.

[handwritten annotation: The Bible, Quran, Torah } guides but not perfect infalible or free from error.]

The Universal Order

The nature of the Universe is ultimately good, constructive, and leans toward balance. Evil is created from a state of imbalance.

Hierarchies and Intermediaries

Divine beings, deities, archangels, angels, and spirits act as links in a chain, the rungs on a ladder that aid the magician in climbing and descending the planes into the higher realms of Being. Golden Dawn magicians are taught to always invoke the Highest first.

The Celestial Pattern

Because Macrocosm and Microcosm are linked, the individual human soul and aura contain a reflection of the Celestial powers. By awakening and purifying this reflection within, the magician is able to (1) effect magical change, and (2) transmute and reorient the soul toward the Divine.

The Work

As part of the discipline needed to return to the Divine, human beings must learn to understand the invisible realms that lie hidden behind the manifest Universe. To that end, it embraces the practices of esoteric spirituality, mysticism, and the magical arts. Armed with knowledge gained from esoteric practices, the highest aspiration of the magician is toward union with the Divine, often called the goal of the Great Work.

Balance and Equilibrium

One of the most repeated themes in the Golden Dawn is the vital importance of balance and equilibrium. The astrological significance of the equinoxes is particularly emphasized in our tradition. The Sun is the light of the visible world, but it also symbolizes the Divine Light. Twice a year at the vernal and autumnal equinoxes when both day and night are of equal length, GD Temples reestablish the magical link between the Sun and the Order. This is just as important for the individual as well; the GD has always admitted men and women on the basis of perfect equality. Furthermore, GD rituals and exercises are designed to foster balance within the soul and psyche of the magician.

Spirituality

The Golden Dawn is *not* a religion, although spiritual principles, ideas, and imagery play a large role in its teachings and magical work. It teaches tolerance for all true life-affirming spiritual paths. As the Neophyte is told: "Hold all religions in reverence, for there is none but contains a ray from the ineffable Light you seek." GD magicians come from a wide variety of religions. The work is meant to complement the magician's religious practice, not replace it.

WHAT THE TEACHINGS ENCOMPASS

The Golden Dawn system of magic was designed to teach its students abstract esoteric concepts as well as the more practical applications of Western ceremonial magic. Egyptian, Judeo-Christian, Greek, Gnostic, Rosicrucian, and Masonic elements can all be found within the Hermetic teachings of the Order. The basics of magic, its language and theory, are taught early on to aspiring students, while the more advanced magical techniques and practices are in the wheelhouse of the advanced magician. The complete curriculum of the Golden Dawn is too extensive to list in its entirety here; however, the major components are described below so that readers can begin to grasp the comprehensive nature of the work.

Qabalah

The Qabalah is the foundation for much of the magic employed by the Golden Dawn. The various grades, officers, and even the layout of a Golden Dawn Temple within the Order setting are all based on a Qabalistic structure. In the higher teachings, basic Qabalistic knowledge permeates every aspect of the work. The following are among the things that aspirants learn:

- The attributes of the ten major energy centers on the Qabalistic Tree of Life

- The energetic paths connecting these ten energy centers

- Correspondences, patterns, and images associated with the Qabalistic energies

- The Hebrew alphabet, the primary symbol-system of Western magic

- Gematria: a Hebrew numerical code used in magic

- Divine Hebrew godnames and words of power

- Qabalistic archangels and angels

- The parts of the soul as defined by Qabalah

- How to use Qabalistic energies for "the Way of Return"

- How to make, consecrate, and use Qabalistic sigils and talismans for magical work

- Four Qabalistic scales of color used in talismans and Spirit Vision Work

- Qabalistic exercises for self-purification, healing, and connecting with the Divine

Elemental, Planetary, and Zodiacal Magic

Next to the teachings of the Qabalah, astrological correspondences are the most prevalent form of esoteric knowledge used in the Golden Dawn. Beginning students learn basic astrological information concerning the zodiac—the twelve signs, the twelve houses, the decanates, the triplicities, and the quadruplicities. Knowledge of the elements and the planets in particular is an essential factor in ceremonial magic. Students learn:

- The attributes and correspondences of the elements

- The attributes and correspondences of the twelve zodiacal signs

- The attributes and correspondences of the seven ancient planets

- Elemental archangels, angels, and Spirits

- Planetary archangels, angels, and Spirits

- Zodiacal archangels, angels, and Spirits

- How elemental and astrological energies reflect inner spiritual realities of the psyche and the aura

- How to manipulate, balance, and cleanse these inner elemental and astrological realities for the purpose of linking with the Divine

- How to construct and interpret a zodiacal chart

- Planetary Hours, the best times for working planetary magic

- How to make, consecrate, and use planetary sigils and talismans for magical work

Divination

Divination is an art and science that seeks to discover the divine significance behind "chance" events. The word "divination" indicates communication from the Divine. This is a receptive skill that must be cultivated. It takes practice for the magician to pay attention to what the Divine is trying to express in a reading. The Golden Dawn excels in symbol divination, which uses a fixed set of divinatory symbols, each with its own meaning and interpretation. The practice of divination aids in the development of psychic awareness. Under this topic, aspirants learn:

- The attributes of the tarot

- Divination through geomancy

- Horary astrology, a form of divination

• Rosicrucian Chess, a divinatory game

• The Ring and Disk, a form of pendulum divination

Spirit Vision Work

One of the most prevalent types of magical work performed by advanced Golden Dawn magicians is Spirit Vision Work, often called *skrying*. This is a form of clairvoyance or foreseeing that usually employs a gazing device such as a crystal or a symbolic portal image to aid a person's concentration, train their psychic abilities, and allow spiritual visions to come through into normal waking consciousness. Magicians learn to skry into various symbols including but in no way restricted to:

• Tarot cards

• Hebrew letters

• Zodiacal symbols

• Planetary symbols

• Geomantic symbols

• Sigils

• Eastern Tattva symbols (or their Western equivalent, the alchemical Triangles of the elements)

• Enochian letters

• Enochian pyramid squares

Enochian

Often considered one of the pinnacles of the Golden Dawn system, Enochian magic is derived from the work of renowned sixteenth-century Elizabethan magician Dr. John Dee and his seer, Edward Kelley. Enochian is the unifying system of magic that combines nearly every other major component of the work mentioned above. Advanced Golden Dawn magicians learn to work with:

• The Elemental Tablets of the Watchtowers

• The Tablet of Union

- The Enochian alphabet

- Enochian angels

- Enochian Calls, a series of invocations

- The Enochian planetary system known as the *Heptarchia*

- The *Tabula Sancta*, or Holy Table of Practice

- The *Sigillum dei Emeth*, or Great Seal

- The creation, consecration, and use of Enochian talismans

- Enochian Spirit Vision Work

There is a great deal of other work that does not fall so neatly into the categories listed here: meditation, the creation of magical implements and Sacred Space, healing, aura control, godform assumption, the projection and movement of energy, dramatic invocation, and ceremonial magic. All of these topics and techniques are vital to the comprehensive magic of the Golden Dawn.

The material contained in these teachings is fundamental to building a solid foundation of knowledge that will steadily become second nature to the aspirant. It enables the magician to perceive more clearly the hidden astral influences that permeate the physical world. The conscious commitment to learn the magical language and symbol-systems of the unconscious mind results in the cultivation of psychic reflexes and "muscle memory," which aid the magician in his or her work. But more importantly, the memorization of magical data changes the very structure of the psyche, which is gradually infiltrated by holy symbols that speak on a subconscious frequency to the Divine Being in each of us. The mind of the magician is steadily cleansed by this process as an increasing percentage of mundane thoughts are supplanted or transformed by spiritual thoughts, just as the body sheds old cells and replenishes them with new ones.

THE ART OF MEDITATION

Few methods are more essential to the successful practice of magic than this seemingly simple activity. Meditation is focused awareness. Once the mind is fixed on a spiritual subject, the higher faculties can be accessed. In Western magic, meditation is a two-part process. The first step is to quiet the conscious mind from all internal chatter. The second is to contemplate a specific topic or image, following all implications, nuances, and meanings while eliminating all nonrelated thoughts. With time and effort the magician improves his or her powers of concentration and mental clarity.

Meditation is also a wonderful exercise in willpower. It trains the brain to examine something intently while at the same time resisting the urge for the mind to wander. In only three days' time, a ten-minute daily routine of meditation will leave you with less stress and more energy and focus.

Before you meditate, perform a relaxation exercise in a room where you will not be disturbed. The following technique is an excellent prelude to any type of meditation or ritual work. We cannot overstate the importance of this practice.

A Relaxation Exercise

1. Lie on your back on a firm, flat surface with arms at the sides of the body. Remain as relaxed as possible with the eyes closed. (This is the reclining position for meditation.)

2. Starting with the top of the head, deliberately tense the muscles of the forehead for a moment as much as possible. Then let go of the tension. Relax the forehead totally. After a brief period, tense the muscles of the face and neck. Then let the tension go fully away. Relax completely.

3. Continue down the rest of the body in the same manner, first tensing then releasing the muscles: the shoulders, arms, chest and back, stomach, buttocks, thighs, calves, and feet. Tense, and then relax.

4. Tense the entire body as much as possible, then relax fully and deeply. Release all tension. Notice how much more relaxed your body is after the balancing effects of flexing and releasing.

5. If tension reemerges anywhere in the body, repeat the entire process.

6. Breathe deeply without strain as you cultivate a sense of peaceful relaxation.

Seated Position for Meditation

Sit upright in a straight-backed chair with your feet flat on the ground and your thighs parallel to the floor. Place your hands on top of your thighs.

Standing Position for Meditation

Stand up straight with your feet hip-width apart, parallel to each other. Arms at your sides.

RHYTHMIC BREATHING

Rhythmic breathing is an effective way to begin a meditation. Focusing on a deep rhythmic breath shifts the mind's awareness inward and activates the body's parasympathetic nervous system which assists relaxation. Two simple breathing exercises are the Two to One Breath and the Fourfold Breath.

Two to One Breath

In this exercise, the exhalation is twice as long as the inhalation. There are no pauses between inhalation and exhalation.

    1. Inhale slowly to the count of one.

    2. Exhale slowly to the count of two.

The Fourfold Breath

The Fourfold Breath is a traditional Golden Dawn exercise for rhythmic breathing.

    1. Empty the lungs and remain empty while counting four.

    2. Inhale, counting four, so that you feel filled with breath to the throat.

    3. Hold this breath while counting four.

    4. Exhale, counting four until the lungs are empty.

This should be practiced, counting slowly or quickly till you obtain a rhythm that suits you, one that is easy and calming. Having attained this, count the breath in this manner for two or three minutes until you feel relaxed, and then proceed with the meditation.

HOW TO MEDITATE

Try to set aside the same time every day for meditation. Your meditative session should take no more than five minutes at first. Eventually you can extend your sessions to ten, fifteen, and twenty minutes.

Choose your meditation posture, whether reclining, seated, or standing. This posture should be balanced but sufficiently comfortable. Perform a few cycles of rhythmic breathing until the body is still and the mind quiet, before returning to your normal breathing. Maintain this state for a few minutes at first, and longer as you get more used to preventing the mind from wandering.

Meditate on the topic at hand.

Think about the topic in a general way at first, then contemplate a specific aspect of the subject or a series of thoughts connected to it. Follow these related aspects out to any ideas that your mind associates with them. Then choose one connected thought or image and follow that to its conclusion.

If your mind wanders off, gently bring it back to the subject of the meditation. You can allow new ideas into your thoughts so long as they have something to do with the chosen topic.

Do not get discouraged if your attention span seems limited. It will improve over time as you persevere.

When finished, perform a few cycles of rhythmic breathing before returning to your normal breathing.

Pre-Ritual Meditation

After a period of time, you will discover a meditation regime that works best for you; you will learn which posture, rhythmic breathing cycle, and time frame delivers the most favorable results. Once this is determined, use your personal meditation regime as part of your standard preparation for ritual work.

MEDITATION: THE POINT

1. Begin with the seated position for meditation. Close your eyes, relax, and proceed with rhythmic breathing.

2. Focus on the idea of a point as described in mathematics: A point is a location in space. It has position but is without size. Take note of the ideas to

which this gives rise. Concentrate your mind on the point as a focus, try to realize the presence of the Divine in every point, every location in nature.

Visualization

Visualization is the practice of imaging something, such as a place or Deity, with intense clarity. It is the ability to formulate a strong, clear mental image. Imagination is the faculty that makes this possible.

Although modern civilization tends to downplay imagination as a fantasy pastime of children, imagination is the ultimate creative ability in human beings and a primary instrument of magic. When we imagine something, we create a picture of it in the psyche. We *image* it. When an inventor constructs an invention, he first creates it in the mind's eye, building up a mental image of the mechanics involved and the shape and dimensions that the invention will take. In this way, the invention becomes a reality on the astral plane before it becomes a reality in the physical plane. The magician uses this same faculty of imagination to build up an image of what he or she desires to accomplish, giving it shape and form in the astral light. The ability to visualize is essential in magic, and learning the art of visualization is fundamental to one's magical training. It also follows that one's power of concentration is vitally important to the magical procedure.

"I Can't Visualize!"

For the artists and craftsmen among us, it is surprising to learn that many people have difficulty in visualizing. This problem can usually be overcome in time with steady and patient practice.

However, some people struggle with *aphantasia*, a little-understood neurological condition in which individuals cannot form images in their imagination, picture things in their mind, or even recall memories as pictures. More medical research must be done to understand the nature of this condition and develop a treatment. Many aphantasiacs are able to dream, but they recall dreams through textual descriptions, rather than imagery. As with many such conditions, there is a huge spectrum of aphantasian experience, from the complete inability to visualize anything, to having blurry or momentary visions. While it is far beyond the scope of this book to treat aphantasia, some aphantasiacs have been able to increase their ability to visualize through Neurolinguistic Programming, image streaming, lucid dreaming, relaxation techniques, exercises for entering a hypnogogic state while awake, listening to guided meditations, or working with negative after-images, a kind of optical illusion in which an image continues to be seen briefly after exposure to the real image has concluded (see the section Negative After-Images in chapter 9).

The following exercise is designed to aid visualization by focusing on simple shapes and colors of everyday items.

Begin with the seated position for meditation. Close your eyes, relax, and proceed with rhythmic breathing. When ready, open your eyes and gaze into the palm of your left hand. Cup the fingers of your hand into a claw. Imagine that you are holding a small apple. Picture its roundness and redness. Once this image is clear in your mind, expand your fingers outward as you imagine that the apple grows to twice its original size. Then draw your fingers back as you imagine the apple shrinking back to its previous size. Play with the size of the apple for a while. Pass the apple to your right hand and then place it somewhere near you.

Repeat this technique and visualize an orange, followed by a green tomato. When finished, place all the visualized items in a row. Then concentrate on dissolving them slowly, one at a time until nothing of the visualized objects remain.

VISUALIZATION EXERCISE: THE LINE

1. Begin with the seated position for meditation. Close your eyes, relax, and proceed with rhythmic breathing.

2. When ready, visualize a point of light as described in space: having position but without size. Contemplate the Divine within this point as it exists within every point in nature and the Universe.

3. Next, visualize the point moving in a single direction. As it moves it traces a straight line. Visualize two points at either end of the line. The line has no thickness—it is one-dimensional. Then imagine that the line extends infinitely in both directions. Strongly visualize this line and meditate upon all its implications.

Vibration

"By names and images are all Powers awakened and reawakened." This often-repeated Golden Dawn quotation clearly states that vibration and visualization are the twin engines that empower magic. Vibration is a method by which divine names and words of power are intoned forcefully and with authority in a strong "vibration" meant to attract the specific energies that are associated with them.

All matter is vibratory energy. There is a physical phenomenon known as *harmonic resonance* that shows that if one object starts to vibrate strongly enough, another object nearby will begin to vibrate or resonate with the first, if both objects share the same natural vibratory rate. The magician vibrates a godname in order to effect a harmonic resonance between Deity as it exists within his or her own psyche and as it exists within the Greater Universe. The aim is to have the psyche "resonate" with the Divine. Not only does this lift the consciousness to a higher, more purified level, it accelerates the purification of the body through the expulsion of old dead cells.

Properly performed, the vibration should be felt throughout the entire body and imagined to be vibrated throughout the Universe. Successful vibration in ritual is often accompanied by a tingling sensation in the hands or face.

In the rituals and exercises presented in this book, any words that are capitalized should be vibrated.

Vibration Exercise: Yod

1. Begin with the seated position for meditation. Close your eyes, relax, and proceed with rhythmic breathing.

2. When ready, visualize a point of white light. Contemplate the Divine within this point as it exists within every point in nature and the Universe.

3. Next, visualize the light growing into the flame-like shape of a *Yod*, the Sacred letter from which all other letters of the Hebrew alphabet are derived (Figure 1).

Figure 1: Yod

4. Inhale deeply and slowly vibrate the word **"YOD"** ten times. Each vibration of the syllable should be between seven to ten beats or seconds long. Keep the image of the letter Yod within your mind as you vibrate.

5. When finished, dissolve the image of the letter. Take note of how you feel and any insights that you may have experienced during the exercise.

MEDITATION: THE TRIANGLE

1. Begin with your personal Pre-Ritual Meditation Practice.

2. Focus on the figure of a Triangle as it exists in geometry, in architecture, in nature, and in spirituality. The Triangle, the first and simplest of all polygons, is the only geometric shape into which all flat plane surfaces can be reduced. All other polygons can be divided into Triangles by drawing lines from their angles to their centers. Contemplate the number three and the triad. Take note of any ideas that develop from this meditation.

VISUALIZATION EXERCISE: THE TRIANGLE

1. Begin with the standing position for meditation. Close your eyes, relax, and proceed with rhythmic breathing.

2. When ready, bring your arm straight up, and extend your index finger as if you were pointing at something directly in front of you. Bring your hand up about a foot and a half higher and visualize a point of white light at the end of your finger. This is your starting point (Figure 2).

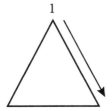

Figure 2: Tracing the Triangle

3. Next, trace a large Triangle in the air, going clockwise from the starting point. Strongly visualize the Triangle as lines of white light.

4. When finished, trace the lines of the Triangle in reverse, starting at the top and proceeding anticlockwise. Mentally dissolve the image. Take note of how you feel and any insights that you may have experienced during the exercise.

VIBRATION EXERCISE: IAO

Hermetic magicians often vibrate the name IAO as the Western equivalent of the Eastern chant OM. IAO was the name of the supreme Deity of the Gnostics, and is derived from the Tetragrammaton, or "Four-Lettered Name" of the Hebrew God embodied by the letters YHVH (sometimes pronounced in the ancient world as Yahweh, Yeho, or Yahu). In the Golden Dawn, the letters of the name IAO are used to represent a triad of Egyptian deities: Isis, Apophis, and Osiris—or the cycle of life, death, and rebirth.

1. Perform the Visualization exercise of the Triangle described above, but add the following: While tracing the first line, inhale deeply then slowly vibrate "**eee**." When tracing the second line, intone "**aahh**." Trace the third line and vibrate "**oohh**."

2. When finished, trace the lines of the Triangle in reverse (once) and mentally dissolve the figure. Take note of how you feel and any insights that you may have experienced during the exercise.

Variations

Try the following variations on the IAO vibration while standing, but do not trace the Triangle.

- *Building energy:* Start vibrating with a low note (tone) and end with a high note.

- *Releasing energy:* Start vibrating with a high note (tone) and end with a low note.

- *Modulating force:* Vibrate in one tone but start out softly, then loudly, then softly again at the end.

- *Visualized vibration:* Bring your hands above your head and as you vibrate "I," start with a higher note. As you vibrate "A," bring your hands slowly down to the level of your throat and deepen the note, visualizing it in your vocal chords. As you vibrate "O," bring your hands slowly down to your heart center and deepen the note, visualizing it in your diaphragm, where it spreads out to your entire body.

VISUALIZATION EXERCISE: THE SQUARE

The square is an important lineal figure that represents stability and balance.

1. Start in the standing position and begin with a brief period of rhythmic breathing.

2. When ready, extend your index finger as if you were pointing at something directly in front of you.

3. Still pointing, bring your hand up about a foot higher and over to the left. Visualize a point of white light at the end of your finger. This is the starting point.

4. Next trace a large square, going clockwise from the starting point (Figure 3). Strongly visualize the square in lines of white light.

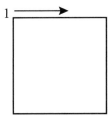

Figure 3: Tracing the Square

5. When finished, trace the lines of the square in reverse, starting at the top and proceeding anticlockwise. Mentally dissolve the image. Take note of how you feel and any insights that you may have experienced during the exercise.

VIBRATION EXERCISE: YHVH—THE TETRAGRAMMATON

Four Hebrew letters, *Yod Heh Vav Heh* (often transliterated as YHVH), stand for the highest Hebrew name for God—a name that is considered unknown and unpronounce-able. YHVH is often referred to as the *Tetragrammaton*, or "Four-lettered Name." It is considered the holiest of the Hebrew names of God. While scholars often pronounce this name as Yahweh and observant Jews replace it with Adonai ("Lord"), Golden Dawn magicians pronounce the name by its four letters, each of which is attributed to one of the four elements: Yod-Fire, Heh-Water, Vav-Air, and Heh Final-Earth.

1. Perform the Visualization exercise of the Square described above, but add the following: While tracing the first line, inhale deeply then slowly vibrate **"YOD."** When tracing the second line, intone **"HEH."** Trace the third line and vibrate **"VAV."** For the final line, vibrate **"HEH."**

2. Repeat the tracing of the square and intoning the name three more times. Visualize it strongly.

3. When finished, trace the lines of the square in reverse (once) and dissolve the figure. Take note of any feelings or insights.

4. Perform the same variations described in the Vibration exercise for IAO.

WILLPOWER EXERCISE: THE OPPOSITE HAND

The human brain is hardwired to use our dominant hand; therefore, it takes willpower to use our subordinate hand.

1. Select a period of time, anywhere from a half-hour to an hour, that you can devote to this exercise.

2. For the period of time allotted, use your nondominant hand for all tasks such as opening doors, reaching for things, etc.

3. Take note of how you feel and any insights that you may have experienced during the exercise.

WILLPOWER EXERCISE: CONTROLLED SPEECH

Changing one's speech is a way to assert mental control over an automatic habit.

1. Select a period of time that you can devote to this exercise.

2. Begin with your personal Pre-Ritual Meditation Practice.

3. For the period of time allotted, don't use part of your vocabulary that you wish to change. Here are some examples:
   • Avoid using the word "I."

   • Try avoiding contractions such as "can't," "won't," and "don't." Say "cannot," "will not," and "do not."

- If you tend to swear, try substituting a humorous word instead.

- Say "Hello" instead of "Hey."

- Try adding new descriptive words to your normal speech, such as "azure," "gossamer," and "erudite."

4. Take note of how you feel and any insights that you may have experienced during the exercise.

The Magical Motto

All Golden Dawn magicians choose a magical motto or mystical name for themselves. This is typically a meaningful word or short aspirational phrase (not a paragraph!) for use in all magical workings. The magical name is taken in order to disassociate oneself from the mundane world for the duration of the magical work at hand. Many magicians choose mottoes that have personal spiritual significance for them. Golden Dawn mottoes are typically rendered in Latin, Greek, Hebrew, or any language that is not the magician's normal speaking language. Examples of mottoes include *Emeth* ("Truth") and *Yehi Aour* ("Let There Be Light").

The Magical Journal

We encourage students to keep a magical journal of all esoteric practice: meditations, exercises, rituals, and readings. The exact format of the journal is not important. What matters is that you develop the habit of recording your work. Your journal will become a valuable resource for your spiritual growth, helping you to determine what works and what doesn't work.

Always include the date, time, and circumstances of the working, along with any results or feelings that occur afterward.

A sample journal entry:

Sunday, 10/29/17
7:30 pm

Banished with the LBRP.
Performed the Meditation on a Point.
Finished with the Middle Pillar exercise.

LBRP was very strong. I had a particularly clear visualization
of Uriel holding sheaves of wheat. Had trouble concentrating
during the point meditation. Finished strong with the Middle
Pillar but got a cramp in my foot from standing too long.
May try to sit after the LBRP next time.

Ended my practice at 8:00 pm.

THE HEALTH OF THE BODY

One of the great disconnects in Western magic and Western spirituality in general is
this: while focus on the health of the mind, soul, and psyche are paramount, the health
of the body receives far less attention. This is an imbalance that needs to be acknowledged and remedied. In recent times, the magical community has addressed this problem and our students are encouraged to do likewise.

One option is to incorporate yoga and its well-known benefits into your overall
spiritual practice. Israel Regardie often suggested that students take up a series of five
Tibetan exercises for rejuvenation that were published in a book by Peter Kelder and
reprinted in Donald Michael Kraig's *Modern Magic*. For those who prefer a more Western path, the physical fitness regime created by Joseph Pilates, which bears his name, is
a great alternative, as is any reasonable fitness program that you are safely able to take
up. Whichever direction you choose will help correct this Western deficiency and bring
a more holistic approach to your magical practice.

Review Questions

1. Who were the three founding members of the Golden Dawn in London?

2. What year was the Order founded?

3. What is the name of the document that contained the outlines of the Order's rituals?

4. What year did the Order split into different factions?

5. What were the names of the Golden Dawn's two main offshoot orders?

6. Define magic.

7. What are the Four Laws of Magic?

8. What is the Hebrew word for angel? What does it mean?

9. Name one of the dangers to watch out for in magic.

10. What is meditation?

11. How often do you meditate?

12. What is your experience of the Meditation on the Point? The Visualization exercise on the Line? The Triangle?

13. What is a magical motto?

14. Have you chosen a magical motto? What is it and what does it mean to you?

15. What is vibration?

16. What is your experience of the Vibration exercise of IAO? Of YHVH?

17. Do you keep a magical journal? Why or why not?

18. Do you incorporate a regime of physical fitness into your practice? Why or why not?

19. Have you determined your own Pre-Ritual Meditation Practice?

20. Why do you wish to practice Golden Dawn magic?

chapter 2

LEARNING THE LANGUAGE OF MAGIC

Before we can proceed to some of the more practical techniques of Golden Dawn magic, it is essential to examine the primary symbol-systems composing the road map magicians use to chart and navigate the magical Universe. The material in this chapter includes the "ABCs" of our tradition: the basic language, symbols, and correspondences that magicians turn to time and time again in their practice. This study work is the foundation of the Hermetic Arts. Within the Order setting, much of this material is taught in the form of grade work handed out in stages to beginning students to aid their theoretical studies. This is in keeping with the paradigm of a school, because the Golden Dawn is a school of the Mysteries. Memorization of this "magical language" is a must. Just as an engineer cannot be expected to apply his craft without first having committed certain rudiments of his trade to memory, so too the magician cannot expect to perform magic effectively without understanding the fundamentals of magic. While memorizing this information might seem difficult at first, constant use of this material guarantees that it will become second nature to the magician. These symbols and correspondences are deeply embedded with profound knowledge and since they reoccur regularly throughout various stages of the magician's work, they should receive frequent meditation and reflection.

MONAD, DYAD, TRIAD, TETRAD

Chapter 1 included meditations and exercises on the point, the line, the Triangle, and the square. Beyond the practical application of these meditations, they were designed to introduce the aspirant to the important concepts of monad, dyad, triad, and tetrad.

The Monad

A Greek term for "unit," monad refers to the central spark of pure divinity at the heart of every living being. It is the Divine Being as well as the Transcendent Deity. Numerous other terms are used to describe this: the Source of All; Ultimate Divinity; Universal Unity, God, the Light Divine, Divine Spirit, Ain Soph, and a host of other titles.

The Dyad

A Greek term for "two," or "otherness." The ancient Greek philosopher Pythagoras taught that the monad was Spirit and the dyad was matter. It is the portal between the One and the many. Inherent to the idea of the dyad is the principle of polarity, which is the state of having two opposite or contradictory tendencies or aspects. The dyad is often represented by a pair of polar opposites: day and night, male and female, work and rest, black and white, etc.

The Triad

The triad, or group of three, represents the first born number, resulting from the natural progression of its "parental" numbers, the monad and the dyad. Three is the only number that is equal to the sum of the previous numbers. It is also the only number whose sum equals the multiplied product of the first three numbers ($1+2+3 = 1 \times 2 \times 3$). Because of its simplicity, the Triangle is the strongest shape in architecture, while the triad is a symbol of harmony reflected in all divine trinities of father, mother, and child.

The Tetrad

The tetrad indicates a group of four, which is the first number by the addition and multiplication of equals ($2+2 = 2 \times 2$). As the first even number produced after the triad, four is considered a feminine number that rounds out the divine family: father, mother, son, and daughter. It is also a number of completion and stability: there are four seasons, four cardinal directions, and four elements.

The tetrad figures prominently in the symbol of the *tetractys* (Figure 4), a Triangle containing ten points distributed into four rows, which points to an esoteric relationship between the numbers four and ten.

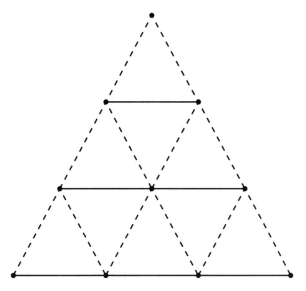

Figure 4: The Tetractys

THE ELEMENTS

One of the most basic divisions of knowledge in magic concerns the four elements: Fire Water, Air, and Earth. It has been a part of Western esoteric practice since the time of the ancient Greeks. Like the dyad of the polarities, the fourfold paradigm is a theme that occurs throughout every area of magic.

The four elements are not simply the physical substances of the same names but rather divisions of nature. They are the basic categories of existence and action—the building blocks of everything in the Universe. Everything contains one or more of these archetypal energies.

In magic, elemental energies are used to affect the physical and etheric levels as well as some of the denser aspects of the astral realm.

Fire

The qualities of Fire are heat and dryness. Fire symbolizes action, movement, vitality, spontaneity, quickness, the beginning, initializing force, and transformation. Fire rules electricity, combustion, radioactivity, leadership, personal power, activity, and physical energy. The direction or cardinal point assigned to Fire is south. The Hebrew name of this element is *Ash*.

Water

Water's qualities are cold and moisture. Water represents receptiveness, responsiveness, creativity, fluidity, fertility, and reproduction. Water governs pleasure, social interactions, emotions, and all liquid physical matter. The direction attributed to Water is west. Its Hebrew name is *Mem*.

Air

Air has the qualities of heat and moisture. Air is the element of speed, communication, expression, mediation, connection, reconciliation, adaptation, abstraction, changeability, and conflict. Air rules the intellect, the weather, illness, suffering, and all gaseous physical matter. The direction corresponding to Air is east. In Hebrew it is called *Ruach*.

Earth

Earth's qualities are cold and dryness. Earth symbolizes stability, solidity, materiality, manifestation, endurance, and productivity. Earth governs agriculture, money, business, employment, and all solid physical matter. North is the direction assigned to Earth. This element is called *Aretz* in Hebrew.

In terms of polarity, Fire and Air are considered masculine, while Water and Earth are seen as feminine. In terms of the human psyche, Fire expresses willpower; Water is emotion, intuition, and the subconscious mind; Air is the intellect and the rational mind; and Earth is sensory perception.

The four elements are symbolized by a series of Triangles (Figure 5).

Figure 5: The Elemental Triangles

Spirit

The four elements are crowned and completed by a fifth—Spirit, which is also known as the quintessence or "fifth essence." The word "spirit" comes from the Latin word *Spiritus,* meaning "breath." Spirit symbolizes the Deity, the Infinite, and the Ever-Present. It is the element of ultimate transcendence and divine essence.

In terms of polarity, Spirit is androgynous. The "direction" assigned to Spirit is the center although it permeates everything. In terms of the human psyche, Spirit represents higher awareness. Its Hebrew name is *Eth*. It is related to the *Pentagrammaton*, or "Five-Lettered Name," discussed later.

The symbols for Spirit include a plain circle and the eight-spoked Spirit Wheel (Figure 6).

Figure 6: The Spirit Wheel

FLASHING COLORS

Color is extremely important in the higher grades of the Golden Dawn system because it is through the proper application of color, as well as through sounds and symbols ("names and images"), that the magician is able to forge a magical link with the divine intelligences.

In addition to creating an elaborate system of color scales, the GD utilized what it called "Flashing Colors." These are essentially the same as complementary colors used by artists. Complementary colors are two colors that lie directly opposite each other on a standard artists' color wheel. Flashing Colors placed next to each other produce an optical "pulsing" effect that is helpful to the magician's practice.

Each of the five elements has its own dyad of hues: a basic color as well as a Flashing Color that is its polar opposite (Table 1).

Table 1: Flashing Colors of the Five Elements

Element	Basic Color (Ground)	Flashing Color (Charge)
Spirit	White	Black
Fire	Red	Green
Water	Blue	Orange
Air	Yellow	Violet
Earth	Black	White

The basic color can be described as the "ground" color associated with a particular magical force. It is often used as the background color on a talisman. The Flashing Color can be called the "charge" color, or the hue used to paint the magical sigil (such as the Fire symbol) on a talisman that has red as its basic color.

The twelve colors on a standard artists' color wheel are listed in Table 2 along with their complementary "flashing" color.

Table 2: Flashing Colors of an Artist's Color Wheel

Basic Color (Ground)	Flashing Color (Charge)
Red	Green
Red-orange	Blue-green
Orange	Blue
Yellow-orange	Blue-violet
Yellow	Violet
Yellow-green	Red-violet
Green	Red
Blue-green	Red-orange
Blue	Orange
Blue-violet	Yellow-orange
Violet	Yellow
Red-violet	Yellow-green

THE QABALAH

While astrology and its related imagery can be defined as the primary symbol-system of the Golden Dawn, the Hermetic Qabalah can be described as the heart and soul of Golden Dawn magical philosophy.

Qabalah is a Hebrew word that means "tradition." It is derived from the root word *qibel* meaning "to receive" or "that which is received." This refers to the ancient custom of handing down esoteric teachings by oral transmission.

The Qabalah is a multifaceted body of occult principles and an essential part of Western Esoteric Tradition. It is a complete spiritual ecosystem of esoteric wisdom that has been called a "filing cabinet" of occult knowledge and "the yoga of the West." This mystical metasystem is used to organize every other existing religious tradition and spiritual path in a manner that reveals the interconnectedness between all of them.

While it contains obvious influences from ancient Greek philosophy, the origins of the Qabalah are found in ancient Hebrew mystical lore. The bulk of the system emerged from the teachings of medieval Jewish occultists in Europe from the third to the sixteenth centuries. Qabalah was then taken up by Christian Hermeticists from the sixteenth to the eighteenth centuries. But it was during the Occult Revival of the late nineteenth century that the Hermetic *Qabalah* of the Western Magical Tradition, as opposed to the more traditional Jewish *Kabbalah*, was developed. The Golden Dawn had a major role in disseminating this Hermeticized Qabalah along with its most notable symbol, the Tree of Life.

For magicians, the Qabalah provides the perfect blueprint for every magical association, concept, and function. Briefly stated, the Qabalah is a model or system of meta-knowledge pertaining to:

- God, the Supreme Being, or Divine Spirit—its nature and attributes

- The cosmology or basic structure of the Universe

- The cosmogony or "origin story" of the Universe

- The *ultimate* reality represented by the Greater Universe or Macrocosm

- The *human* reality represented by the Lesser Universe or Microcosm

- The relationship that exists between the Macrocosm and the Microcosm (between Divinity and humanity)

- The *involution* of Spirit into matter, and the *evolution* of matter back into Spirit (its source)

- The origin and structure of the various unseen Spirit realms

- The nature and function of angels and other Spirits

- The nature and evolution of the human soul

- The transcendental symbolism of numbers and other correspondences

- The equilibrium of opposites

- A system of practical magic and mysticism

It would be a mistake to assume that the Qabalah is only relevant to the monotheistic faiths. This system is deeply entwined with the Western Esoteric Tradition; it is not the exclusive property of any single religion. Its framework and philosophic concepts belong to all students of the mysteries, no matter what their faith. Qabalistic principles are basic and universal. Today's Qabalah is a vibrant, living, philosophy that includes the birth of the Cosmos, the eternal mind of God, and the spiritual development of humankind. Study of the mystical Qabalah is a discipline not a doctrine—it is pragmatic and experiential.

Simply stated, the Qabalah is a structured system that guides the student toward a mystical understanding of the Divine Universe and how to effectively interact with it.

The Qabalah is usually classified under four heads that sometimes overlap:

- **The Dogmatic Qabalah**—the study of ancient Hebrew literature such as the Torah and medieval Qabalistic texts.

- **The Practical Qabalah**—involves the construction of talismans and other methods of ceremonial magic.

- **The Literal Qabalah**—looks at gematria or the relationship between numbers and the letters of the Hebrew alphabet. It uncovers hidden meanings of Hebrew words and names.

- **The Unwritten Qabalah**—refers to the knowledge of the primary symbol of the Tree of Life.

Benefits of the Qabalah

As the Hermetic student begins to contemplate and experience the energies of the Tree of Life, he or she will find that they develop into genuine forces that become animated within the psyche. These newly awakened forces will initiate a process of reorganization in the mind of the student, gathering up disjointed elements of the divine powers that lie dormant in the average person. They begin to structure themselves in accordance with the Tree of Life, permitting the student to tap into a previously unknown source of divine inspiration that is kept alive and energized through meditation and active ritual work.

The Qabalah has often been called the "Ladder of Lights" because it depicts cosmic generation, which is the descent of the Divine into the physical. But it also defines how the individual may employ this ladder for spiritual ascent by purifying both body and mind through ceremony, contemplation, and prayer, until at length one achieves that pristine state of consciousness that is necessary to attain union with the Higher Self.

THE HEBREW ALPHABET

One of the first things that a Golden Dawn student learns is the Hebrew alphabet, the primary symbolic language of Western magic. Many students feel intimidated by the prospect of having to commit this to memory and question the necessity for it. The importance is this: The letters of the Hebrew alphabet are Sacred symbols. Each letter has a literal meaning, an esoteric meaning, a numeral value, a color, a sound, and a host of other connected meanings. Hebrew is the language of the Qabalah, its associated symbols, levels, godnames, angel-names, talismanic seals, and more. Beginners should not get discouraged over this—the twenty-two letters of the Hebrew alphabet are studied throughout the GD system; they will quickly become familiar through constant use. Golden Dawn magicians are not expected to be able to read a newspaper in Tel Aviv, but they should be able to read and write divine and angelic names in Hebrew on a talisman.

Table 3 lists basic information on the Hebrew letters that the student should commit to memory. For example, the first letter is named Aleph, which means "ox." It is pronounced by Hermetic magicians as "a" as in "father" and has the numerical value of 1. The first column in the table shows the proper form of the letter while the second column shows a simplified version that can be used for a quick, legible rendition of the letter using a pen or pencil.

Five of the letters (Kaph, Mem, Nun, Peh, and Tzaddi) have a final form, which means they have a different shape and numeral value when these letters come at the end of a word.

Table 3: The Hebrew Alphabet

Letter	Simplified	Name	Meaning	Sound	Value	Final
א	א	Aleph	Ox	A (ah)	1	
ב	ב	Beth	House	B	2	
ג	ג	Gimel	Camel	G, Gh	3	
ד	ד	Daleth	Door	D, Dh	4	
ה	ה	Heh	Window	H	5	
ו	ו	Vav	Pin, nail, hook	O, U, V	6	
ז	ז	Zayin	Sword, armor	Z	7	
ח	ח	Cheth	Fence, enclosure	Ch	8	
ט	ט	Teth	Serpent	T	9	
י	י	Yod	Hand	I, Y	10	
כ	כ	Kaph	Fist, palm of the hand	K, Kh	20	ך 500
ל	ל	Lamed	Oxgoad	L	30	
מ	מ	Mem	Water	M	40	ם 600
נ	נ	Nun	Fish	N	50	ן 700
ס	ס	Samekh	Prop, support	S	60	

Letter	Simplified	Name	Meaning	Sound	Value	Final
ע	ע	Ayin	Eye	Aa	70	
פ	פ	Peh	Mouth	P, Ph	80	ף 800
צ	צ	Tzaddi	Fishhook	Tz	90	ץ 900
ק	ק	Qoph	Ear, back of the head	Q	100	
ר	ר	Resh	Head	R	200	
ש	ש	Shin	Tooth	S, Sh	300	
ת	ת	Tau	Cross	T, Th	400	

The letters of the Hebrew alphabet are further divided into three groups: the three *Mother Letters,* the seven *Double Letters,* and the twelve *Simple Letters.* The three Mothers Letters are Aleph, Mem, and Shin. They represent the most ancient of the elements: Air, Water, and Fire. (Earth is assigned to the letter Tau, one of the Double Letters. Both Fire and Spirit are assigned the letter Shin.) According to Qabalistic lore, everything in the manifest Universe sprang from the three Mother Letters.

The seven Double Letters and the twelve Simple Letters are attributed to the seven planets and the twelve signs of the zodiac, respectively.

Finally, Hebrew words are written from right to left. For example, we would transliterate the word "Qabalah" into its Latin-letter equivalents as QBLH, which in Hebrew would be composed of the letters *Qoph, Beth, Lamed,* and *Heh,* written as קבלה.

GEMATRIA

The method of assigning numbers to each of the Hebrew letters is known as *gematria.* The ancient Hebrews did not have a separate set of figures to describe numbers. Instead, they used the letters of their alphabet. Gematria developed as a process of ascribing meaning to numbers and determining the meanings of words from the numerical value of their letters. Words converted into numbers can be compared to the values of other words to acquire a new perspective on the original meaning. Words that share the same numerical value are said to have a significant relationship to one another.

For example, the Hebrew name *Ruach Elohim* (the Spirit of God/Gods) in Hebrew has a numeral value of 300 (Ruach = Resh: 200, Vav: 6, Cheth: 8 = 214, Elohim = Aleph: 1, Lamed: 30, Heh: 5, Yod: 10, Mem: 40 = 86). Three hundred is the same as the value of the Hebrew letter Shin, which incidentally is the symbol of the Ruach Elohim.

In another case, the Hebrew word *achad,* which means "one" or "unity," has the numeral value of 13, the same value as the word *ahevah,* "love." Therefore, a relationship exists between these Hebrew words.

Readers may find numerous cases of sublime names sharing numerical values with low and demonic ones. The student is advised to consider this as a further example of the truth "As above, so below." Even the highest heavens have their equivalents in the lowly abode of shells.

Aiq Beker

One important tool used in gematria for the conversion of letters into numbers is the method known as *Aiq Beker,* also called the Qabalah of Nine Chambers (Figure 7). This diagram shows three rows and three columns of numbers grouped together according to similarity. The name Aiq Beker comes from reading the Hebrew letters in the first two chambers from 1 to 200: Aleph, Yod, Qoph, and Beth, Kaph, Resh. Using this chart, magicians can reduce the numbers of the Hebrew letters to their lowest common denominators so that they can be used to create sigils on magical squares. This process is described in chapter 10.

300	30	3	200	20	2	100	10	1
ש	ל	ג	ר	כ	ב	ק	י	א
600	60	6	500	50	5	400	40	4
ם	ס	ו	ך	נ	ה	ת	מ	ד
900	90	9	800	80	8	700	70	7
ץ	צ	ט	ף	פ	ח	ן	ע	ז

Figure 7: Aiq Beker

Another way of using Aiq Beker is to take one of the three letters in any given section of the Aiq Beker diagram and exchange it for one of the other two letters in that section. Thus in the first box, the letter Qoph could be substituted for either the letter Aleph or the letter Yod. The result could be used as a type of code or cypher.

Notariqon

This technique derives its name from the Latin word for "shorthand writer," *notarius*. It is a method for finding acronyms.

One form of notariqon is expansive, meaning that every letter in a single word is used to create the first initial of another word in a sentence. Take the word *Berashith*, the first word in Genesis, for example. Every letter of this word can be made an abbreviation of another word, yielding the sentence *Berashith Rahi Elohim Sheyequebelo Israel Torah*, which means "In the Beginning God(s) saw that Israel would accept the law."

The second form of notariqon is contractive, the complete reversal of the first. In this case, the first letter of each word in a sentence is taken to create a single word that is the synthesis of the entire sentence. One example of this is a word found in the Lesser Ritual of the Pentagram, AGLA. The letters of this word are taken from the sentence *Atah Gibor Le-Olahm Adonai*, which means "Thou art great forever, my Lord." Another example is the word "ARARITA," constructed from the sentence *Achad Rosh Achdotho Rosh Ichudo Temurahzo Achad*, meaning "One is his beginning, One is his individuality, his permutation is One."

Another example is the commonly used word AMEN, written in Hebrew as Aleph, Mem, Nun, which stands for the phrase *Adonai Melekh Na'amon* or "Lord, Faithful King."

Notariqons may also be formed using letters other than the initial ones, such as the final or middle letters.

THE TREE OF LIFE

The diagram of the Tree of Life (Figure 8) is essential to one's understanding of the Hermetic Qabalah. According to tradition, the Universe emanated from the Three Veils of Negative Existence or stages of abstract "nothingness": *Ain* ("Nothing"), *Ain Soph* ("Limitless"), and *Ain Soph Aur* ("Limitless Light"). The Unknowable Infinite, called God by some and Ain Soph by the Qabalists, began to manifest its energy into the Universe through ten stages, or "emanations," known as the *Sephiroth*, which were reservoirs or containers of divine energy. A single emanation is called a *Sephirah*. Each successive Sephirah became denser than the previous one, acquiring substance as energy

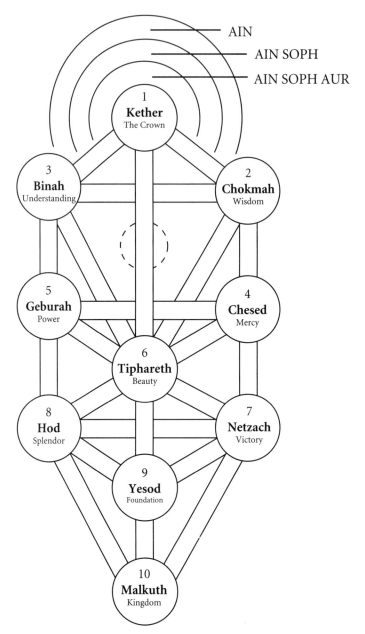

Figure 8: The Tree of Life

descended into the various stages of manifestation. Eventually the energies solidified at the tenth and final level of emanation, resulting in the physical Universe as we know it.

The ten Sephiroth are placed on the diagram of the Tree of Life in perfect juxtaposition so that each Sephirah counterbalances its polar opposite. Why ten? Because ten is a perfect number that includes every digit without repetition—it contains the total essence of all numbers. These ten Sephiroth, along with the twenty-two paths that connect them, called *Navitoth*, compose what is known as the Thirty-Two Paths of Wisdom.

THE SEPHIROTH

The Sephiroth are represented on the Tree of Life as ten circles or spheres. Each of these "Sacred vessels" is a power, energy, or instrument of the Eternal, although not separated from the Eternal like human instruments are. These holy emanations express abstract ideals of God; divine essences organized into an archetypal blueprint for everything in the Universe and the cosmology of Creation. The energetic patterns implied on the Tree underscore the whole of existence, and so the attributes of the Sephiroth may be found in any branch of knowledge. Although characteristic of the Divine, the Sephiroth also describe the human soul and humanity's experience of and relationship with Deity.

Each Sephirah issued forth in succession as if "one candle were lit from another without the emanator being diminished in any way" and in a specific order. In this analogy, the original candle is not lessened in any respect, although it gives of its essence to the candles that follow. But unlike the candle, the Sephiroth are not seen as being separated from the source. They are one with Deity yet they are also distinct from one another, and therefore they are more easily comprehended by human beings who wish to approach the Divine through meditation. The ten emanations are the diverse expressions and mind-states of a single Divine Unity as well as containers of the divine essence. Each Sephirah represents one specific aspect of god-energy or a particular level of consciousness, while the paths that connect them are the conduits from one form of god-energy to another, as well as the routes that we can take to arrive at these different levels.

The ten Sephiroth, along with their names, meanings, and qualities are:

1. **Kether** (כתר)—"the Crown." Oneness, unity.

2. **Chokmah** (חכמה)—"Wisdom." Force, expansion.

3. **Binah** (בינה)—"Understanding." Form, contraction.

4. Chesed (חסד)—"Mercy." Construction.

5. Geburah (גבורה)—"Power." Might, severity.

6. Tiphareth (תפארת)—"Beauty." Balance, awareness.

7. Netzach (נצח)—"Victory." Emotion, desire.

8. Hod (הוד)—"Splendor." Intellect, reason.

9. Yesod (יסוד)—"Foundation." Astral blueprint, matrix.

10. Malkuth (מלכות)—"the Kingdom." Physical manifestation.

1. Kether

The first and highest Sephirah is Kether, "the Crown," so called because it is above all the other spheres. Sometimes called "the Ancient," Kether represents the Infinite as opposed to the finite. Kether is the point, the moment that the Universe as we know it was conceived, containing all that was, is, and will be. It is the place of first emanation and ultimate return. The Crown is the sphere of pure spiritual being: the point of Absolute Unity without division—ultimate peace and oneness. It is also the Sephirah of the *Primum Mobile* or "First Whirlings" (in Hebrew *Rashith ha-Gilgalim*) that represent the birth of the Universe.

2. Chokmah

From this unity emanate two principles, contrary in outward aspect, yet inseparable in essence. The second Sephirah is Chokmah, "Wisdom." If Kether can be described as a point, then Chokmah could be portrayed as a straight line: an extension of the point into space. It is considered male in an abstract sense, the archetypal "Divine Father" principle that is active, and expansive. Within Chokmah lies the first masculine expression as opposed to the androgynous Kether. Whereas Kether is the calm center point of the Universe, Chokmah is complete action and movement—the vital energizing element of existence. It is also the Sephirah of the zodiac (*Mazzaloth* in Hebrew).

3. Binah

The third Sephirah is Binah, "Understanding." Understanding is the ability to grasp the ideas that are intrinsic to Wisdom. This sphere is considered female in an abstract sense—passive and contractive (or formative). Receptivity is a feminine function and just as in the case of Chokmah's masculinity, we are referring to sexual functions in the most basic and unmanifested of concepts.

In mathematics any three points in three-dimensional space determine a plane. Therefore, Binah, the "Divine Mother" principle, is the great archetypal form-builder; it receives the overflow of the divine energy from Chokmah and organizes it for the first time under the concept of Form. It is also the Sephirah affiliated with the planet Saturn (*Shabbathai* in Hebrew).

Daath

Together, Kether, Chokmah, and Binah form what is called the *Supernal Triad*, a high state of divine consciousness that transcends human awareness. They are separated from the lower part of the Tree by a chasm known as the *abyss*, a boundary in levels of being wherein is the quasi-sephirah of Daath ("knowledge"), which is not a true Sephirah but rather a passageway across the Abyss.

The rest of the Sephiroth, seven in number, serve to build the world of matter. Like the preceding spheres they emanate in triads—two extreme forces often described in terms of masculine and feminine energies, bound together by a third that unites and harmonizes between them.

4. Chesed

The Fourth Sephirah is Chesed, or "Mercy." In mathematics four points that are not all on the same plane define a space. Therefore, Chesed is the first emanation of the physical world and contains the structural support of everything in the manifest Universe. It begins the process of realizing the abstract energies of the three previous spheres.

The patterns of the Tree of Life repeat themselves after the initial three spheres are formed; therefore, Chesed is the same type of force as Chokmah, but on a lower, denser level.

The energy of Chesed is often symbolized by beneficent sky deities and merciful Kings. This Sephirah is represented by the planet Jupiter (*Tzedek* in Hebrew).

5. Geburah

The natural order of the Universe depends upon the concept of opposites in balance, thus the benevolence, mercy, and form-building functions of Chesed are countered by the harsh, destructive actions of the Fifth Sephirah of Geburah, which is "Power." Often described as fiery, Geburah's other titles include "Judgment" and "Severity." Chesed expands, Geburah contracts. One gives life, the other takes it. Geburah places boundaries on the unrestricted expansion of Chesed. These forces cannot be separated, for the Cosmos could not exist if they were.

The energy of Geburah is commonly represented by warrior and martial deities, and is represented by the planet Mars (*Madim* in Hebrew).

6. Tiphareth

The fourth and fifth spheres are balanced by the sixth Sephirah, Tiphareth, or "Beauty," which is the expression of all that is harmonious. Lying at the very heart of the Tree, Tiphareth is in line with Kether and mirrors much of the pureness of the Crown above, but on a more tangible level. Through the union of Mercy and Justice, Beauty is obtained.

Because of its position, Tiphareth is seen as a connecting link between higher and lower states of consciousness, and as a result Golden Dawn magic places a great deal of focus here. It is a point of transition, reconciling "That Which Is Above" to "That Which Is Below." Tiphareth intercedes between these different levels of being.

The sixth Sephirah is considered an especially mystical sphere. Its energy is personified by redeemer, dying-and-resurrected, and savior deities. It is also the Sephirah represented by the luminary of Sol (*Shemesh* in Hebrew).

7. Netzach

The remaining Sephiroth can be better described by the effects they have on human consciousness than by polarities alone. The four lowest Sephiroth are representative of the Lower Self or personality.

The seventh, eighth, and ninth Sephiroth are dynamic; they represent Deity as the generative principle of all life, and of all things in the manifest Universe. The seventh Sephirah, Netzach, or "Victory," is a dynamic force that inspires us. It is a reflection of the fiery Geburah but at the level of the human personality, mediated by Tiphareth, the Fire becomes desire and devotion, instinct and emotion. Art, music, dance, and poetry are all expressions of this, as are love, hate, and the full range of human emotion.

The energy of Netzach is symbolized by deities of love and patrons of the arts, and this sphere is represented by the planet Venus (*Nogah* in Hebrew).

8. Hod

Balancing Netzach on the opposite side of the Tree is Hod, or "Splendor," the sphere of reason and intellect. This is the rational mind, which organizes and categorizes. All expressions of writing, language, communication, science, and magic are assigned to Hod, as are all magical names and words of power. Hod is a lower form of the energy found in Chesed, but mediated through Tiphareth.

Hod and Netzach cannot function properly one without the other. Intellect needs the balance of emotion to drive it, otherwise the words and science of Hod become cold labelings, dead and uninspired. Likewise, emotions need the discipline of intellect to stabilize them and keep their dynamic energy from being squandered.

The energy of Hod is commonly represented by deities of wisdom, magic, and communication. This Sephirah is represented by the planet Mercury (*Kokab* in Hebrew).

9. Yesod

The ninth Sephirah is Yesod, or "Foundation." The spiritual experience of Yesod is said to be the "Vision of the Machinery of the Universe." This sphere is the receptacle of influences from all of the preceding Sephiroth, which are then combined into a type of divine blueprint for everything in the Universe just prior to the act of creation. It is the astral matrix upon which the physical Universe is built. All events whether natural or manmade occur in the aethers of Yesod before they occur in the physical world. The ninth Sephirah is the pregnant final stage that precedes the full manifestation of form.

Yesod's energy is personified by deities of the sky, wind, and Air. It is also the Sephirah represented by the luminary of the Moon (*Levannah* in Hebrew).

10. Malkuth

The tenth and final Sephirah, Malkuth, is the "Kingdom"—the world of physical manifestation and the receptacle of all forces and energies passed down from the other nine Sephiroth. It receives the etheric framework of manifestation from Yesod then completes the building process by grounding the energy in matter. While the other Sephiroth are kinetic and mobile, Malkuth is the only sphere that has achieved stability and rest. This is the material Universe as we know it, complete with the planets, stars, and constellations.

The physical representation of Malkuth is the planet Earth, our own terra firma. It is the seat of all matter. Yet Malkuth is more than simply the ground beneath our feet, it is also the Sephirah in which all four elements are based.

Because Malkuth is a lower reflection of Kether, the Tenth Sephirah is seen as the completion of the Tree of Life in one sense, and the beginning of a new Tree in another.

The energy of Malkuth is often symbolized by chthonic deities of Earth, vegetation, and the Underworld. Therefore, it is represented by the planet Earth—the sphere of the elements also called the World of Foundations (*Olam Yesodoth* in Hebrew).

MAGICAL ATTRIBUTES OF THE SEPHIROTH

The powers of the Sephiroth can be used in magic to invoke the qualities, attributes, and areas of influence that they represent (Table 4).

Table 4: Magical Attributes of the Sephiroth

Sephirah	Attributes
Kether	Illumination, spirituality, peace, tranquility, completion, synthesis, Divine Light, Higher and Divine Genius
Chokmah	Initiative, stimulating energy, vitalizing force, Divine Wisdom, Paternal Wisdom
Binah	Secrets, strength through silence, understanding of sorrows and burdens, organization, structuring, containing, setting limits, faith, Maternal Understanding
Chesed	Financial gain, abundance, prosperity, justice, fairness, new opportunities, obedience to higher power, government, generosity, laughter, good outlook on life
Geburah	Energy, courage, fortitude, protection, change, getting rid of what is outmoded, cleansing, purifying, critical judgment, war and discord
Tiphareth	Devotion, illumination, mystic visions, harmony, balance, glory, healing, life and success, Christ consciousness, Higher Self
Netzach	Creativity, the arts, love and passion, social consciousness, idealism, sexuality, energy and understanding in relationships, unselfishness
Hod	Communication, learning, teaching, writing, magic, skill, dexterity, ability to "wheel and deal," truthfulness, ability to detect falsehood, journeying, commerce

Sephirah	Attributes
Yesod	Intuition, psychic abilities, dreams and visions, prophecies, mental health, independence, confidence, understanding of the cycles of change
Malkuth	Materialization, solidity, physical environment, completion, physical health, overcoming inertia, self-discovery, discrimination

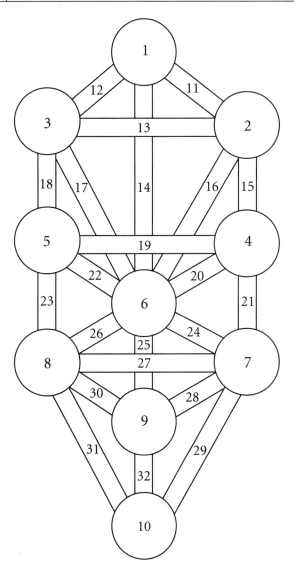

Figure 9: The Thirty-Two Paths of Wisdom on the Tree of Life

THE NAVITOTH

The ten Sephiroth are connected by the twenty-two Navitoth, or "paths," which are assigned to the twenty-two letters of the Hebrew alphabet. While the Sephiroth as a group are considered receptive (passive and feminine) vessels of god-energy, the paths are seen as projective (active and masculine) conduits of god-force. These twenty-two pathways are the forces and methods the magician uses to transition from one level of consciousness to the next.

Together, the ten Sephiroth and the twenty-two paths are known as the Thirty-Two Paths of Wisdom (Figure 9). After the Sephiroth, the numbering of the Navitoth runs from 11 to 32, beginning with the letter Aleph and ending with Tau.

THE SWORD AND THE SERPENT

Each Sephirah issues forth in rapid succession as if "one candle were lit from another without the emanator being diminished in any way" and in a specific order, often called the *Lightning Flash* or *Flaming Sword*. It is pictured as a jagged sword that is bent in such a way that its hilt starts in Kether and its tip ends in Malkuth.

The natural order of the twenty-two Navitoth is depicted as the Serpent of Wisdom, which touches every path leading from Malkuth back to Kether. This is the reflux current of energy that aspires after the Divine (Figure 10).

The Flaming Sword is the descending current of divine energy that facilitates the manifestation of the Universe. It is the Way of Involution or the descent of Spirit into matter. The Serpent of Wisdom, on the other hand, is the counterbalancing ascent of materialized energy. This is the Way of Evolution from matter back to its Divine Source.

THE PILLARS

One of the main principles of the Tree of Life is that of equilibrium. This idea is exemplified in the formation of the three pillars of the Tree created by the natural succession of the Sephiroth (Figure 11). The Left-Hand Pillar, also called the Pillar of Severity, consists of the spheres of Binah, Geburah, and Hod. The Right-Hand Pillar, known as the Pillar of Mercy, is composed of the spheres of Chokmah, Chesed, and Netzach. The central spheres of Kether, Tiphareth, Yesod, and Malkuth form the Middle Pillar, or the Pillar of Mildness.

Figure 10: The Sword and the Serpent

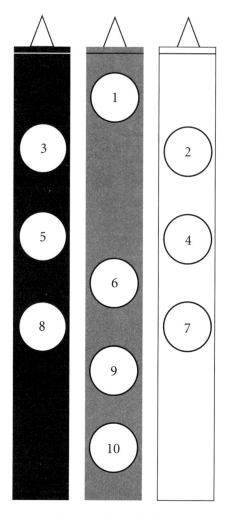

Figure 11: The Pillars

The Right-Hand or White Pillar is described as masculine, positive, and active. It is also known as the Pillar of Force. The Left-Hand or Black Pillar is feminine, negative, and passive. This Pillar is also called the Pillar of Form. The Black and White Pillars represent the two great contending forces in nature, and their descriptions are not meant to imply that one is good and the other evil, but rather that magnetic energy exists between these two universal polar opposites. The whole of the Cosmos depends upon the perfect balance of these polarities.

The Qabalah stresses a middle way between these two rival columns—the avoidance of one-sided extremes that can lead to spiritual and psychological imbalance. The extremes point out the need for harmonizing these opposites in a new and higher integrity. The Middle Pillar is symbolic of the "Way of Return," or the path of redemption as it were, back to the Source.

The Middle Pillar is therefore the Pillar of Mildness and the Pillar of Balanced Forces; equilibrating the other two columns. In a Golden Dawn Temple, only the Left and Right Pillars are physically symbolized by actual pillars. The Middle Pillar is represented by the aspirant standing between them.

THE FOUR WORLDS

The Qabalistic Universe is separated into four distinct worlds, planes, or levels. With the creation of the Sephiroth, these Four Worlds came into being; each realm evolved from the one before it, becoming more substantial and increasing in density as the levels descend from the spiritual to the physical. Each of these worlds envelopes its predecessor like the layers of an onion; the highest spiritual world at the center is progressively Veiled from the lowest world, which forms the outer layer.

Each Qabalistic World is symbolized by one of the letters of the Tetragrammaton, or "Four-Lettered Name" of God, and one of the four elements, reinforcing the concept of the fourfold model of the Universe :

1. Atziluth: The Divine or Archetypal World

2. Briah: The Archangelic or Creative World

3. Yetzirah: The Angelic or Formative World

4. Assiah: The Material World or World of Action

Atziluth

Atziluth is the first and highest world and is attributed to Yod, the first letter of Tetragrammaton. This World of pure Deity and primordial Fire gave birth to the other three worlds in a descending scale of light. Some traditions assign it to the three Sephiroth of Kether, Chokmah, and Binah, while others ascribe to it only the sphere of Kether.

Briah

Briah is the second World, the World of Creation. Heh, the second letter of Tetragrammaton and primordial Water are ascribed here. Water represents the fluid, inventive mind, thus Briah is described as the World of Pure Intellect. It is also known as the realm of the archangels. Some assign only Chokmah and Binah to this world, while others show it with the spheres of Chesed, Geburah, and Tiphareth.

Yetzirah

Yetzirah is the third World, the World of Formation and the realm of groups of angels. The third letter of Tetragrammaton, Vav, is assigned here, making Yetzirah the realm of primordial Air. This world is approximate to the astral plane and the etheric framework behind the physical Universe. While some ascribe only Netzach, Hod, and Yesod to this world, others place seven of the Sephiroth from Chesed to Yesod in the Yetziratic World.

Assiah

Assiah is the fourth and final World, the World of Materiality and Action. This world consists only of Malkuth and the final letter Heh of Tetragrammaton is attributed here. It is the world of primordial Earth, but in Assiah the four elements that make up the physical Universe exist both in sensation and in the hidden properties of matter and energy. This is the corporeal world where tangible activity can take place. It is the realm of substance and of humanity, yet it is also the world of "shells," made up of the denser portions of the three preceding worlds. Assiah is also the abode of demons, known to the Qabalists as the qlippoth.

THE QLIPPOTH

One of the consequences of the Universe coming into being was the creation of the *qlippoth*, which means "shells" or "husks." The qlippoth (singular form is *qlippah*) are chaotic and unbalanced forces, otherwise known as evil demons or fallen Spirits. Although there are qlippoth attributed to the twelve signs of the zodiac and the elements, the best known of these demons are the ten types of qlippoth that correspond to the ten Sephiroth on the Tree of Life. Whereas the Sephiroth symbolize progressive evolution and spiritual reunion with the Divine, the qlippoth represent de-evolution and spiritual disintegration. They are the unstable polar opposites of the harmonious Sephiroth and are said to form a second tree that is called evil. The qlippotic tree is usually represented as a mirror image of the Tree of Life, reflected from the base of Malkuth.

Formed when a prototypal but precarious version of the Tree of Life first came into being before shattering, the power of the qlippoth is based upon all forms of overindulgence, harmful excess, and imbalance in general. They are the destructive and unequilibrated aspects of the holy Sephiroth. Just as every Sephirah is said to have a virtue, there is a corresponding "vice" that is embodied in the associated qlippah. This point is driven home to the candidate in the Neophyte ceremony when the Hierophant explains that "Unbalanced power is the ebbing away of life. Unbalanced mercy is weakness and the fading out of the will. Unbalanced severity is cruelty and the barrenness of mind."

THE FOUR SCALES OF COLOR

The Golden Dawn created an elaborate system of color scales that represent the Thirty-Two Paths of Wisdom in each of the Four Qabalistic Worlds. These colors can be used to project or receive the energy of the various Sephiroth and their connecting paths. Like the Four Worlds, these color scales are each assigned one of the letters of the Tetragrammaton. The color scales and their attributes are:

1. **The King Scale:** Atziluth, Yod, Fire, masculine

2. **The Queen Scale:** Briah, Heh, Water, feminine

3. **The Prince Scale:** Yetzirah, Vav, Air, masculine

4. **The Princess Scale:** Assiah, Heh Final, Earth, feminine

The King and Prince Scales are both considered masculine and projective, while the Queen and Princess Scales are feminine and receptive. Of these, the King and Queen Scales are of primary importance to the construction of talismans and flashing Tablets. They are also paramount in the Golden Dawn's standard Tree of Life diagram referred to as the *Minutum Mundum,* or the "Small Universe," which depicts the colors of the receptive Sephiroth in the Queen Scale along with the colors of the projective Navitoth in the King Scale. A complete list of the Four Color Scales can be found in other books. Here we need only consider the King and Queen Scale colors of the Sephiroth (Table 5).

Table 5: Colors of the Sephiroth

Sephirah	King Scale Color (Projective)	Queen Scale Color (Receptive)
1. Kether	Brilliance	White
2. Chokmah	Soft Blue	Gray
3. Binah	Deep Red-Violet	Black
4. Chesed	Deep Violet	Blue
5. Geburah	Orange	Red
6. Tiphareth	Rose Pink	Yellow
7. Netzach	Yellow-Orange	Green
8. Hod	Violet	Orange
9. Yesod	Blue-Violet	Violet
10. Malkuth	Yellow	Citrine, Olive, Russet, and Black

When considering Daath, which is not a true Sephirah, the King Scale color is lavender and the Queen Scale color is gray-white.

King Scale colors can be used to *project* Sephirotic energy outward, such as when sending healing energy to another person. The colors of the Queen Scale are used whenever you want to *receive* these energies.

GODNAMES AND SPIRITUAL HIERARCHIES

Each of the Sephiroth has various divine names (known as the spiritual hierarchies) assigned to them. This categorizing of divine, archangelic, and angelic names defines different levels of Being under the Four Qabalistic Worlds.

Godnames are potent divine names or "words of power" used to invoke the highest aspects of Deity, especially those holy names assigned to the ten Sephiroth of the Tree of Life. Many of these names are presented in the Hebrew Scriptures as the various Sacred names of God. They are often referred to in the Golden Dawn as the *divine names* and represent the supreme expressions of the Sephiroth. Under the scheme of the Four Qabalistic Worlds, divine names are attributed to the archetypal world of Atziluth.

The godnames of the ten Sephiroth are listed in Table 6.

Table 6: Godnames of the Sephiroth

Sephirah	Godname	Meaning
Kether	Eheieh	I am
Chokmah	Yah	Lord
Binah	YHVH Elohim	The Lord God
Chesed	El	God
Geburah	Elohim Gebur	God of Power
Tiphareth	YHVH Eloah Ve-Daath	Lord God of Knowledge
Netzach	YHVH Tzabaoth	Lord of Armies
Hod	Elohim Tzabaoth	God of Armies
Yesod	Shaddai El Chai	Almighty Living God
Malkuth	Adonai Ha-Aretz	Lord of Earth

These godnames are vibrated in various Golden Dawn rituals such as the Middle Pillar exercise given later in this chapter.

ARCHANGELS AND ANGELS OF THE SEPHIROTH

Next in the hierarchy are the archangels, which correspond to the Creative World of Briah (Table 7). Archangels organize and direct the forces intrinsic to their respective Sephirah into action. Forces marshaled include the groups of angels, often called angelic hosts, who are responsible for implementing the actual mechanics or workings of a Sephirah. These angelic armies fall under the Formative World of Yetzirah.

Table 7: Archangels and Angels of the Sephiroth

Sephirah	Archangel	Meaning	Angelic Host	Meaning
Kether	Metatron (Greek)	Next After the Throne	Chayoth Ha-Qadesh	Holy Living Creatures
Chokmah	Raziel	Herald of God	Ophanim	The Wheels
Binah	Tzaphqiel	Beholder of God	Erelim	The Thrones
Chesed	Tzadqiel	Righteousness of God	Chashmalim	Shining Ones
Geburah	Khamael	Severity of God	Seraphim	Flaming Ones
Tiphareth	Raphael	Healer of God	Melakim	The Kings

Table 7: Archangels and Angels of the Sephiroth

Sephirah	Archangel	Meaning	Angelic Host	Meaning
Netzach	Haniel	Grace of God	Elohim	The Gods
Hod	Michael	Perfect of God	Beni Elohim	Children of the Gods
Yesod	Gabriel	Strength of God	Kerubim	Strong Ones
Malkuth	Sandalphon (Greek)	Fellow Sibling	Ashim	Souls of Fire

These divisions can be likened to an army; at the top is the Commander-in-Chief, who holds a divine (Atziluth) title. Under him is a general known as an archangel (Briah) who commands various legions. These legions are made up of numerous foot soldiers known as angels (Yetzirah). In Golden Dawn magic, the Highest is always petitioned first and the rest of the hierarchy follows in turn.

The best way to learn this material is to make several copies of a blank Tree of Life diagram. Then write down the divine and angelic names in their proper order on the spheres representing the Sephiroth. Do this several times until you have committed it to memory.

DIVINE NAMES AND OFTEN-USED WORDS OF POWER

Hermetic magicians may pronounce Hebrew divine names in a slightly different manner than a Jewish rabbi would. While Hebrew has no letters that are officially vowels, some letters such as Aleph, Yod, and Vav are considered vowel stand-ins or vowel approximates. For Hermetic magicians intoning Hebrew names and words of power in ritual, "a" usually sounds like "ah" as in father; "e" sounds like "ay" as in "may"; "i" sounds like "ee" as in "sweet"; "o" sounds like "oh" as in "aloha"; and "u" is pronounced "oo" as in "cool."

For Enochian words and names, the rules are different because many words are composed solely of consonants—no vowels. The Golden Dawn developed two ways to approximate vowels by adding the vowel sounds of the consonant's name. The first method uses the sound of the name of the letter in English, where "m" is pronounced "em and "r" is pronounced "ar." The second method uses the sound of the name of the letter in Hebrew, where "m" is pronounced "meh" as in Mem and "r" is pronounced "reh" as in Resh.

The list below provides the meanings and pronunciations of certain Hebrew, Greek, and Enochian words and divine names commonly used in Golden Dawn ritual, as well as rituals and exercises presented in this book.

Adonai: (Ah-doh-nye—the last syllable rhymes with "high") Hebrew—"Lord."

Adonai ha-Aretz: (Ah-doh-nye Hah-Ah-retz) Hebrew—"Lord of the earth." The divine name of Malkuth.

AGLA: (Ah-gah-lah) Hebrew notariqon or acronym for *Atah Gibor Le-Olahm Adonai*, which means "Thou art great forever, my Lord."

ARARITA: (Ah-rah-ree-tah) Hebrew notariqon or acronym—*Achad Rosh Achdotho Rosh Ichudo Temurahzo Achad*—"One Is His Beginning; One Is His Individuality; His Permutation Is One."

Atah: (Ah-tah) Hebrew—"Thou art."

Bitom: (Bay-ee-toh-em) Enochian name for the Spirit of Fire.

Eheieh: (Eh-hey-yay) Hebrew—"I am."

El (or Al): Hebrew—"God." Divine name of Chesed.

Elohim: (El-oh-heem) Hebrew—"God" as well as "Gods."

Elohim Gibor: (El-oh-heem Gee-boor) Hebrew—"God of Power." Divine name of Geburah.

Elohim Tzabaoth: (El-oh-heem Tzah-Bah-oth) Hebrew—"God of Armies." Divine name of Hod.

Emor Dial Hectega: (Ee-mor Dee-ahl Heck-tay-gah) Enochian—The Three Great Secret Names of God born upon the Banners of the North.

Empeh Arsel Gaiol: (Em-pay Ar-sell Gah-ee-ohl) Enochian—The Three Great Secret Names of God born upon the Banners of the West.

Exarp: (Ex-ar-pay) Enochian name for the Spirit of Air.

Hcoma: (Hay-koh-mah) Enochian name for the Spirit of Water.

Hekas, Hekas, Este, Bebeloi: (Hay-kahs, hay-kahs, es-stay bee-beh-loy!) Greek—Traditional proclamation that a ritual is about to start.

HRU: (Her-roo) Said to be the angel of the tarot. Its source may be the Egyptian word *hru* meaning "day." Since the Order's documents sometimes list this name as H.R.U., it may also be based on an unknown notariqon.

IAO: (Ee-ah-oh) Supreme Deity of the Gnostics. Similar to YHVH.

I.N.R.I.: (letters pronounced separately) Latin initials with many meanings. (See the Analysis of the Key Word, chapter 8.)

Khabs Am Pekht: (Khobs ahm Peckt) Egyptian—"Light in Extension."

Konx Om Pax: (Kohnx ohm Pahx) Greek—"Light in Extension."

Le-Olahm, Amen: (lay-oh-lahm ah-men) Hebrew—"Forever, unto the ages."

LVX: (letters pronounced separately, pronounced together as "lukes") Latin— "Light."

Malkuth: (Mahl-kooth) Hebrew—"The Kingdom."

Nanta: (En-ah-en-tah) Enochian name for the Spirit of Earth.

Oip Teaa Pedoce: (Oh-ee-pay Tay-ah-ah Pay-doh-kay) Enochian—The Three Great Secret Names of God born upon the Banners of the South.

Oro Ibah Aozpi: (Or-oh Ee-bah-hay Ah-oh-zohd-pee) Enochian—The Three Great Secret Names of God born upon the Banners of the East.

Ruach: (Roo-ah'ch). Hebrew for "breath" as well as "spirit."

Ruach Elohim: (Roo-ah'ch El-oh-heem). Hebrew for "Spirit of God."

Shaddai El Chai: (Shah-dye El Chai) "Almighty Living God." Divine name of Yesod.

Ve-Gedulah: (v'ge-doo-lah) Hebrew—"and the glory."

Ve-Geburah: (v'ge-boo-rah) also (v'ge-voo-rah) Hebrew—"and the power."

Yah: (Yah) Hebrew—"Lord." Divine name of Chokmah.

Yeheshuah: (Yeh-hay-shoo-ah) Hebrew—The Pentagrammaton or Five-Lettered Name of God. Transliterated from Hebrew as YHShVH.

Yehovashah: (Yeh-ho-vah-shah) Hebrew—A variation of the Pentagrammaton. Transliterated from Hebrew as YHVShH.

YHVH: (Yod-heh-vav-heh) Hebrew—the Tetragrammaton or Four-Lettered Name of God. It may be derived from an ancient form of the Hebrew verb "to be." It has similarities to the Roman Jove and the Gnostic IAO.

YHVH Eloah Ve-Daath: (Yod-heh-vav-heh El-oh-ah V'-Dah-aath) Hebrew—"Lord
God of Knowledge." Divine Name of Tiphareth.

YHVH Elohim: (Yod-heh-vav-heh El-oh-heem) Hebrew—"The Lord God." Divine
Name of Binah, also used for Daath.

YHVH Tzabaoth: (Yod-heh-vav-heh Tzah-bah-oth) Hebrew—"Lord of Armies."
Divine Name of Netzach.

ESOTERIC ASTROLOGY

The study of the stars is one of the oldest known sciences. Golden Dawn magicians
study two branches of astrology—exoteric and esoteric. The first involves delineating
and interpreting a horoscope and the mathematics involved with it. For instructions on
this, readers should consult our book *Self-Initiation into the Golden Dawn Tradition*.

Esoteric astrology deals with the mysteries of the Universe itself—the spiritual,
moral, intellectual, and physical dynamics of the Cosmos. Esoteric astrology reveals the
universal pattern of living and the means by which human beings can align themselves
with the blueprint of the Divine. It is a system for understanding Celestial energies and
a method for viewing the Universe as a symmetrical whole. This is also the system that
magicians utilize in virtually all types of magical practice. Next to the teachings of the
Qabalah, astrological correspondences are the most prevalent form of esoteric knowledge used in the Golden Dawn.

THE PLANETS

Planet, or "wandering star," developed as a term to describe any Celestial body visible
from the earth that appeared to move or "wander" in a regular orbit against the back-
drop of stars in the night sky. The ancients recognized seven planets, including the lumi-
naries of the Sun and the Moon (Sol and Luna). Planetary energies are used to affect the
astral realm, the subtler planes above it, and the physical realm below it. The planets also
represent aspects of the human soul.

In magic and traditional astrology (as opposed to modern astrology), the seven
ancient planets are widely utilized for their extensive symbolism, more so than the
twelve zodiacal signs. This is because planets are agents of change. As the "movers and
shakers" of astrology, it is their function to act, move, and initiate change. In a zodiacal
chart, it is the position and effect of the planets over the signs and houses that they rule
that takes precedence over every other aspect of the chart.

In planetary magic, the symbols and powers of the planets are invoked to effect change in their associated sphere of influence and rulership.

Saturn ♄

Named after the Roman God of agriculture, this planet was known as the Greater Malefic due to its harsh qualities. Saturn is the planet of organization, discipline, responsibility, structure, goals, limitations, conservatism, restrictions, delays, theories, orthodoxy, tradition, depth, patience, truth, wisdom, and solidification. This planet rules agriculture, old age, sorrow, death, time, the past, and abstract thought. Its energy is slow and enduring. In the Qabalah it is assigned to Binah, the third Sephirah.

Jupiter ♃

Named after the primary Roman God, this planet was called the Greater Benefic because of its helpful aspects. Jupiter is the planet of expansion, growth, prosperity, wealth, good fortune, luck, opportunity, assimilation, indulgence, optimism, big business, morality, higher education, ambitions, and philosophy. This planet rules leisure time, charity, and rites of passage and other formal ceremonies. Jupiter's action is orderly and efficient and fosters growth and increase. On the Tree of Life it corresponds to Chesed, the fourth Sephirah.

Mars ♂

Named after the Roman God of War, the ancients referred to this planet as Lesser Malefic by reason of its severe energy. Mars is the planet of conflict, aggression, dynamic action, force, power, strife, strain, adversity, destruction, work, achievement, and competition. This planet rules animal nature, weapons, war, male sexuality, accidents, violence, surgery, tools, iron, and steel. The action of Mars is sudden, forceful, and disruptive. The energy of Mars can be used destructively, or with courage and fortitude. In the Qabalah it is assigned to Geburah, the fifth Sephirah.

Sol (the Sun) ☉

Sol is named after the Invincible Sun God of ancient Rome. Sol rules over equilibrium, balance, harmony, reconciliation, mediation, and success in all endeavors. The Sun represents the primary masculine principle and men in general. It is also the fundamental expression of the individual, displaying qualities of success and leadership. Sol governs health, vitality, personal fulfillment, energy, essential principles, authority, command, rank, office, title, advancement, achievement, justice, identity, and capacity for experience. The energy of Sol is energizing and stimulating. On the Tree of Life it is attributed to Tiphareth, the sixth Sephirah.

Venus ♀

Named after the Roman Goddess of Love, Venus was nicknamed the Lesser Benefic due to its pleasant qualities. This planet governs emotional life, natural love, marriage, unions, sensuality, female sexuality, sociability, attraction, social interactions, enjoyments, pleasure, art, music, poetry, drama, song, culture, beauty, possessions, jewelry, and adornment. Its action is mild and harmonious. Qabalistically, Venus is connected to Netzach, the seventh Sephirah.

Mercury ☿

Named after the fleet-footed Roman Messenger God, Mercury is the planet of communication, language, reason, intellectual pursuits, rationalization, awareness, perceptions, learning, opinions, transmission, words, speaking, writing, mailings, messages, and all means of expression. In addition, Mercury deals with medicine, healing, family, day-to-day activities, travel and transportation, commerce, economics, and gambling. This planet also governs theft and deception. Mercury's action is rapid, unpredictable, changeable, and explosive. In the Qabalah it is associated with Hod, the eighth Sephirah.

Luna ☽

Identified with Diana, Roman Goddess of the Moon, Luna embodies the primary female principle and women in general. The Moon rules over instincts, moods, feelings, habits, the subconscious, the unknown, tides, liquids, Water, phases, biological cycles, reproduction, childbirth, reflexes, reflections, alternations, and receptivity. Luna rules needs, dreams, desires, personal interests, magnetism, impressionability, fertility, visions, mysticism, and psychic phenomena. The Moon's action changes and fluctuates. On the Tree of Life, Luna is attributed to Yesod, the ninth Sephirah.

HEBREW LETTER ATTRIBUTIONS

The seven planets are each assigned to one of the seven Double Letters of the Hebrew alphabet (Table 8). (NOTE: the letter Tau pulls double duty: it is attributed to Saturn as well as the element of Earth.)

Table 8: Hebrew Letters Assigned to the Planets

Planet	Letter
Mercury	Beth
Luna	Gimel
Venus	Daleth
Jupiter	Kaph
Mars	Peh
Sol	Resh
Saturn	Tau

The ancients also assigned certain planetary values to the North and South Nodes of the Moon, the points in Celestial longitude where the Moon crosses over the ecliptic or path of the Sun.

The North Node (☊) of the Moon is called *Caput Draconis,* or "Head of the Dragon." This is a point of gain, increase, and added self-assurance.

The South Node (☋) of the Moon is known as *Cauda Draconis,* or the "Tail of the Dragon." The South Node is a point of release, decrease, and letting go.

PLANETARY HIERARCHIES

The planets also have certain godnames and angels associated with them. Hebrew god-names affiliated with the Sephiroth are also attributed to the seven planets to which they correspond (Table 9).

Table 9: Hebrew Names and Godnames of the Planets

Planet Name (in English and Hebrew)	Godname
Saturn (Shabbathai)	YHVH Elohim
Jupiter (Tzedek)	El
Mars (Madim)	Elohim Gebur

Planet Name (in English and Hebrew)	Godname
Sol (Shemesh)	YHVH Eloah Ve-Daath
Venus (Nogah)	YHVH Tzabaoth
Mercury (Kokab)	Elohim Tzabaoth
Luna (Levannah)	Shaddai El Chai

The workings of the planetary hierarchies are similar to those of the Sephiroth. Each plane has an archangel, an intelligence, and a Spirit. (Intelligences are planetary angels under a different name.) The administrative force is the planetary archangel. The intelligence of a planet is seen as an evolutionary, nurturing, inspiring, or guiding entity, while the Spirit is traditionally viewed as a blind or "raw" energy force without guidance or intelligence. When invoking these entities in magic, the Spirit must always be guided by the intelligence, under the control of the archangel (Table 10).

Table 10: Angels and Spirits of the Planets

Planet	Archangel	Intelligence	Spirit
Saturn	Kassiel	Agiel	Zazel
Jupiter	Sachiel	Iophiel	Hismael
Mars	Zamael	Graphiel	Bartzabel
Sol	Michael	Nakhiel	Sorath
Venus	Anael	Hagiel	Qedemel
Mercury	Raphael	Tiriel	Taphthartharath
Luna	Gabriel	Shelachel	Chasmodai

The names of many of these spiritual beings are derived from planetary talismans known as magic squares (Figure 15).

A couple of archangels on this list, Raphael and Michael, are attributed to *both* a Sephirah *and* a planet, which may seem puzzling. Try not to confuse the Sephirotic, planetary, and elemental hierarchies. Different angels, like different people, can have the same name. It is helpful to call these angels in accordance with their specific titles and functions, such as *Michael Shemeshel* (Michael, archangel of the Sun) as opposed to *Michael Hodael* (Michael, archangel of Hod).

GEOMETRIC FIGURES

Geometric figures, also called *polyangles*, play an important role in Golden Dawn magic. Triangles, Crosses, Pentagrams, Hexagrams, and other lineal figures are regularly traced during ritual to call forth the energies identified with them. These figures are traced in the air and visualized in the astral light by the magician.

Polyangles come in two forms, both of which can be used in magic: *polygrams* and *polygons*. Polygrams are described as figures consisting of many intersecting lines that resemble stars. Polygons are closed plane figures having three or more sides. For example, the polygon of Geburah and Mars is known as a pentangle. The two forms of a Mars pentangle are the Pentagram and the pentagon. Tiphareth and Sol have two forms of the hexangle: the Hexagram and the hexagon.

The two forms of a polyangle produce different magical effects. The polygon represents the distribution of a force, while the polygram signifies the concentration and sealing of a force. Used together, the two polyangles assigned to a Sephirah or a planet can initiate the whirl of the desired force and seal it into a talisman.

The lineal figures appropriate to the planets are based upon their Qabalistic correspondences (Table 11).

Table 11: Lineal Figures of the Planets

Number	Sephirah	Planet	Polygram	Polygon	Other
1	Kether	-	-	-	The Point
2	Chokmah	-	-	-	Line/Cross
3	Binah	Saturn	-	Triangle	
4	Chesed	Jupiter	-	Square	Cross
5	Geburah	Mars	Pentagram (5 points)	Pentagon	
6	Tiphareth	Sol	Hexagram (6 points)	Hexagon	
7	Netzach	Venus	Heptagram (7 points)	Heptagon	
8	Hod	Mercury	Octagram (8 points)	Octagon	
9	Yesod	Luna	Enneagram (9 points)	Enneagon	
10	Malkuth	Earth	Decagram (10 points)	Decagon	

A few other lineal figures need to be mentioned.

Vesica

A vesica (Figure 12) is a pointed oval formed by the intersection of two circles. It is the common ground shared by both circles, and is often used to symbolize a state of transition, transference, or transcendence. The *vesica piscis* or pointed oval aureole was used by medieval artists to enclose holy figures.

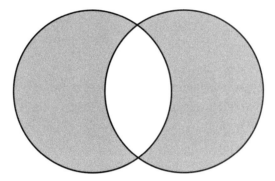

Figure 12: The Vesica

Rhombus

A rhombus (Figure 13) is an equilateral parallelogram, or four-sided figure whose opposing sides are parallel and equal, with no right angles. In such a figure, each side is identical to the side opposite it. A diagonal line drawn between two opposite points on the rhomboid would form two congruent Triangles. The rhombus is very similar to the vesica, both in shape and in function.

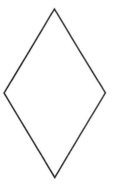

Figure 13: The Rhombus

Dodecangle

The two forms of this twelve-sided figure include the dodecagram and the dodecagon. Both refer to the whole of the zodiac. Although they are not allied through number, the dodecangle can be used to some extent with the second Sephirah of Chokmah, to which the zodiac is referred.

MAGIC SQUARES

Magic squares, also called *qameoth* (singular *qamea*), are potent mystical diagrams and talismans that relate to the planets and their energies. These diagrams are ancient and probably of Persian origin.

A magic square is formed from a grid of numbers arranged so as to yield the same number each way—horizontally, vertically, and diagonally. The sum of each column of figures and the sum total of all the numbers of the square are specifically attributed to the planet in question. The number of grid units that make up one of the rows or columns of the qamea determines which planet it is associated with through the number of its corresponding Sephirah on the Tree of Life (Table 12).

Table 12: Number Associations of the Planets

Planet or Power	Sephirah	Qamea Units per Row
Saturn	Binah	3
Jupiter	Chesed	4
Mars	Geburah	5
Sol	Tiphareth	6
Venus	Netzach	7
Mercury	Hod	8
Luna	Yesod	9
Earth	Malkuth	10
Zodiac		12

The number of the planet Saturn is 3 (Binah). Three squared is 9, the total number of grid units in the Saturn qamea. The sum of each column and each row is 15. And the total sum of all the numbers on the Saturn square is 45. Every qamea contains many such numbers that are used to create divine, angelic, and Spirit names, which correlate to their assigned planetary energies.

The *planetary seal* (Figure 14) is a sigil of the planet, a symbol designed in such a manner that its traced lines touch every number or unit square of that planet's qamea. It symbolizes the governing force of the planet.

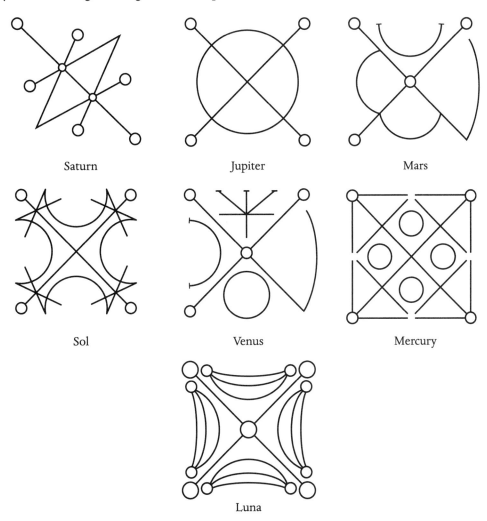

Figure 14: Planetary Seals

Magic squares of the planets (Figure 15) are important in the designing of sigils and planetary talismans—magical objects that are ceremonially consecrated to attract a particular force for a specific goal.

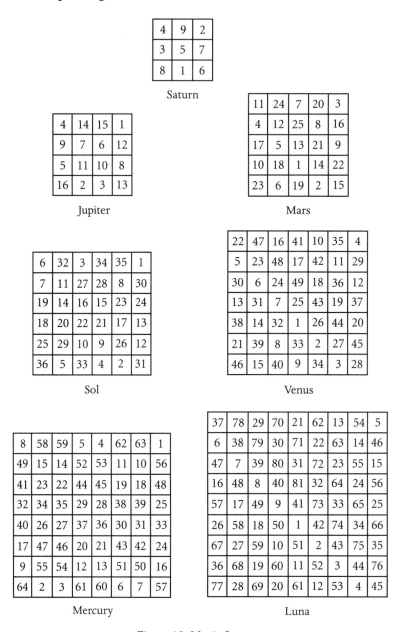

Figure 15: Magic Squares

The modern-day Golden Dawn has also added two more magical squares to our tradition: the qamea of Malkuth and the elements and the qamea of Mazzaloth (Figure 16). The first can be used to create talismans aligned with the tenth Sephirah as well as the four elements, while the second can be used to design talismans for the twelve zodiacal signs.

10	92	8	94	5	96	97	3	99	1
11	19	83	17	85	86	14	88	12	90
71	22	28	74	26	25	77	23	79	80
40	62	33	37	65	66	34	68	69	31
51	49	53	44	46	45	57	58	42	60
41	59	48	54	56	55	47	43	52	50
70	39	63	67	35	36	64	38	32	61
30	72	78	24	76	75	27	73	29	21
81	89	13	87	16	15	84	18	82	20
100	2	98	7	95	6	4	93	9	91

The Qamea of Malkuth and the Elements

12	134	135	9	8	138	139	5	4	142	143	1
121	23	22	124	125	19	18	128	129	15	14	132
109	35	34	112	113	31	30	116	117	27	26	120
48	98	99	45	44	102	103	41	40	106	107	37
60	86	87	57	56	90	91	53	52	94	95	49
73	71	70	76	77	67	66	80	81	63	62	84
61	83	82	64	65	79	78	68	69	75	74	72
96	50	51	93	92	54	55	89	88	58	59	85
108	38	39	105	104	42	43	101	100	46	47	97
25	119	118	28	29	115	114	32	33	111	110	36
13	131	130	16	17	127	126	20	21	123	122	24
144	2	3	141	140	6	7	137	136	10	11	133

The Qamea of Mazzaloth

Figure 16: Magic Squares of Malkuth and Mazzaloth

MAGICAL TIMING

It can be beneficial to perform planetary meditations and magic in accordance with assigned days and magical hours. The days of the week are attributed to the seven ancient planets and the Gods who represented them (Table 13). (Note: There is no special day for Earth.)

Table 13: Planetary Days

Sunday	Monday	Tuesday	Wednesday	Thursday	Friday	Saturday
Sol	Luna	Mars	Mercury	Jupiter	Venus	Saturn

Magical or Planetary Hours are not the same as regular hours. To determine the magical hours for a particular day (or night), you must know the exact times for sunrise and sunset at your location. In years past, you would have to check the local paper for fishing times or a publication such as the *Old Farmer's Almanac*. Today you can check online for sunrise and sunset calculators.

Divide the total time between sunrise and sunset by 12. This will give you the length of the Magical Hours of the day. Dividing the time between sunset and sunrise by 12 will give you the length of the Planetary Hours of the night. The hours of the day and night will be of different lengths except on the equinoxes (Tables 14 and 15).

Table 14: Table of Planetary Hours: Day Hours

	Sun.	Mon.	Tues.	Wed.	Thurs.	Fri.	Sat.
Sunrise							
Hour 1	Sol	Luna	Mars	Mercury	Jupiter	Venus	Saturn
Hour 2	Venus	Saturn	Sol	Luna	Mars	Mercury	Jupiter
Hour 3	Mercury	Jupiter	Venus	Saturn	Sol	Luna	Mars
Hour 4	Luna	Mars	Mercury	Jupiter	Venus	Saturn	Sol
Hour 5	Saturn	Sol	Luna	Mars	Mercury	Jupiter	Venus
Hour 6	Jupiter	Venus	Saturn	Sol	Luna	Mars	Mercury
Hour 7	Mars	Mercury	Jupiter	Venus	Saturn	Sol	Luna
Hour 8	Sol	Luna	Mars	Mercury	Jupiter	Venus	Saturn
Hour 9	Venus	Saturn	Sol	Luna	Mars	Mercury	Jupiter
Hour 10	Mercury	Jupiter	Venus	Saturn	Sol	Luna	Mars
Hour 11	Luna	Mars	Mercury	Jupiter	Venus	Saturn	Sol
Hour 12	Saturn	Sol	Luna	Mars	Mercury	Jupiter	Venus

Table 15: Table of Planetary Hours: Night Hours

	Sun.	Mon.	Tues.	Wed.	Thurs.	Fri.	Sat.
Sunset							
Hour 1	Jupiter	Venus	Saturn	Sol	Luna	Mars	Mercury
Hour 2	Mars	Mercury	Jupiter	Venus	Saturn	Sol	Luna
Hour 3	Sol	Luna	Mars	Mercury	Jupiter	Venus	Saturn
Hour 4	Venus	Saturn	Sol	Luna	Mars	Mercury	Jupiter
Hour 5	Mercury	Jupiter	Venus	Saturn	Sol	Luna	Mars
Hour 6	Luna	Mars	Mercury	Jupiter	Venus	Saturn	Sol
Hour 7	Saturn	Sol	Luna	Mars	Mercury	Jupiter	Venus
Hour 8	Jupiter	Venus	Saturn	Sol	Luna	Mars	Mercury
Hour 9	Mars	Mercury	Jupiter	Venus	Saturn	Sol	Luna
Hour 10	Sol	Luna	Mars	Mercury	Jupiter	Venus	Saturn
Hour 11	Venus	Saturn	Sol	Luna	Mars	Mercury	Jupiter
Hour 12	Mercury	Jupiter	Venus	Saturn	Sol	Luna	Mars

PLANETARY COLORS

The planetary colors most often used in Golden Dawn magic are the King and Queen Scale colors listed in Table 16. King Scale colors are used to project the forces of the planets, while the Queen Scale colors are employed to receive these energies.

Table 16: Planetary Colors

Planet	King Scale Color	Queen Scale Color
Saturn	Blue-violet	Black
Jupiter	Violet	Blue
Mars	Red	Red
Sol	Orange	Yellow
Venus	Green	Sky-blue
Mercury	Yellow	Violet
Luna	Blue	Silver

THE ZODIACAL SIGNS

The word "zodiac" is taken from a Greek word meaning "circle of animals." This refers to the circle traced by the Sun in its movement through the heavens from the perspective of Earth. The zodiac is divided into twelve sections named after the twelve constellations that the circle is seen to pass through (Figure 17).

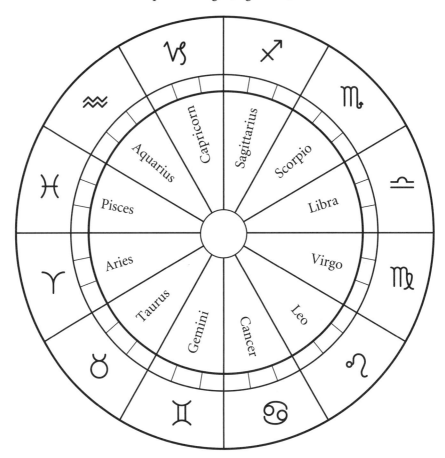

Figure 17: The Wheel of the Zodiac

Unlike the planets, the signs do not effect change. Instead, they are envisioned as regions, realms, or territories that the planets move through. A sign is similar to a specific area, while a planet is something that can inhabit that area. A planet moving through one of these heavenly terrains alters its operation accordingly. Some signs weaken the influence of a particular planet while strengthening others. Different signs may intensify the manner in which a planet's energies are expressed.

While each sign is ruled by one of the planets, the signs have their own set of attributes that determine how the planets operate within the different signs (Table 17). In zodiacal magic, the characteristics and powers of the signs are invoked and utilized, as are the energies of the planets as they move through and are influenced by the signs. Magical work with the various signs is a way by which the magician can fine-tune the planetary energies as filtered through the signs themselves.

Table 17: The Zodiacal Signs

Sign and Symbol	Meaning	Rules from	Ruled by
Aries ♈	Ram	Mar. 21–April 19	Mars
Taurus ♉	Bull	April 20–May 20	Venus
Gemini ♊	Twins	May 21–June 20	Mercury
Cancer ♋	Crab	June 21–July 22	Luna
Leo ♌	Lion	July 23–Aug. 22	Sol
Virgo ♍	Virgin	Aug. 23–Sept. 22	Mercury
Libra ♎	Scales	Sept. 23–Oct. 22	Venus
Scorpio ♏	Scorpion	Oct. 23–Nov. 21	Mars
Sagittarius ♐	Archer	Nov. 22–Dec. 21	Jupiter
Capricorn ♑	Sea-goat	Dec. 22–Jan. 19	Saturn
Aquarius ♒	Water-bearer	Jan. 20–Feb. 18	Saturn
Pisces ♓	Fish	Feb. 19–Mar. 20	Jupiter

THE TRIPLICITIES: GROUPED BY ELEMENT

The twelve signs are distributed among four triplicities or sets of three signs. Each of these triplicities is attributed to one of the four elements, and they represent the operation of the elements in the zodiac.

△ **Fire Signs:** Aries, Leo, and Sagittarius
Traits: energy, enthusiasm, ambition, spontaneity, and enterprise

▽ **Water Signs:** Cancer, Scorpio, and Pisces
Traits: sympathetic, receptive, intuitive, and complex

△ **Air Signs:** Libra, Aquarius, and Gemini
Traits: communicative, sociable, intellectual, and changeable

▽ **Earth Signs:** Capricorn, Taurus, and Virgo
Traits: practical, industrious, patient, sensual, and stable

THE QUADRUPLICITIES: GROUPED BY QUALITY

The twelve signs are also divided into three quadruplicities or groups of four signs. Each of these quadruplicities is attributed to one of three qualities: Cardinal, Kerubic (Fixed), and Mutable.

Notice that in the triplicities, the first sign given in all the elemental groupings is a Cardinal Sign, the second is a Kerubic Sign, and the third is a Mutable Sign. We represent these qualities with the initial letters C, K, and M.

C Cardinal Signs: Aries, Cancer, Libra, and Capricorn

These signs rule the change of seasons: Aries—spring; Cancer—summer; Libra—fall; and Capricorn—winter. They are also attributed to the four cardinal points of the compass: Aries—east; Cancer—north; Libra—west; and Capricorn—south.

Qualities: active, quick, creative, enthusiastic, ambitious

K Kerubic Signs: Leo, Scorpio, Aquarius, and Taurus

These fixed signs govern the middle month of each season. Unlike the Cardinal Signs that herald the transition between seasons, the Kerubic Signs are solidly established in the heart of each season.

Qualities: stable, steady, determined, tenacious, inflexible

M Mutable Signs: Sagittarius, Pisces, Gemini, and Virgo

These signs rule the closing month of each season. Also called Common Signs, they govern the completion of the work of one season while looking ahead to the next.

Qualities: clever, changeable, versatile, volatile, quick, intuitive, complex

The following provides a quick look at the twelve signs and some of their keywords:

1. Aries
Cardinal Fire
Keywords: beginning, initiative, executive, impulse, energy, activity, enterprise

2. Taurus
Kerubic Earth
Keywords: Stability, materiality, practicality, possessions, determination

3. Gemini
Mutable Air
Keywords: Versatility, dexterity, skill, expression, communication, intelligence

4. Cancer
Cardinal Water
Keywords: domesticity, sensitivity, familial, empathy, tenacity

5. Leo
Kerubic Fire
Keywords: charisma, magnetism, drama, idealism, ambition, optimism

6. Virgo
Mutable Earth
Keywords: discrimination, analytical, methodical, precise, science, service

7. Libra
Cardinal Air
Keywords: Balance, harmony, fairness, companionship, cooperation, diplomacy, persuasion

8. Scorpio
Kerubic Water
Keywords: transformation, regeneration, intensity, motivation, secrecy

9. Sagittarius

Mutable Fire

Keywords: Aspiration, idealism, philosophy, spirituality, education, freedom, liberty,
exploration

10. Capricorn

Cardinal Earth

Keywords: ambition, conservation, pragmatism, organization, responsibility, business

11. Aquarius

Kerubic Air

Keywords: Imagination, knowledge, invention, philanthropy, independence,
humanitarian

12. Pisces

Mutable Water

Keywords: compassion, understanding, emotion, intuition, instincts, introspection,
charity, mysticism, the arts

The Qabalah assigns the twelve signs of the zodiac or *Mazzaloth* to the second
Sephirah of Chokmah on the Tree of Life. The magic square of the Mazzaloth can be
used to create zodiacal sigils and talismans.

HEBREW LETTER ATTRIBUTIONS

The twelve signs are each assigned to one of the twelve Simple Letters of the Hebrew
alphabet. These are shown in Table 18 along with the Hebrew names of the signs.

Table 18: Hebrew Letter Attributions of the Signs

Sign	Hebrew Name of Sign	Hebrew Letter
Aries	Ṭaleh	Heh
Taurus	Shor	Vav
Gemini	Teomim	Zayin
Cancer	Sarṭon	Cheth

Sign	Hebrew Name of Sign	Hebrew Letter
Leo	Ari	Teth
Virgo	Betulah	Yod
Libra	Moznaim	Lamed
Scorpio	Akrab	Nun
Sagittarius	Qasshat	Samekh
Capricorn	Gedi	Ayin
Aquarius	Deli	Tzaddi
Pisces	Dagim	Qoph

ELEMENTAL AND ZODIACAL HIERARCHIES

Like the planets, the signs of the zodiac also have spiritual hierarchies. Godnames of the zodiacal signs are those of the triplicates and are the same as the godnames of the four elements (Table 19).

Table 19: Elemental Godnames, Archangels, and Angels

Element	Godname	Archangel	Angel
Fire	Elohim	Michael	Ariel
Water	El	Gabriel	Taliahad
Air	YHVH	Raphael	Chassan
Earth	Adonai	Uriel	Phorlakh

The archangels of the zodiacal signs are listed in Table 20.

Table 20: Zodiacal Archangels and Angels

Sign	Archangel	Angel
Aries	Malkhidael	Sharahiel
Taurus	Asmodel	Eraziel
Gemini	Ambriel	Serayel
Cancer	Muriel	Pakhiel
Leo	Verkhiel	Sheratiel
Virgo	Hamaliel	Shelathiel

Table 20: Zodiacal Archangels and Angels (continued)

Sign	Archangel	Angel
Libra	Zuriel	Chadaqiel
Scorpio	Barkhiel	Sayitziel
Sagittarius	Adnakhiel	Saritaiel
Capricorn	Hanael	Semaqiel
Aquarius	Kambriel	Tzadmaqiel
Pisces	Amnitziel	Vakhabiel

Hebrew spellings for all of the angels and archangels listed in this book can be found in our text *Tarot Talismans: Invoke the Angels of the Tarot.*

ZODIACAL COLORS

The colors most often attributed to the zodiacal signs are provided in Table 21. The King Scale colors project zodiacal force; Queen Scale colors receive it.

Table 21: Zodiacal Colors

Sign	King Scale Color	Queen Scale Color
Aries	Red	Red
Taurus	Red-orange	Deep blue-violet
Gemini	Orange	Pale mauve
Cancer	Yellow-orange	Maroon
Leo	Yellow	Deep violet
Virgo	Yellow-green	Slate gray
Libra	Green	Blue
Scorpio	Blue-green	Dull brown
Sagittarius	Blue	Yellow
Capricorn	Blue-violet	Black
Aquarius	Violet	Sky blue
Pisces	Red-violet	Buff, flecked silver-white

Another set of colors that may be useful for readers to consider is the King and Queen Scale colors of the Elements, shown in Table 22.

Table 22: Elemental Colors

Element	King Scale Color	Queen Scale Color
Spirit	White	Deep purple
Fire	Red	Vermilion red
Water	Blue	Sea-green
Air	Yellow	Sky-blue
Earth	Citrine, olive, russet, black	Yellow-orange

GEOMANCY

One final symbol system that must be addressed is *geomancy,* or "Earth divination." Geomancy uses sixteen figures, each of which consists of four lines of dots often called *tetragrams*. Each of the four lines of a tetragram is composed of either one or two dots. Geomantic divination is done by generating the binary lines of the tetragrams through one of any number of random processes, such as flipping a coin, rolling dice, or poking holes in the ground a random number of times with a stick. An odd number of holes equals one dot while an even number equals two.

Golden Dawn students are required to learn how to perform geomantic divinations, but we will not dwell on the topic here. However, the sixteen tetragrams (Figure 18 on the next page) are important symbols in their own right, and they are often inscribed on planetary and zodiacal talismans. They signify Celestial as well as terrestrial energies.

3-D VISUALIZATION EXERCISE: CIRCLE AND SPHERE

This exercise is designed to hone the student's skill in manipulating a visualized image.

1. Start in the standing position and begin with a brief period of rhythmic breathing.

2. When ready, extend your index finger as if you were pointing at something directly in front of you.

3. Still pointing, bring your hand over to the left, and visualize the starting point of white light at the end of your finger.

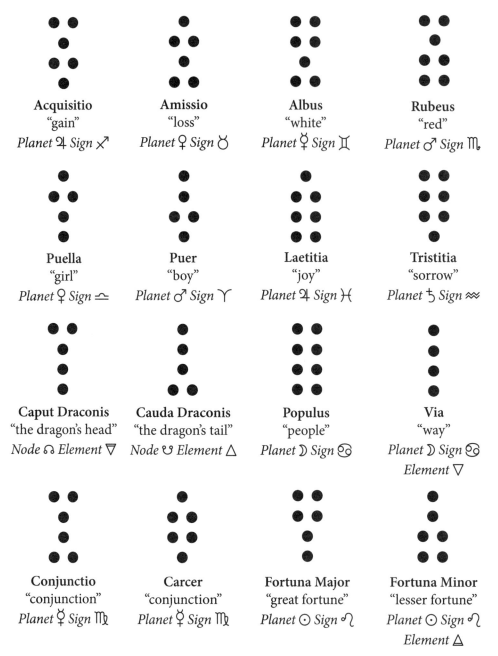

Figure 18: The Tetragrams of Geomancy

4. Trace a circle clockwise from the starting point, until you complete the circle at its point of origin (Figure 19). Visualize the white outline of the circle strongly.

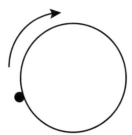

Figure 19: Tracing the Circle

5. Then place the palm of your hand, fingers upward, at the center of the circle, as if you were feeling the surface of a wall.

6. Now visualize the outline filling up with white light, so that your hand rests against a completely filled-in white circle.

7. Next, keeping your hand in the same position, pull your arm back toward you about a foot. As you do so, visualize the part of the circle that your hand touches bulging out as it moves with your hand, resulting in a convex bubble resting against your hand.

8. Extend your arm out again, and see the convex bubble flatten again as if against a wall.

9. Pull your arm back toward your body again. This time visualize the circle bulging out toward your hand and bulging out away from you on the opposite side of the circle, becoming a sphere. It should resemble a balloon expanding with Air.

10. Strongly visualize this sphere. See its three-dimensional form shaped by the interplay of light, shadow, and perspective. If you want, cup the fingers of your hand and give a slight flick of your hand to the right, sending the sphere spinning slowly in place.

11. When finished, place your palm against the sphere to stop its spin. Extend your arm and compress the sphere back into a flat circle.

12. Visualize the white light fading from the center of the circle, leaving only a white outline.

13. Point your index finger back at the starting point on the left. This time, trace the circle counterclockwise, completely dissolving the circle as you return to the point of origin.

14. Take note of how you feel and any insights that you may have experienced during the exercise.

AN INTRODUCTION TO THE MIDDLE PILLAR EXERCISE

The exercise of the Middle Pillar (sometimes abbreviated as MP) is designed to establish the Sephiroth of the central pillar, the Pillar of Mildness, within the aura of the person performing it. It brings a sense of calmness and harmony and also acts to increase vitality.

This one ritual has many variations and uses. In the basic exercise, the magician visualizes the Middle Pillar superimposed over his or her body, specifically the four Sephiroth: Kether, Tiphareth, Yesod, Malkuth, along the so-called "invisible Sephirah" of Daath, which is used here as a conjunction of the powers of Chokmah and Binah (Figure 20). The godnames of these five energy centers are vibrated a number of times in conjunction with the visualizations.

Using the imagination, the student builds up a replica of the Tree of Life in the aura that interpenetrates and surrounds the physical body. The Pillar of Severity is on the aspirant's right side, the Pillar of Mercy is on the left, and the Pillar of Mildness is in the center of the aspirant's body. The astral construction of the Middle Pillar within the aura should be practiced regularly as part of a lifelong spiritual routine.

Israel Regardie, the magician most responsible for crafting the Golden Dawn's Middle Pillar exercise in its current form, held that this simple exercise can increase one's field of attention, aid in the achievement of balance and equilibrium, and provide the student with a remarkable wellspring of power and spiritual perception. Practice of the Middle Pillar exercise is concurrently stimulating and relaxing—it releases points of tension in both mind and body, often leaving one feeling joyful, rested, and energized.

It is also a wonderful technique for healing, consecrating Sacred objects, raising and radiating energy, and for aligning oneself with the divine forces inherent in the godnames of the Tree of Life.

THE MIDDLE PILLAR (MP) EXERCISE

This exercise can be performed either standing, sitting, or lying down. Begin with closed eyes and rhythmic breathing.

Vibration of the Sephiroth Godnames

1. Imagine a sphere of white light just above your head. Vibrate the name **"EHEIEH"** (Eh-hey-yay) three times or more until it is the only thought in your conscious mind.

2. Imagine a shaft of light descending from your Kether (crown) center to your Daath center at the nape of the neck. Form a sphere of light at the Daath center. Vibrate the name **"YHVH ELOHIM"** (Yode-heh-vav-heh El-oh-heem). Intone the name the exact number of times that you vibrated the previous name.

3. Bring a shaft of light down from the Daath center to the Tiphareth center around your heart. Form a sphere of light there. Vibrate the name **"YHVH ELOAH VE-DAATH"** (Yode-heh-vav-heh El-oh-ah v'-Dah-ath) the same number of times as before.

4. See the shaft of light descending from the Tiphareth (heart) center into the Yesod center in the groin region. Imagine a sphere of light formed there. Intone the name **"SHADDAI EL CHAI"** (Shah-dye El-Ch-eye) several times as before.

5. Visualize the shaft of light descending from the Yesod (groin) center into your Malkuth center at the feet and ankles. Vibrate the name **"ADONAI HA-ARETZ"** (Ah-doe-nye ha-Ah-retz) the same number of times as before.

6. Imagine the Middle Pillar complete. Then circulate the light you have brought down through the Middle Pillar around the outside of your body to strengthen your aura. (Perform each circulation a number of times.)

Visualized Circulation of Breath

7. *Side to Side:* Using the cycles of rhythmic breathing, bring the light down one side of the body and up the other, from Kether to Malkuth and back to Kether. Exhale and visualize the light descending the left side of the body. Inhale and imagine the light ascending the right side of the body back to Kether.

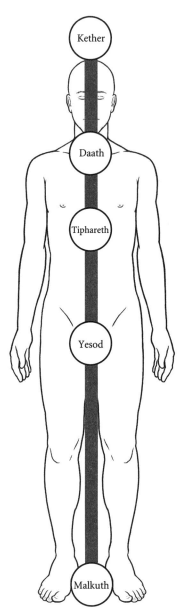

Figure 20: The Middle Pillar

8. *Front to Back:* After performing this for a short space of time, imagine the ribbon of light descending from Kether down the front of your body to Malkuth and rising up your back, returning again to Kether. Inhale for rising, exhale for descending.

9. *The Shower of Light:* Still employing rhythmic breathing, visualize the sphere of Malkuth, then see the light rise again in a ribbon that spirals around the shaft of the Middle Pillar in the center of your body from Malkuth to Kether. When it reaches Kether, imagine a shower of light cascading down the outside of your body as it descends to Malkuth again. Circulate the light in this manner for some time.

Closing

10. Finally, focus some of the energy in Tiphareth, the heart center, before ending the exercise.

REVIEW QUESTIONS

1. What does "quintessence" refer to?

2. What are Flashing Colors?

3. What does the Unwritten Qabalah refer to?

4. What does the Literal Qabalah refer to?

5. How many Hebrew letters have a final form? Which letters are they?

6. Which Hebrew letter means "oxgoad"? Which one means "fishhook"? Which one means "camel"?

7. Which Hebrew letter has a value of 5? 40? 80? 900?

8. What is Aiq Beker?

9. What is a notariqon?

10. What are the Sephiroth? List them.

11. What are the Navitoth?

12. What are the Four Worlds? Describe each one.

13. What are the Four Color Scales?

14. What does the term "Minutum Mundum" refer to?

15. What is a godname? Give an example.

16. List the archangels of the ten Sephiroth.

17. List the archangels of the seven planets.

18. How are planets different from zodiacal signs?

19. What are the two forms of a polyangle? How do they differ in function?

20. What is a qamea?

21. What is a triplicity? List the signs in the triplicities.

22. What is a quadruplicity? List the signs in the quadruplicities.

23. What is your experience of the Middle Pillar exercise? How often do you practice it?

24. What planet is attributed to Tuesday?

25. What is a tetractys?

chapter 3

UNDERSTANDING THE
ORDER SYSTEM

Even solitary Golden Dawn magicians should have a basic understanding of the various grades or levels of initiation, as well as the officers involved in group work performed within a functioning Order. "Why?" you might ask. "I don't need to be initiated in an order, I just want to do the magic!"

The answer is that the Order system itself is intimately connected to the practical, personal magic of the aspirant. The layout of the Temple; the energies, symbols, and functions connected with the officiating magicians; and the forces invoked during the various grade initiation ceremonies are fully utilized in most of the advanced workings of Golden Dawn magicians. Various magical techniques and formulas are hidden and sometimes clearly displayed in the movements, composition, and speeches of the rituals and their structural supports.

Traditionally, Golden Dawn magic was only taught within the confines of the Order system. Its teachings were simply not available to seekers outside of the official Order setting. That began to change in 1937 when Israel Regardie published the bulk of the Order's curriculum in *The Golden Dawn: The Original Account of the Teachings, Rites and Ceremonies of the Hermetic Order*. This opened the floodgates for esoteric students eager to work the system on their own. Regardie was a vocal champion of the idea that students could initiate themselves through the various grades of the Golden Dawn. It was his opinion that through repeated performance of such rituals as the Middle Pillar exercise and the Opening by Watchtower, the aspiring magician could effectively be considered an initiate of the Golden Dawn's magical current.

The Dreaded "H" Word

Some make the mistake of thinking that the Golden Dawn system is authoritarian because there is a hierarchy of structured grades and supervising officers. Remember that the Golden Dawn is a school of the Mysteries. Within the order setting there is a hierarchy like that of any other school, wherein the administration and faculty (not the student body!) sets the agenda and course material. A hierarchical system allows experienced officers and more advanced students to guide and advise beginners. But some will always prefer the route of the solo practitioner and self-initiation.

Even today it is difficult to become a member of an initiating Golden Dawn order due to the fact that, compared to other spiritual paths that exist with the aid of large organized religions, Golden Dawn magicians compose a tiny niche. And while there are far more Golden Dawn Temples operating in the world today than in any previous time, they simply don't exist everywhere. They were never meant to. Therefore, it is not always possible for prospective students to find a Temple close to them. Some groups offer useful correspondence courses and mentoring to long-distance members, while others offer more dubious practices such as astral initiation by proxy, by telephone, or over the internet. The value of an initiation performed when the student is not physically present in a Sacred Space purified and consecrated by an initiating team trained to move energy within the aspirant's auric sphere is, of course, highly questionable. This is one of the primary reasons that we wrote *Self-Initiation into the Golden Dawn Tradition* for solo practitioners who wish to experience a more traditional practice designed for solitary work.

The main construct at the core of the Order system has already been introduced—the Qabalah! The various grade initiations and even the officers who implement them correlate to other spiritual energies and cosmic principles that we now examine.

SOME COMMON TERMS

Golden Dawn ceremonies are held in a room often called a Hall but also commonly referred to as a Temple. A male initiate is a *frater*, or brother, and a female is a *soror*, or sister. The plural forms are fratres and sorores. Someone preparing for their first initiation is called a candidate.

GRADES AND DEGREES

When we refer to the Golden Dawn system, we are actually referring to two different Orders that are interconnected. The First or Outer Order is the *Hermetic Order of the Golden Dawn*. The Second or Inner Order is the *Ordo Rosae Rubeae et Aurea Crucis*, usually referred to as the R.R. et A.C. The two Orders serve as outer and inner courts of the mysteries.

The ten grades of the Golden Dawn system correspond to the Sephiroth on the Qabalistic Tree of Life. These grades are divided into three separate groups known as the First, Second, and Third Orders. The grades (from lowest to highest) are listed in Table 23.

Table 23: The Grades

Grade	Symbol	Sephirah	Element	Planet
Neophyte	⓪=⓪	–	–	–
Zelator	①=⑩	Malkuth	Earth	Earth
Theoricus	②=⑨	Yesod	Air	Luna
Practicus	③=⑧	Hod	Water	Mercury
Philosophus	④=⑦	Netzach	Fire	Venus
Portal	–		Spirit	–
Adeptus Minor	⑤=⑥	Tiphareth	–	Sol
Adeptus Major	⑥=⑤	Geburah	–	Mars
Adeptus Exemptus	⑦=④	Chesed	–	Jupiter
Magister Templi	⑧=③	Binah	–	Saturn
Magus	⑨=②	Chokmah	–	–
Ipsissimus	⑩=①	Kether	–	–

The First Order consists of the grades from Neophyte through Philosophus. The grade of Neophyte is a probationary period that is not assigned a Sephirah on the Tree of Life. A person of this grade would be considered a member of the Order, but not yet a full initiate. And yet in one sense this is the most important grade, because it is the one grade that all initiated Golden Dawn members share. *We are all Neophytes.*

The grades from Zelator through Philosophus are known as the elemental grades, and are each attributed to one of the four elements: Fire, Water, Air, Earth. Advancement through the grades of the First Order is designed to expose the initiate to the four elemental principles of nature. But more importantly, the student advancing through these grades learns to recognize, cleanse, and rebalance the four elements as they exist within his or her own psychological makeup. These inner elements can be characterized as distinct sections of the subconscious mind and the auric sphere. In our tradition these elements are symbolized by the Egyptian God Osiris who was killed, dismembered, reassembled, and resurrected into a pure spiritual form. The keywords of the entire First Order could easily be rendered as "purify and balance."

Between the grades of the Philosophus and Adeptus Minor there is an additional initiation ceremony that is not assigned to a Sephirah on the Tree of Life. The Portal is not properly a grade, but it is in fact another probationary period between the First and Second Orders. The Portal is attributed to the fifth element of Spirit, which crowns and completes the other four elements. It is also a period of incubation; the initiate who has equilibrated the four elements within the psyche undergoes a symbolic nine-month interval of gestation before being "born" as an Adept of the Second Order.

The Second Order consists of grades from Adeptus Minor to Adeptus Exemptus, and it is here that the initiate begins the practice of ceremonial magic. The grade of Adeptus Minor or the "Lesser Adept" is the grade where the majority of the published magical work of the system takes place. This is fitting because the initiate who advances to the higher grades assigned to Geburah and Chesed must *always* be able to return to the balanced sphere of Tiphareth on the Middle Pillar and the humble title of the "Lesser Adept."

It would be far better if we could simply drop the word "adept" from our lexicon entirely, because at the point of initiation into the ⑤=⑥ grade, what exactly is it that the aspirant is adept at? The theoretical knowledge of the Outer Order! He or she is just beginning the practical magic of the Inner Order!

The higher grades are divided into various subgrades that mirror the grades of the Outer Order: Neophyte Adeptus Minor (NAM), Zelator Adeptus Minor (ZAM), Theoricus Adeptus Minor (ThAM), and so on. In similarity with the Neophyte Grade, the Neophyte Adeptus Minor is the one grade that all adepts share.

While the First Order can be seen as Osirian in emphasis, the Second Order is Rosicrucian. Rosicrucianism is a mystical and philosophical movement that emerged in Germany during the seventeenth century and was said to have been created by the mythical founder, Christian Rosenkreutz. The Rosicrucian movement spawned several groups concerned with the study of religious mysticism, philosophical and religious doctrines, alchemy, Qabalah, spiritual transformation, and general esotericism. Whereas other Rosicrucian groups are oriented toward mysticism, the Golden Dawn's Inner Order is the preeminent *magical* manifestation of the Rosicrucian impulse.

The Second Order guides and teaches the First Order, and is likewise guided and taught by the Third Order.

The Third Order, consisting of grades from the Magister Templi to Ipsissimus, is made up of nonphysical beings—inner planes contacts—who are guardians of the entire current represented by the Golden Dawn. It is not possible for a living adept to attain these high grades since it entails crossing the abyss and entering the realm of the Supernal Triad. These grades are not attained by living initiates, although some Orders give out these high titles honorarily, a practice we disagree with because it tends to inflame the ego—working against the psychic balance that all adepts should strive for.

There are numerical symbols attached to each grade, such as (0)=[0] or (2)=[9]. The first number refers to the number of steps or initiations symbolically taken on the Qabalistic Tree of Life to attain that grade. The second number refers to the exact Sephirah or sphere on the Tree of Life represented by that grade.

THE THREE DEGREES

The three degrees of the Golden Dawn are often mistakenly identified with the three Orders. The terms "grades," "orders," and "degrees" are entirely distinct within the structure of the Golden Dawn and should not be confused.

The First Degree is composed of the five grades of the Outer Order from Neophyte through Philosophus. It is attributed to the Black Pillar of Severity on the Tree of Life.

The Second Degree consists of one grade only, that of the Portal. This probationary degree corresponds to the White Pillar of Mercy on the Qabalistic Tree.

The Third Degree encompasses the three grades of the Inner Order of the R.R. et A.C. This degree is assigned to the Middle Pillar on the Tree of Life.

THE TEMPLE

One of the most common setups of the Temple space is known as the Hall of the Neophytes (Figure 21), the first arrangement that a candidate sees and one that will form the blueprint for much of his or her magical work from that point forward.

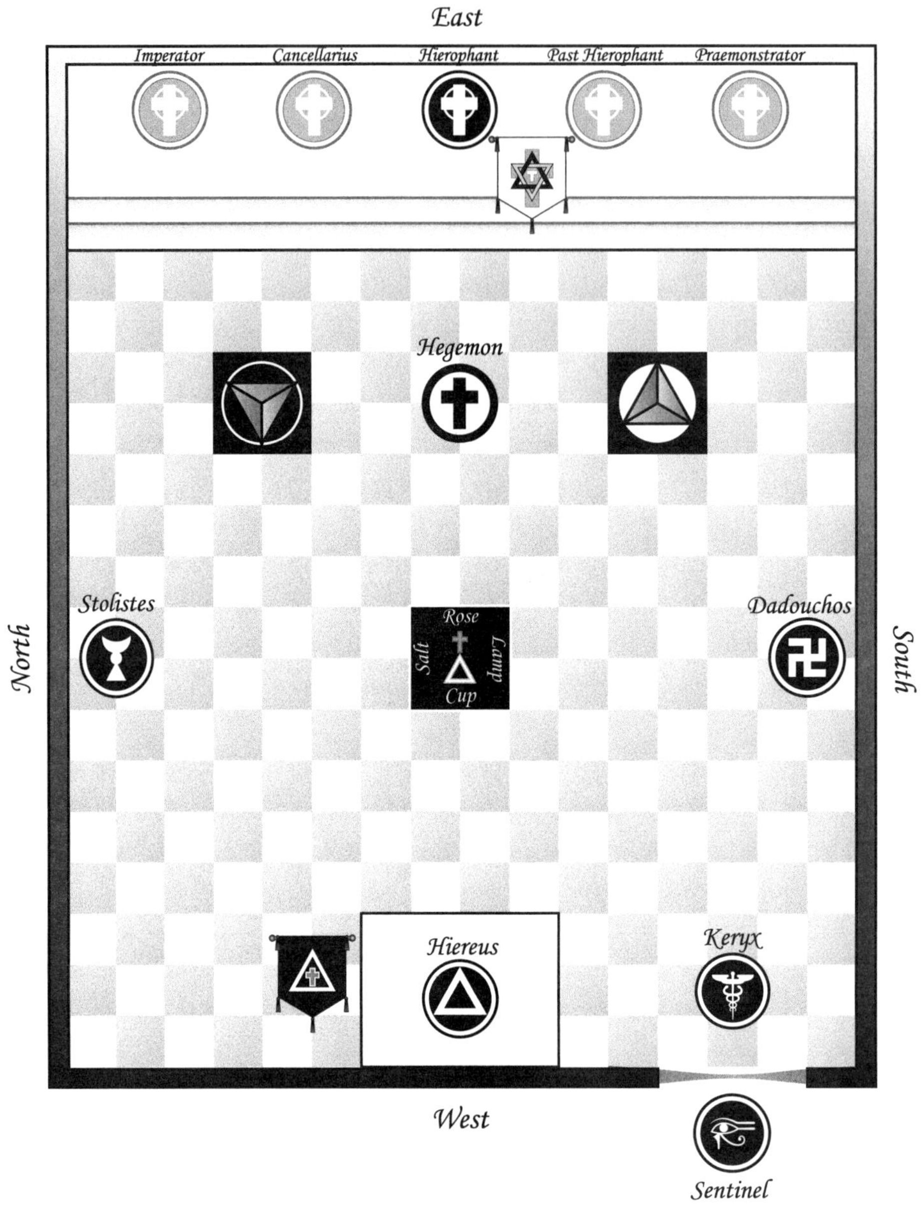

East

Imperator   Cancellarius   Hierophant   Past Hierophant   Praemonstrator

North

South

Hegemon

Stolistes

Dadouchos

Rose
Salt   Lamp
Cup

Hiereus

Keryx

West

Sentinel

Figure 21: Neophyte Temple

Symbolically, the Temple is situated on the bottom portion of the Qabalistic Tree of Life with Malkuth in the far west and Yesod just east of the Altar. The Pillars of Mercy and Severity are represented by physical columns, one black and the other white. A veil behind the dais in the east represents a demarcation on the Tree, behind which is symbolically Tiphareth.

THE OFFICERS

The Greatly Honored Chiefs

The Hermetic Order of the Golden Dawn was founded and organized along the lines of a hierarchical system. It is headed and directed by three individuals known as the *Greatly Honored Chiefs.* These offices, like any other office in the Order system, can be filled by persons of either gender.

Besides their administrative duties, the G.H. Chiefs take on the godforms of certain Egyptian deities and act as magical batteries or channels that intercede between specific inner planes contacts and the rest of the membership.

The G.H. Chiefs include the Praemonstrator, the Imperator, and the Cancellarius. They are seated on a dais in the east—the direction of the dawning Sun that all Golden Dawn Temples are oriented toward.

In addition to wearing Lamens of the Circled Cross (a stylized form of the Rose Cross) these three officers wear the emblem of the Order they govern, the Cross and Triangle, on their outer cloaks. (Figure 54 in chapter 6.)

The Temple Chiefs

Individual Temples are governed by three adepts known as the Temple Chiefs, who answer unto the G.H. Chiefs and represent them in the Temple, assuming their Dias stations and symbolism when the G.H. Chiefs are not present. Temple Chiefs also go by the titles of Praemonstrator, Imperator, and Cancellarius, but they should not be confused with the G.H. Chiefs, as their administration extends only to the respective Temple placed in their care.

Præmonstrator

Præmonstrator is Latin for "guide" and "one who prophesies." The feminine form is *Præmonstratrix.* This officer is the teacher or instructor and symbolizes Water and the Qabalistic Sephirah of Chesed. The Egyptian Deity associated with this officer is Isis, premier Goddess and patron of magic. The ceremonial regalia worn by the Præmonstrator is primarily blue. He bears a scepter topped by a Maltese Cross. This officer also represents the grade of Adeptus Exemptus.

Imperator

Imperator is Latin for "commander, leader." The feminine form is *Imperatrix*. This officer is the lawgiver and symbolizes Fire and the Qabalistic Sephirah of Geburah. The Egyptian Deity associated with this officer is Nephthys, sister of Isis. The ceremonial regalia worn by the Imperator is primarily red, and he bears a red sword. This officer also represents the grade of Adeptus Major.

Cancellarius

Cancellarius is Latin for "chancellor," indicating a high official in a church or university. It originally meant "doorkeeper." Its implied meaning is an intermediate or someone who occupies a middle position. The feminine form is *Cancellaria*. This officer is the scribe, secretary, or recorder who is in charge of all written records, archives, and communications. The Cancellarius symbolizes Air and the Qabalistic Sephirah of Tiphareth. The Egyptian Deity associated with this officer is Thoth, the ibis-headed scribe of the Gods. The ceremonial regalia worn by the Cancellarius is primarily yellow and he bears a scepter topped by a Hexagram. This officer also represents the grade of Adeptus Minor.

THE SEVEN

Except for astral work, all ritual in the Temple is carried out by seven active officers who perform specific duties in the ceremonies of the Outer Order. They are: Hierophant, Hiereus, Hegemon, Keryx, Stolistes, Dadouchos, and Phylax. These titles are derived from those of officiating priests of the Eleusinian Mysteries in ancient Greece.

Many of these officers also represent various First Order grades, and while it is preferable that they hold the grade they represent (at a minimum) it is not usually required that they do so.

Hierophant

Hierophant comes from the Greek *Hierophantes*, "he who shows Sacred things" or "initiating priest." Its implied meaning is one who teaches spiritual matters, especially with regard to adorations and sacrifices. The feminine form is *Hierophantissa*. The Hierophant sits at the center of the dais in the east. He is the presiding officer and the inductor to the Mysteries, and also represents the Portal grade. His Lamen symbol is the circled Cross (like those of the three Chiefs), and his ritual implements are the crown-headed scepter and the white Banner of the East. The Egyptian Deity associated with the Hierophant is Osiris, the slain and resurrected god.

Of the seven active officers, only the Hierophant is required to be a member of the Second Order and, at a minimum, hold the grade of ZAM.

(Note: The member who served in the office of Hierophant for the semester immediately preceding the current one is known as the Past Hierophant. He is seated on the dais to the left of the Hierophant and partakes of the same symbolism. The Egyptian Deity associated with the Past Hierophant is Horus the Elder.)

Hiereus

Hiereus means "priest," which implies one who performs sacrifices in the Temple. The feminine form is *Hiereia*. Stationed in the west, the Hiereus is the sword-bearing Guardian of the Sacred Mysteries who protects the Hall from the profane and banishes all that is evil or unbalanced. His Lamen symbol is the Triangle, and his ritual implements are a sword and the black Banner of the West. The Egyptian Deity associated with the Hiereus is Horus, the hawk-headed avenger of the Gods. This officer also represents the grade of Philosophus.

Hegemon

Hegemon is Greek for "guide, leader." Its implied meaning is one who proceeds first on a path. The feminine form is *Hegemone*. Stationed between the two pillars just east of the Hall's center, the Hegemon is the Guardian of the Threshold of Entrance and Preparer of the Way for the Enterer. He guides the candidate through the Temple during initiation. His Lamen symbol is the cross, and his ritual implement is a miter-headed wand. The Egyptian Deity associated with the Hegemon is Ma'at, Goddess of justice and balance. This officer also represents the grade of Practicus.

Keryx

Keryx is Greek for "herald." Its implied meaning is one who announces, calls the meeting to order, and delivers messages. The feminine form is *Kerykissa*. Stationed in the

Southwest, the Keryx is the Warder within the Temple who guards against intrusion. He makes all proclamations and leads all processions around the Hall. His Lamen symbol is the caduceus, and he carries a red lamp and a caduceus staff. The Egyptian Deity associated with the Keryx is Anubis. This officer also represents the grade of Theoricus.

Stolistes

Stolistes means "preparer" or "decorator." Its implied meaning is one who sees that all ritual clothing and ornamentation are in readiness. The feminine form is the same. His station is in the north. The implement of the Stolistes is the Cup of Water, and he is in charge of all ritual purifications. His Lamen symbol is also the Cup. The Egyptian Deity associated with the Stolistes is Mut, the mother Goddess. This officer also represents the grade of Zelator.

Dadouchos

Dadouchos is Greek for "torch bearer." In the Eleusinian Mysteries, this officer was a woman who held the torch as a symbol of the way by which Demeter searched for her daughter. The feminine form is *Dadouche*. His station is in the south. The implement of the Stolistes is the Censer of Incense, and he is in charge of all ritual consecrations. His Lamen symbol is the Fylfot Cross or swastika, an ancient emblem of whirling forces. The Egyptian Deity associated with the Dadouchos is Neith, a Goddess of wisdom and war. Like the Stolistes, this officer also represents the grade of Zelator.

An Alternative symbol for the Dadouchos
The cross potent

Some readers might find the ancient emblem of the Fylfot Cross, otherwise known as the swastika, to be problematic for obvious reasons. It is highly unfortunate that this millennia-old Sacred symbol was misappropriated in the mid-twentieth century by Nazis, racists, and modern extremist political groups for their own corrupt, evil purposes. Such heinous purposes are entirely antithetical to the spiritual ideals of the Hermetic Order of the Golden Dawn.

Bear in mind that the whirling motion of the Dadouchos' Fylfot Cross, as indicated by the arm positions, was to the right. The Nazis used a tilted and reversed version of the symbol. However, it may still be too difficult for some to use the traditional symbol of the Dadouchos.

Luckily, there is an alternative symbol for magicians who simply cannot use the Fylfot Cross in their spiritual work: the Cross Potent (Figure 22). Like the Fylfot Cross, the Cross Potent is composed of 17 units derived from the 25-unit qamea of Mars and so it can fit many aspects of the esoteric symbolism the Order teachings require.

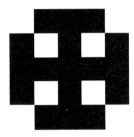

Figure 22: Cross Potent

___

Phylax

Phylax is Greek for "sentinel, guardian." The feminine form is *Phylakissa*. The Phylax is stationed in the Pronaos or antechamber to guard the outer side of the door and keep out intruders. His Lamen symbol is the all-seeing eye and his implement is a sword. The Egyptian Deity associated with the Phylax is Opowet, a wolf-headed God associated with Anubis and sometimes referred to as Anubis of the West. This officer also represents the grade of Neophyte.

All the officers work together to transmit the proper magical force in any initiation rite. The seven Outer Order officers are appointed to serve for a period of six months, from equinox to equinox. The Temple is magically reconsecrated at this time and the members are given a new password for the ensuing semester. See Figure 23 for the Lamen symbols for each officer.

Praemonstrator, Imperator, Cancellarius,
Hierophant, Past Hierophant

Figure 23: Lamen Symbols of the Officers

RITUAL DRAMA AND INITIATION

The initiation ceremonies of the Golden Dawn are a series of mystery plays or ritual dramas infused from beginning to end with various techniques and formulae of magic. The officers reenact specific mythologies essential to the Western Esoteric Tradition, including the spiritual legends of the ancient Egyptians, Hebrews, Greeks, and the Rosicrucians. The Neophyte Grade reenacts Egyptian legend of the "Weighing of the Soul" in the Hall of Truth. The mythological narrative that acts as the background for the Zelator Ceremony is the ancient Hebrew Tabernacle in the Wilderness described in the Book of Exodus. The Theoricus endures a ritualized passage through the Underworld. The Practicus allegorically undergoes the Samothracian Mysteries of Ancient Greece. The Philosophus witnesses a drama revolving around a Biblical account of the battle between good and evil, order and chaos. The Portal ceremony features elemental reintegration and balancing. And the Adeptus Minor is introduced to the story of Christian Rosenkreutz.

To effect a psychospiritual change in the awareness of the candidate, the ritual officers work as a team using the magical methods of divine theurgy—symbols and correspondences, manipulation of the astral light, and the faculties of willpower, visualization, and imagination—to give the ceremony its magical potency. Whether or not the candidate is made aware of the narrative drama underlying the ritual, every initiation ceremony is the focus of subtle manipulations of the astral light intended to help the candidate in his or her quest for spiritual growth.

A Golden Dawn initiation ceremony requires that certain magical forces be activated within the candidate's sphere of sensation. Because of this, it is crucial that a team of initiators be qualified and competent. They must be able to transmit the proper magical energies into the candidate's aura.

All of the symbols and movements in a Golden Dawn initiation ceremony, including the various signs, grips, gestures, and passwords, are designed to enhance and reiterate the purpose of the ritual—the quest for the Divine Light. Not all of the intricate symbolism is fully comprehended by the candidate, but that makes little difference in the long run, because the inherent value of such symbolism is that it has an autosuggestive effect on the candidate that is perceived at a deep, subconscious level.

If the entire initiatory process is successful, the candidate will have been given an infusion of divine energy, in the hope that he or she will indeed attain the increased awareness that is needed to exalt the soul and achieve the completion of the Great

Work. The objective of the entire system is to bring the Divine Light into all aspects of the soul and psyche. "For it is by that Light that the golden Banner of the inner life may be exalted; it is in light where lies healing and the power of growth." Although the initiating officers can provide the necessary magical impetus for this end, it is up to the individual aspirant to travel the path of initiation with heart and determination.

THE PSYCHOLOGY OF INITIATION

We often use the term "psyche" to indicate not only the soul but also the intellect, the Spirit, and the totality of all psychic processes. This includes the two primary divisions of the human psyche: the conscious and the unconscious.

Consciousness is that component of waking awareness perceptible to a person at any given instant. Consciousness is not merely "thinking" but also feeling, will, fantasy, and all other facets of waking life. It includes the ego—that portion of the psyche that governs thought and behavior. As a defense mechanism, the ego often creates a false front or outer persona—a mask that it presents to the outer world as reality, but which in fact conceals the true nature of the individual.

The unconscious can be further divided into the collective unconscious and the personal unconscious. Swiss psychologist Carl Jung's idea of the *collective unconscious*, or the mental patterns and psychic structures that are universally shared by all of humanity, comes very close to Eliphas Levi's idea of the astral light.

The impulses and content of the *personal unconscious*, on the other hand, are unique to the individual. The personal unconscious is the often-cited "evil twin" of the human psyche, containing all the repressed, forgotten, or rejected memories and drives that make up the *shadow*, a type of alter ego whose unconscious inclinations run opposite to those of the ego.

In magic, the shadow is analogous to the *qlippoth*—the unbalanced, and corrupted energies that offset the balanced, orderly, and positive aspects of the Sephiroth. The qlippoth are often symbolized collectively by the figure of a terrible red dragon. Rather than confronting their own shadow, their own "personal demon," many people project the attributes of the shadow onto someone else. Repressed psychic material not dealt with in an appropriate fashion will usually leak out in ways that are both unwanted and unhealthy.

The personal unconscious also includes the *animus* and *anima*, masculine and feminine soul images. The proper role of either one is to act as a *psychopomp* or "soul guide"—the mediator between the conscious and the unconscious.

One of the goals of the initiatory process is integration. This integration takes place on three levels: magical, alchemical, and psychological. All three can be said to involve three stages of progression, the purposes of which are similar, and overlap in different areas. In magic these stages can be called purification, consecration, and union. In alchemy they are called separation, purification, and recombination. In psychology these stages can be called analysis, confronting the shadow, and individuation or self-realization. These terms are merely different facets of the same goal: to achieve one's highest potential as a human being.

Golden Dawn initiation ceremonies are designed to instill within the candidate an awareness of his or her own divine nature, providing a means by which the magician can consciously release the psyche from the bondage of the repressed and projected shadow and facilitate integration of the newly purified portions of the psyche.

One objective of the initiation ceremonies is to gradually bring about a higher state of awareness that is essentially threefold: it encompasses the ideas of spiritual illumination, psychological health, and wholeness of being.

In an initiation ceremony, the officers represent the various component parts of the candidate's psyche all working together to effect a change in consciousness. Thus, the Keryx symbolizes the candidate's Ruach or intellectual mind leading the way on the path toward the Divine Light. He represents the lower part of the reasoning mind functioning in obedience to the Higher Will.

The active will of the candidate is represented by the Hiereus, who protects against all evil and imbalance.

The Hegemon is analogous to the highest part of the reasoning mind, working in combination with the divine soul. This officer symbolizes the Neshamah—the aspiring, compassionate, and intuitive consciousness that seeks to bring about the rise of the Light, and the one who guides the candidate along the way.

The Higher and Divine Genius is represented by the Hierophant. Symbolizing the supreme spiritual soul, this officer is stationed in the east, the place of the dawning Sun and the symbolic direction of the heavens. It is through him that the higher powers are brought into the Temple.

While an initiation ritual is certainly an artificial method for expressing the abstract psychological principles inherent with the human Spirit, a well-performed initiation can accelerate growth of consciousness and spiritual awareness within the candidate.

HIDDEN FORMULAS OF MAGIC

Another important aspect of the initiation rituals is this: hidden within them are countless formulas for practical magical work. These include techniques for evocation, consecration of talismans, spiritual development, and more, and are grouped together under the title of the Magic of Light (covered in chapter 10).

PURIFICATION EXERCISE 1: ELEMENTAL BALANCING

One of the essential steps in our theurgic process is to bring to the aspirant an awareness of the inner elemental makeup of his or her psyche in conjunction with the cleansing and balancing of these elements within the mind and aura.

In this exercise, the elements are imaged in the aura to mirror the placement of the elements in Malkuth. They are activated within the auric sphere of the magician by physical actions, visualizations, and vibration of godnames associated with the lower Sephiroth on the Tree and their associated elements.

1. Begin with your personal Pre-Ritual Meditation Practice.

2. Imagine a brilliant light above your head. Reach up with your right hand as if to touch this light and bring it down to your forehead. Imagine the yellow Triangle of Air superimposed over the upper part of your body. Vibrate **"SHADDAI EL CHAI"** (Shah-dye El Chai) a number of times until the vision and the vibration are clear and strong.

3. Then picture the black Triangle of Earth covering the lower portion of your body. Bring your hand down as if pointing to the ground and vibrate **"ADO-NAI HA-ARETZ"** (Ah-doh-nye Hah-Ah-retz) a number of times as before.

4. Visualize the red Triangle of Fire superimposed over the right side of your body. Touch your right shoulder and intone **"YHVH TZABAOTH"** (Yode-Heh-Vav-Heh Tzah-Bah-oth) several times as before.

5. Imagine the blue Triangle of Water covering the left side of your body. Touch your left shoulder and intone **"ELOHIM TZABAOTH"** (El-oh-heem Tzah-Bah-oth) several times.

6. Bring both hands together, interlocking the fingers, palms outward with the thumbs pointing down, and touch the area of your heart with your knuckles. Imagine the Spirit Wheel in white at the center of your body, uniting the

four elemental Triangles. Imagine the brilliant light above your head connected with this sigil of Spirit. Vibrate **"ETH"** until the vision and the vibration are clear and strong.

7. Begin the following visualizations with the rhythmic breathing of the Fourfold Breath:

   • *Inhale:* imagine the Fire Triangle

   • *Full Hold:* imagine the Water Triangle

   • *Exhale:* imagine the Air Triangle

   • *Empty Hold:* imagine the earth Triangle

8. Breathe normally. Strongly imagine all of the elemental Triangles within your psyche balanced and harmonized under the guidance of Spirit.

9. When finished, take note of how you feel and any insights that you may have experienced during the exercise.

The Exercise of the Three Pillars

This variation of the Middle Pillar exercise expands the basic exercise to include all the Sephiroth on the Tree of Life, bringing all of the divine energies of the Tree into the magician's aura.

The exercise can be performed standing, sitting, or lying down. Begin with closed eyes and rhythmic breathing.

Vibration of Sephiroth Godnames

1. Imagine a sphere of white light just above your head. Vibrate the name **"EHEIEH"** (Eh-hey-yay) three times or more until it is the only thought in your conscious mind.

2. Then imagine a shaft of white light descending from your Kether center to your Chokmah center at the left Temple of your forehead. Visualize a sphere of gray light there. Intone the name of **"YAH."** Keep vibrating the name the same number of times as before.

3. Bring a shaft of white light horizontally across from your Chokmah center to your Binah center at the right Temple of your forehead. Form a sphere of

black light there. Vibrate the name **"YHVH ELOHIM"** (Yode-heh-vav-heh El-oh-heem) a number of times as before.

4. Now bring a shaft of white light down diagonally from your Binah center to your Daath center at the nape of your neck. Visualize a sphere of gray-white light there. Vibrate the name **"YHVH ELOHIM."** Intone the name a number of times as before.

5. Next, visualize a shaft of white light down diagonally from the Daath center to your Chesed center at your left shoulder. Form a sphere of blue light there. Vibrate the name **"EL"** a number of times as before.

6. Bring a shaft of white light horizontally from Chesed to your Geburah center at your right shoulder. Visualize a sphere of red light there. Vibrate the name **"ELOHIM GIBOR"** (El-oh-heem Ge-boor). Intone the name a number of times as before.

7. Now bring a shaft of light diagonally across from Geburah to your Tiphareth center at your heart. Form a sphere of yellow light there. Vibrate the name **"YHVH ELOAH VE-DAATH"** (Yode-heh-vav-heh El-oh-ah V'-Dah-ath) a number of times.

8. Next, visualize a shaft of white light down diagonally from Tiphareth to your Netzach center at your left hip. Form a sphere of green light there. Vibrate the name **"YHVH TZABAOTH"** (Yode-heh-vav-heh Tzah-bah-oth) a number of times.

9. Bring a shaft of white light horizontally from Netzach to your Hod center at your right hip. Form a sphere of orange light there. Vibrate the name **"ELOHIM TZABAOTH"** (El-oh-heem Tzah-bah-oth). Intone the name a number of times as before.

10. Now see the shaft of white light descending diagonally from Hod into the Yesod center in the genital region. Imagine a sphere of violet light formed there. Intone the name **"SHADDAI EL CHAI"** (Shah-dye El-Chai) several times as before.

11. Next, visualize the shaft of light descending straight down from Yesod into your Malkuth center at the feet and ankles. Imagine a sphere of light formed there in the colors of citrine, russet brown, olive green, and black.

Vibrate the name **"ADONAI HA-ARTEZ"** (Ah-doe-nye Ha-Ah-retz) a number of times as before.

Visualized Circulation of Breath

Imagine the Tree of Life complete. Then circulate the light you have brought down through the various Sephiroth around the outside of your body to strengthen your aura. Use the same steps for visualizing the circulation of light and breath as you did for the basic Middle Pillar exercise (side to side, front to back, and in a shower of light).

Closing

12. Finally, center some of the energy in Tiphareth, the heart center, before ending the exercise.

VISUALIZATION EXERCISE: SWORD AND SERPENT

This visualization can be substituted for the Visualized Circulation of Breath at the end of the exercise of the Three Pillars.

1. After the Sephirah Malkuth has been established in your aura by visualization and vibration of the godname, visualize the Serpent of Wisdom slowly climbing the Tree of Life from its base in Malkuth, wending its way along the Navitoth, starting with the Path of Tau, and ending with the Path of Aleph. While imaging the slow ascent of the Serpent, begin a long, slow inhale of breath.

2. As you visualize the Serpent of Wisdom reaching the Path of Aleph at the top of the Tree, give a rapid exhale of breath and visualize the Flaming Sword striking all of the Sephiroth from Kether to Malkuth nearly simultaneously, bringing the ten spheres to vibrant life.

3. Repeat steps 1 and 2 for several cycles, with a slow inhale and ascent of the Serpent, followed by a rapid exhale and descent of the Flaming Sword. Imagine the flow of energy between the two polarities of Kether and Malkuth, Spirit and Matter, evolution and involution.

4. Finally, center some of the energy in Tiphareth, the seat of balance, before ending the exercise.

REVIEW QUESTIONS

1. The name of which officer originally meant "doorkeeper"?

2. Which officer is associated with Chesed?

3. Where do the names of the seven active officers come from?

4. What is the name of the Second Order?

5. Which grade is assigned to Water?

6. Which grade is assigned to Yesod?

7. Which grade is assigned to Sol?

8. What is the most important grade?

9. The three Orders are often mistaken for what?

10. What does the Second Degree consist of?

11. Define the word "psyche."

12. What is the shadow?

13. What term means "soul guide"?

14. What is the goal of initiation?

15. What is your experience of the exercise of the Three Pillars?

16. What is your experience of the Sword and Serpent exercise?

chapter 4

fIRST STEPS IN RITUAL

Until now, we have supplied students with basic information, meditations, and exercises that are a prerequisite to practicing Golden Dawn magic. We will continue to do so throughout this book. However, in this chapter we introduce the aspirant to the practice of ritual magic, culminating in one of the only rituals ever taught to students of the First Order in a traditional Order setting. This rite supplemented theoretical studies with a simple, yet highly effective ritual that is one of the hallmarks of the Golden Dawn tradition—the Lesser Ritual of the Pentagram. It is much more than a brief ceremony taught to Neophytes in order to slake their thirst for a bit of real magic. The magician performs this powerful little rite many times over during the course of his or her practice.

Ritual magic refers to any type of magic that follows a basic pattern or formula, whether simple or complex. It employs a ceremonial style as its main approach to working with spiritual entities and magical forces. Western ceremonial magic has long been interlaced with the wisdom of the Qabalah and Hermeticism. These two streams power the engine of our tradition.

Previous chapters have shown readers glimpses of ritual magic, through energized visualization, rhythmic circulation of breath, and vibration of godnames in such exercises as the Middle Pillar. Performance of the Lesser Ritual of the Pentagram takes this praxis one step further by invoking archangels to aid the magician's work.

A ritual must be practiced many times in order to be effective. So it is important not to get discouraged early on. An effective ritual is an astrally empowered piece of performance art: a working symbiotic relationship between the magician and the Divine. With every repetition the ritual changes slightly. You may notice something different, a new insight or visualization, an extended feeling of balance and calm, or an impression of the Presence of God. You may be surprised to find that after several performances of the same ritual with little effect, suddenly a clear channel opens up between you and Divinity, even if for just a few moments. For an instant your will is in alignment with Deity, and it is at this point of union that true magic happens. Only through practice can we extend those moments and manifest magical force to produce noticeable change and transformation.

At this point we present the reader with ritual tools that can be used for the exercises and rituals that follow.

THE BANISHING DAGGER

A banishing is a ritual designed to get rid of unwanted energies or entities. Banishing rituals often call for the magician to use a simple black-hilted dagger when tracing Pentagrams (Figure 24). This type of ritual dagger is mentioned in medieval grimoires such as *The Greater Key of Solomon* and later it became the model for the Wiccan athame. As its name implies, this dagger is only used for banishings.

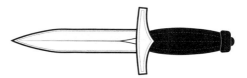

Figure 24: The Banishing Dagger

THE OUTER WAND OF DOUBLE POWER

In magic, a wand represents the magician's willpower. It can be used whenever the magician wishes to focus and direct energy. The Golden Dawn utilizes many different wands for various purposes.

The Outer Wand of Double Power (Figure 25) is a simple wand that beginners can employ for the basic Golden Dawn techniques of invoking and banishing. Half of the wand is painted black, the other half white. To invoke, grasp the wand by the center and point with the white. To banish, grasp the center and point with the black.

Figure 25: Outer Wand of Double Power

Just because this wand is simple in design does not mean it is less powerful than more advanced tools such as the Lotus Wand. It will become consecrated through frequent use and is an effective general-purpose wand for any ritual in this book.

COLOR VISUALIZATION EXERCISE: THE CROSS

For this exercise, you can use your index finger or the Outer Wand of Double Power.

1. Start in the standing position and begin with a brief period of rhythmic breathing.

2. When ready, extend your arm in front of you. Trace a vertical line straight down in bright yellow light (Figure 26). As you do so, vibrate **"YOD HEH."**

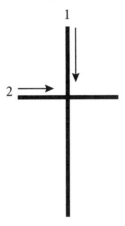

Figure 26: Tracing the Cross

3. Then trace a horizontal line that intersects above the middle of the first line, also in yellow light. As you do so, vibrate **"VAV HEH."** Strongly visualize the yellow Cross you have created.

4. Turn to your right. Follow the same steps as before and trace another Cross in the air, but this time imagine the lines of the figure in bright red. Visualize the red Cross vividly.

5. Turn left, back to your original position, then turn left again. Follow the same steps as before and trace another Cross, but this time imagine the lines of the figure in bright blue. See it clearly.

6. Return to your original central position and see the three Crosses you have created, hanging in the air. This time do not dissolve them.

7. Take note of how you feel and any insights that you may have experienced during the exercise.

An Introduction to the Qabalistic Cross

The Qabalistic Cross (often abbreviated as QC) is a potent little rite that establishes a Cross of Divine Light within the aura of the practitioner. The gestures given are similar to the Christian Cross, and the words are taken from the last few phrases of the Lord's Prayer, which is in turn based upon a Qabalistic Hebrew prayer.

This Cross is Qabalistic because it is associated with the Sephiroth of Kether, Malkuth, Geburah, Chesed, and Tiphareth. These Sephirotic energy centers are activated within the magician's auric sphere by physical gestures, visualizations, and vibration of names and words of power. These spheres also represent a balancing of the four elements within the magician's aura: Kether-Air, Malkuth-Earth, Geburah-Fire, and Chesed-Water. And although the name of Tiphareth is not vibrated, the balancing element of Spirit is indicated by the placing of the hands over the heart.

You may notice that in tracing the cross upon yourself, the right shoulder is touched before the left shoulder, which is opposite from the way that the Christian Cross is traced on the body. This is because you are tracing the Tree of Life *within* your auric body. To do this, visualize yourself with your back to the Tree of Life as if it were one with your spine. Your right shoulder is Geburah and your left shoulder is Chesed (also called *Gedulah*).

The Qabalistic Cross fortifies the aura and establishes balance within the psyche. Continued repetition of this rite alone will bring a measure of equilibrium and calm.

This simple ritual is often placed at the beginning or end of more complex rituals such as the Lesser Ritual of the Pentagram. It is also performed in the middle of many complex rituals. It is impossible to perform this powerful little rite too often. There is always time for it.

The Qabalistic Cross is the epitome of the magician's personal search for light that forms the basis of the Great Work. Properly performed, this single rite can do more to accomplish that work than hosts of more complicated methods.

The Qabalistic Cross (QC)

1. Stand and face east. Imagine a brilliant white light touching the top of your head. Reach up with the index finger or the white end of the Outer Wand of Double Power to connect with this light and bring it to the forehead.

2. Touch the forehead and vibrate **"ATAH"** (Ah-tah, meaning "Thou art").

3. Touch the breast and bring the white end of the wand or index finger down until it touches the heart or abdominal area, pointing down slightly to the ground. Imagine the light descending from the forehead to the feet. Vibrate **"MALKUTH"** (Mal-kooth, meaning "the Kingdom").

4. Touch the right shoulder and visualize a point of light there. Vibrate **"VE-GEBURAH"** (veh-Ge-boor-ah, meaning "the Power").

5. Touch the left shoulder and visualize a point of light there. See the horizontal shaft of light extending from the opposite shoulder to join this point of light. Vibrate **"VE-GEDULAH"** (veh-Ge-doo-lah, meaning "the Glory").

6. Imagine a completed Cross of light running from head to feet and shoulder to shoulder.

7. Bring the hands outward, away from the body, and finally bring them together again, clasped on the breast as if praying. See a point of light shining at the center of the brilliant Cross. Vibrate **"LE-OLAHM"** (bow your head) **"AMEN"** (Lay-oh-lahm, Ah-men, meaning "Forever, unto the Ages").

Expanded Visualization of the QC

To experience the Qabalistic Cross in its most potent form, add the following visualizations:

As you reach up above your head, imagine your astral self growing ever larger. Within your mind's eye, see yourself growing taller and taller until your form is like that of a vast angelic being whose head towers against the infinite expanse of the starry heavens. Picture your feet standing upon the earth, which is reduced to a tiny globe revolving beneath you. When this vision is clear in your mind, formulate a ray of brilliant white light descending upon your head. This Divine Light emanates from the infinite Kether of the Macrocosm beyond the stars and descends to connect with your Kether.

As you intone the words and mark your forehead and breast, see this divine white brilliance descending down the center of your body to your feet in an enormous shaft of light. This grounds the light in the earth, represented by your physical body, as Spirit joins with matter.

As you mark your shoulders while intoning the names, trace the horizontal Crossbar of this enormous Cross of white brilliance, equilibrating the light within your aura.

After completing the Qabalistic Cross, imagine your body returning to its normal size, but maintain the visualized connection with the shaft of Divine Light from the infinite Kether of the heavens.

THE PENTAGRAM

The most common and recognizable symbol in all of magic is the Pentagram or "five-pointed star." It is sometimes called the "Blazing Star," "wizard's foot," the "Star of the Magi," and the "Star of the Microcosm." It is known as the *pentalpha* because it can be constructed out of five Greek alphas (A) (Figure 27).

Figure 27: The Pentagram and the Elements

No one knows the exact magical origins of the Pentagram, but for centuries the five-pointed star has been used as a symbol of protection and an amulet for health and well-being. It was popular among the Babylonians, Egyptians, Assyrians, and Hebrews. According to Eliphas Levi, magicians of old used to draw the symbol upon their doorsteps, to keep malevolent Spirits out and beneficent Spirits in. As early as the sixth century B.C.E., Pythagoras, the Greek philosopher-mystic, used the Pentagram as a holy symbol for his followers.

Taken together, the Pentagram and the pentagon display a mathematic proportion called the Golden Ratio or *phi*, named after the Greek letter. One of the most important principles in Sacred geometry, the Greeks considered phi a symbol of harmony and accord; its proportion is most pleasing to the human eye.

The Pentagram is attributed to the five elements of Fire, Water, Air, Earth, and Spirit, the metaphysical building blocks of all that exists. The fifth element of Spirit, also called the *quintessence* or "fifth essence," crowns and connects the other four. This Divine spark transcends the other elements and makes the whole of the Pentagram greater than the sum of its parts. The five points of the Pentagram are assigned to the five elements as shown in Figure 27.

But Spirit is the divine and guiding principle. This is one reason magicians stress the importance of keeping the Spirit point of the Pentagram upward. In this fashion, it represents the figure of a man with arms and legs outstretched, his head guided by Spirit. To reverse it would be to subject Spirit to the governance of matter. Thus the inverted Pentagram signifies chaos and evil.

Through the number five, the Pentagram is connected to the Hebrew letter Heh and Great Supernal Mother *Aima*, the Divine Feminine in the Qabalah. It is also attributed to Geburah on the Tree of Life and through its corresponding planet, Mars. This makes the figure a most potent magical symbol for defense and protection.

THE PENTAGRAMMATON

In conjunction with our discussion on the Pentagram, we must mention the *Pentagrammaton,* which is Greek for "Five-Lettered Name." This refers to the Hebrew name of Jesus, YHShVH, as rendered by Christian Qabalists of the Renaissance. There are two pronunciations for this name: *Yeheshuah*, usually spelled as Yod Heh Shin Vav Heh (YHShVH), and *Yehovashah*, spelled as Yod Heh Vav Shin Heh (YHVShH). In both cases, the name refers to the Tetragrammaton (YHVH) with the letter Shin placed in the center of the name to represent the descent of the quintessential Spirit into the realm of the four elements. Along with Eth (essence), Ruach (breath), and Eheieh (I am), the Pentagrammaton is one of the Hebrew names closely connected with the element of Spirit (Figure 28).

Figure 28: The Pentagrammaton

Note: In the Hebrew spellings of YHVH and YHShVH, magicians often like to place a dot in the center of the final letter Heh, ה to differentiate Heh-Water from Heh-Earth.

PENTAGRAM EXERCISES

The following exercises are designed to familiarize students with tracing the figure of a Pentagram combined with the various magical techniques that enliven and empower this symbol on the astral.

A: Visualization Exercise

1. Begin with your personal Pre-Ritual Meditation Practice.

2. When ready, stand and extend your arm straight out in front of you. Pointing with your index finger, bring your hand up higher and visualize a point of white light at the end of your finger. This is your starting point.

3. Trace the five lines of a large Pentagram in white light as shown in Figure 29. (After the fifth line, you will have reached the starting point.)

Figure 29: First Pentagram

4. Strongly visualize the figure in white light for a few moments. When you are satisfied with the strength of your vision, slowly let it fade.

5. When finished, point directly at the lower left point of the Pentagram that you previously created. This is the starting point. Trace the five lines of the Pentagram as shown in Figure 30.

Figure 30: Second Pentagram

6. Strongly visualize the figure in white light for a few moments. When you are satisfied with the strength of your vision, slowly let it fade.

7. Take note of how you feel and any insights that you may have experienced during the exercise.

B: Vibration Exercise

1. Perform steps 1 and 2 as in the previous exercise.

2. In tracing the first Pentagram, vibrate the names of the Hebrew letters associated with the five elements as you trace each line of the Pentagram, beginning with the starting point at the top: **"SHIN. HEH. HEH. VAV. YOD"** (Figure 31).

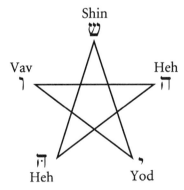

Figure 31: Hebrew Letters on the Pentagram

3. Repeat the tracing of the Pentagram and the intoning of the letters three more times. Take note of any feelings or insights gained through adding vibrations to the basic exercise.

4. When finished, slowly dissolve the figure. Take note of any feelings or insights.

5. Repeat the process with the second Pentagram by vibrating the letters of the five points as you trace each line, beginning with the starting point at the bottom: **"HEH. SHIN. YOD. VAV. HEH."**

6. When finished, slowly dissolve the figure. Record your impressions.

C: Color Visualization Exercise

1. Perform steps 1 through 7 as in exercise "A" on Pentagram visualization, but change the following:

2. As you trace the two Pentagrams, visualize them in red lines, instead of white.

3. Repeat the entire exercise using blue lines. Repeat again with yellow lines, and again with black lines.

D: Color Visualization Exercise

1. Perform steps 1 through 7 as in exercise "A" but change the following:

2. As you trace the two Pentagrams, visualize them in black lines.

3. Then "color between the lines" by imagining all the interior portions of the Pentagram in red. Then imagine all interior portions between the lines in blue, followed in turn by white, yellow, and black.

E: Color Visualization Exercise

1. Perform steps 1 through 7 as in exercise "A" but change the following:

2. As you trace the two Pentagrams, visualize them in black lines.

3. Then "color between the lines" by imagining the interior sections of the five outer angles of the Pentagram in the color of their respective elements as indicated in Figure 32.

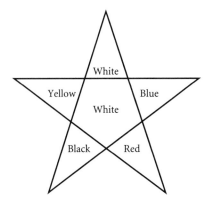

Figure 32: Colors of the Pentagram

F: Intention Exercise

1. Perform steps 1 through 7 as in exercise "A" on Pentagram visualization, but add the following:

2. When tracing the first Pentagram, imagine that the figure is like a key that opens a door. State the following magical intention: **"To all that is Sacred, balanced, harmonious, and beneficial to me at this time; be welcomed."** Pause for a few moments to take in any images, thoughts, or feelings before allowing the figure to fade.

3. When tracing the second Pentagram, imagine that the figure is like a key that closes a door. State the following magical intention: **"To all entities present at this time, go with peace and blessings back to your abodes and habitations."** Allow the image to fade.

4. After you have completed the exercise, take note of any feelings or insights.

G: Divine Light Exercise

1. Perform steps 1 through 7 as in exercise "A" but add the following:

2. After your personal Pre-Ritual Meditation Practice, perform the Qabalistic Cross with the Expanded Visualization given earlier in this chapter.

3. In tracing the Pentagram, picture the shaft of light at your Kether center receiving more energy from the Macrocosmic Kether and welling up from

your Malkuth to gather at your Tiphareth center, where the light is at its strongest. Will and visualize the light going down your arm and out your hand to inscribe the Pentagram.

4. Add the QC to any of the previous exercises listed above.

5. After you have completed an exercise, take note of any feelings or insights.

INTRODUCTION TO THE LESSER RITUAL OF THE PENTAGRAM

Traditionally, only one magical rite was ever given to Outer Order students for their own personal use—the *Lesser Ritual of the Pentagram* (sometimes shortened to the *Lesser Pentagram Ritual* for convenience). While probably the best-known of the Golden Dawn's practices, this little ritual is actually quite powerful and contains most of the techniques used in more complicated magical work. Simply put, it is one of the staples of Golden Dawn practice.

There are two forms of this ritual, one for invoking energies and one for banishing them. Respectively, they are the *Lesser Invoking Ritual of the Pentagram* and the *Lesser Banishing Ritual of the Pentagram*. A banishing ritual is often performed as a prelude to more complex rituals, to "clear" the area beforehand. An invoking ritual has the opposite effect—it is designed to summon forces into the Temple space.

We often use abbreviations in place of long ritual names. Readers have already encountered some of these: the Qabalistic Cross (QC) and Middle Pillar (MP). In this chapter you will come across the following, listed in Table 24.

Table 24: LRP Abbreviations

LRP	Lesser Ritual of the Pentagram
LBRP	Lesser Banishing Ritual of the Pentagram *(a form of the LRP)*
LIRP	Lesser Invoking Ritual of the Pentagram *(a form of the LRP)*

While some magicians assume that one form of the LRP is more important than the other, both are *equally* important for the beginner to memorize and use. They are two halves of the same coin. The Invoking form is the on-switch, the Banishing form is the off-switch. To stress one above the other creates imbalance.

That being said, the novice should concentrate on the Banishing form daily for the first three months of one's practice. Beginners have a tendency to light up on the astral and unknowingly attract all manner of elementals at this early stage of the work.

Therefore, it is far more important for the newcomer to know how to banish. Anyone can attract an elemental, Spirit, or energy. Getting rid of the same can be more difficult.

Performing the LBRP exclusively for three months has the added effect of sweeping out the astral cobwebs and residual "junk" from one's personal magical circle, leaving the practitioner and their Sacred Space ordered, balanced, and uncluttered. Only then should the beginner commence a regular practice employing the LIRP to open and the LBRP to close a magical working.

Anytime a magician (beginner or adept) intends to work in a space that doubles as someone's bedroom, living room, or library, the Lesser Banishing Ritual of the Pentagram should be used as a preliminary cleansing rite. The same is true for an active Temple space that has recently been used for magical work that is different in energy from the work at hand. This also applies to the magician's personal auric circle if they have been engaged in nonmagical, mundane, or stressful activities for much of the day (and who hasn't!), to purify themselves before beginning their magical practice. In all of these cases, performing the LBRP as a cleansing procedure prior to a ritual or other magical working (without the accompanying LIRP) could be more accurately referred to as a preliminary clearing rather than banishing. It can also be used to shut down a ritual at the conclusion of the working, and to bid farewell to the divine and angelic forces that have been invoked.

Many students make the mistake of thinking that the Lesser Ritual of the Pentagram is used to invoke or banish the elements, particularly the element of Earth. This is understandable since the figure of the Pentagram relates to the five elements. The invoking and banishing Pentagrams used in the LRP are identical with the invoking and banishing Earth Pentagrams used in more advanced elemental rituals, so it is common for students to erroneously identify these as Earth Pentagrams.

However, the Lesser Ritual of the Pentagram is used for general purpose invocations and banishings, particularly in the Sephirah of Malkuth in the Qabalistic world of Assiah, the physical, active realm. This is the world in which we live and function. Malkuth is said to contain the four elements of the manifest Universe, which is why in many drawings Malkuth is shown divided into four sections. These sub-elements are: Air of Malkuth, Water of Malkuth, Fire of Malkuth, and Earth of Malkuth. With respect to the entire Tree of Life, Malkuth is the only Sephirah that corresponds to the element of Earth. This is why the earth Pentagram in particular is used throughout the LRP. However, in this instance it would be better to refer to the Pentagram used in the LRP as the *Lesser Pentagram* to avoid confusion. Here Pentagrams are used to invoke or banish energies associated with all four quarters or sub-elements of Malkuth, the material world, especially as they relate to the magician's physical and psychic environment.

There are four parts to the LRP:

1. Opening: The Qabalistic Cross

2. Tracing the Pentagrams

3. The Conjuration of the Four Archangels

4. Closing: The Qabalistic Cross

THE LESSER INVOKING RITUAL OF THE PENTAGRAM (LIRP)

This ritual uses only one form of the Pentagram, the Lesser Invoking Pentagram (Figure 33). The elements are assigned to the directions in accordance with the "four winds" attributions of the ancients: Air–east, Fire–south, Water–west, and Earth–north.

Figure 33: Lesser Invoking Pentagram

1. Use your index finger or the white end of the Outer Wand of Double Power to trace the Qabalistic Cross and the Pentagrams.

Opening: The QC

2. Go to the eastern side (or the center) of the Temple and perform the Qabalistic Cross.

Tracing the Pentagrams

3. Trace a large Lesser Invoking Pentagram. Thrust the implement through the center of the Pentagram and vibrate **"YHVH"** (Yod-hey-vav-hey). Keep your arm extended throughout, never let it drop. The Pentagrams should be visualized in white light.

4. Turn and walk clockwise to the south and trace the same Pentagram there. Charge the figure as before, intoning **"ADONAI"** (Ah-doh-nye).

5. Go to the west and trace the same Pentagram. Charge it with **"EHEIEH"** (Eh-hey-yay).

6. Go to the north and draw the same Pentagram, this time intoning the word **"AGLA"** (Ah-gah-lah).

Conjuration of the Four Archangels

7. Keep the arm extended. Turn to face the east. Extend both arms out in the form of a Tau Cross (a "T" shape) and say, **"Before me, RAPHAEL"** (Rah-fah-yel). Visualize before you the great archangel of elemental Air rising out of the clouds, dressed in flowing yellow and violet robes, and carrying a caduceus wand (Figure 34).

Figure 34: Raphael

8. Behind you, visualize another figure and say, **"Behind me, GABRIEL"** (Gah-bree-el). See the winged archangel of elemental Water stepping out of the sea like the Goddess Venus, dressed in robes of blue and orange, with cup in hand (Figure 35).

Figure 35: Gabriel

9. To your right, see another winged figure, the archangel of elemental Fire, dressed in flaming red and green robes carrying a mighty sword. Say, **"On my right hand, MICHAEL"** (Mee-kah-yel) (Figure 36).

Figure 36: Michael

10. See the great winged archangel of elemental Earth at your left, rising up from the vegetation of the ground in earth-toned robes of citrine, olive, russet, and black, holding stems of ripened wheat. Say, **"On my left hand, URIEL"** (Ur-ee-el) (Figure 37).

Figure 37: Uriel

11. Then say, **"For about me flames the Pentagram, and in the column shines the Six-Rayed Star."**

Closing: The QC

12. Repeat the Qabalistic Cross as in the beginning.

The Lesser Banishing Ritual of the Pentagram (LBRP)

The main difference between this ritual and the preceding one is that instead of tracing four Lesser Invoking Pentagrams in the four quarters, trace the *Banishing* form pictured in Figure 38.

Figure 38: Lesser Banishing Pentagram

1. Use your index finger, a Banishing Dagger, or the Outer Wand of Double Power. If using the wand, point with the black end to trace the Pentagrams.

Opening: The QC

2. Go to the east (or center) of the Temple and perform the Qabalistic Cross.

Tracing the Pentagrams

3. Go to the eastern edge of the Temple. Trace a large Lesser Banishing Pentagram toward the east. Thrust the implement through the center of the Pentagram and vibrate **"YHVH"** (Yod-hey-vav-hey). Keep the right arm extended throughout; never let it drop. The Pentagrams should be visualized in white light.

4. Turn and walk clockwise to the southern limits of the Temple and trace the same Pentagram there. Charge the figure as before, intoning **"ADONAI"** (Ah-doh-nye).

5. Go to the western boundary of the Temple and trace the same Pentagram toward the west. Charge it with **"EHEIEH"** (Eh-hey-yay).

6. Go to the northern edge of the Temple and draw the same Pentagram toward the north, this time intoning the word **"AGLA"** (Ah-gah-lah).

Conjuration of the Four Archangels

7. Keep the arm extended. Turn to face the east. Extend both arms out in the form of a Tau Cross (a "T" shape) and say, **"Before me, RAPHAEL"** (Rah-fah-yel). Visualize the archangel as you did in the LIRP.

8. Behind you, visualize another figure and say, **"Behind me, GABRIEL"** (Gah-bree-el). See Gabriel as you have previously envisioned the angel.

9. To your right, picture the fiery archangel Michael. Say, **"On my right hand, MICHAEL"** (Mee-kah-yel).

10. Visualize Uriel, the great archangel of elemental Earth at your left. Say, **"On my left hand, URIEL"** (Ur-ee-el).

11. Then say, **"For about me flames the Pentagram, and in the column shines the Six-Rayed Star."**

Closing: The QC

12. Return to the east (or center of the Temple). Repeat the Qabalistic Cross as in the beginning.

EXPANDED VISUALIZATION OF THE LESSER PENTAGRAM RITUAL

To experience the Lesser Pentagram Ritual in its most potent form (both invoking and banishing versions), add the following visualization:

After opening with the Qabalistic Cross, maintain the vision of the shaft of Divine Light blending Spirit and matter within you. As you trace the Pentagrams, picture this shaft of light at your Kether center receiving more energy from the infinite Kether beyond, yet grounded in the Malkuth center at your feet—pulling the divine energy back upwards in a reflux current toward the center of your being. Picture the light at its strongest around your Tiphareth center. Will and visualize the light going down your arm and out your hand or implement to inscribe the Pentagrams that should be about three or four feet from point to point.

When tracing the Pentagrams, visualize them as blazing white stars in the four quarters surrounding you. See them connected by a white ring of astral Fire studded in the four cardinal directions with stars of white flame.

As you intone the divine names, imagine that the force of your vibrations extends to the ends of the Universe in the four directions.

Take time to visualize the four archangels, focusing on their color and elemental attributions. Your vision of them may not be exactly the same as someone else's. Just be sure that they are consistent with each other as a group.

Uses of the Pentagram Ritual

In addition to the uses of the Lesser Pentagram Ritual already mentioned, both the invoking and Banishing forms can be employed to enhance your skill at visualization. You should be able to visualize a banishing Pentagram every bit as strongly as you would an invoking one!

Both forms of the LRP can be used as exercises in concentration. While seated or lying down, visualize yourself robed and standing while holding a dagger or wand. Place your consciousness in this astral form and go to the east of your Temple space. In your mind's eye, make yourself *feel* as if you were there by touching the wall, stamping on the floor, etc. Let your astral form execute the ritual, circumambulating the room and mentally vibrating the words. Finish in the east and try to see your results astrally, then walk back, stand behind your physical body, and let your astral body be reabsorbed.

In a small space, the magician can simply stand and turn in place to draw the Pentagrams in the respective quarters. In a larger Temple setting, the magician may perform the Qabalistic Cross standing in the eastern part of the Temple, or directly west of the Altar facing east, but should go to the eastern part of the Temple and walk around the perimeter of the room to trace the Pentagrams.

Here are some of the uses of the LRP:

- General invoking and banishing of energies

- Building and dismantling a magic circle

- Purifying one's personal auric circle

- Strengthening one's skill in visualization, vibration, and willpower

- Protection against negativity and unwanted energies

- Creating a link with the Divine (through the QC)

- Linking with the great archangels of the elements and cardinal points

- Grounding, centering, and calming

- Creating structures (Pentagrams) within the psyche that will permit easier access to the higher planes

- Daily work with this ritual is a form of self-initiation that mirrors on a Microcosmic level the work of the First Order within the magician's aura

After three months of doing just the LBRP for the reasons we stated earlier, you can switch to the regime suggested in the Golden Dawn manuscripts: perform the LIRP in the morning to invoke energy at the start of the day and the LBRP at night to close the energies down.

The Banishing form can be used as a protection against the impure magnetism of others. It is also a way to rid one's self of obsessing or disturbing thoughts. Give a mental image to your particular thought or disturbance and visualize it before you. Cast it out of your aura with the Projection Sign described at the end of this chapter, and when it is away from you, prevent its return with the Sign of Silence. Then imagine the unwanted form in the east and perform the LBRP. See the form dissolving on the outside of your ring of flaming Pentagrams.

SYMBOLISM AND ALCHEMY OF THE LRP

The initial Qabalistic Cross signifies the magician striving to connect with the Higher and Divine Genius, which is discussed in chapter 9. After the QC, the magician traces the Lesser Pentagram in all four quarters, beginning in the east and walking clockwise.

After returning to the east, the magician stands with arms extended in the form of the cross, identifying him- or herself with the Tau Cross of life, a symbol of knowledge gained through sacrifice, but also related to the ideas of mercy and justice. Next comes the invocation of the four archangels, who represent the Divine Creator governing the four elements and the four directions: Raphael, the "Healer of God," is assigned to Air and the east. Gabriel, the "Strong One of God," is assigned to Water and the west.

Michael, "He who is like God," is assigned to Fire and the south. Uriel, "Light of God," is assigned to Earth and the north. These mighty beings will be among the magician's most constant of angelic companions. While the Pentagrams were drawn for *purification* of the circle, the archangels are invoked to *consecrate* the circle with the forces of the Divine Light.

Then comes the statement, "For about me flame the Pentagrams, and in the column shines the Six-Rayed Star." The Six-Rayed Star is the Hexagram or "Star of David," which is the star of the Macrocosm or Greater Universe. It is formed from the two Triangles of Fire and Water, and it symbolizes perfection and total balance. While the Pentagram is the symbol of man, the central Hexagram is the symbol of perfected or purified man, balanced within the Greater Universe.

Like the physical world, the astral realm is not simply a flat plane; it exists in three dimensions. The same is true of the Qabalistic Tree of Life. It is extremely useful to consider the Tree of Life as a two-dimensional road map that stretches in front of or above us. This is by far the easiest way to visualize and incorporate the Tree into our practice. But there are a few times when the magician can imagine the Tree of Life in three dimensions projected onto a model of what astronomers know as the Celestial Sphere or star globe. This is a representation of the stars and constellations divided into two parts at the earth's equator into northern and southern hemispheres, like two great dish-shaped convex bowls that cover our planet, seen from the inside looking out, as if you were in a planetarium. Think of the Celestial Sphere as the earth's aura, complete with its own Middle Pillar. Kether is at the North Pole, Malkuth is at the South Pole, and Tiphareth is at its central core. Sephiroth *not* on the Middle Pillar are duplicated within this aura, resulting in four outer pillars (two black and two white) that mark four directions in space.

These star maps can be found in Israel Regardie's *The Golden Dawn*.[6] But for our purposes, you need only refer to the drawing of the three-dimensional Tree of Life in Figure 39. It is derived from the Order's teachings on the star maps, but applies equally to the individual human aura.

---

6. Israel Regardie, *The Golden Dawn*, 7th edition (Woodbury, MN: Llewellyn Publications, 2015), 751, 760-761.

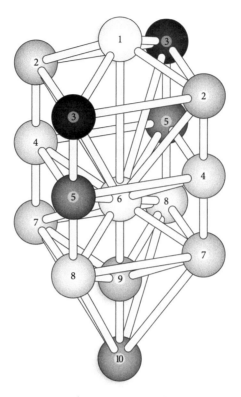

Figure 39: Three-Dimensional Tree of Life

The Lesser Ritual of the Pentagram functions as a type of self-initiation rite that, practiced over time, imprints the three-dimensional Tree of Life as it exists within the magician's sphere of sensation. Each tracing of the Pentagram cleanses and purifies the aura four times—once for each outer pillar in the aura. The magician's purified Middle Pillar sits at the center, symbolized by the "six-pointed star" between the columns (Figure 40).

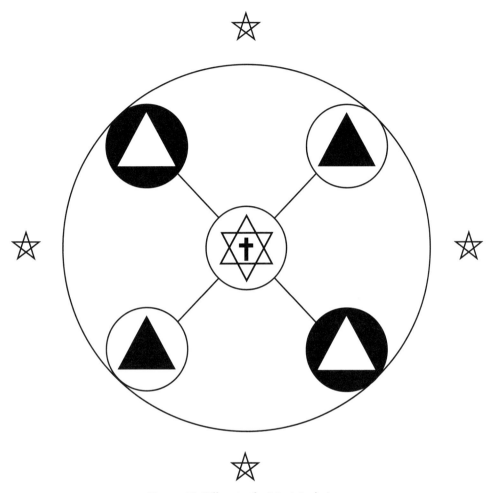

Figure 40: Pillars in the Magician's Aura

Figure 40 shows the pillars of the Tree of Life as projected into a three-dimensional sphere (a kind of star map) within the magician's aura. There are different variations on this diagram; however, this particular version helps the beginner understand how the Sephiroth correspond to the human body in such rites as the Qabalistic Cross. Four pillars, two black and two white, surround the magician who stands at the center, at the position of the Middle Pillar indicated by the Hexagram. The top of the diagram represents the east and the auric pillars that are before the magician. The bottom of the diagram represents the west and the auric pillars that are behind the magician. The Pentagrams are those that are traced in the four quarters during the LRP.

Golden Dawn magicians view the usual diagram of the Tree of Life as the face or front side of the Divine that stands before us. This image of the Tree is then mirrored back to us as though we were backing into a drawing of the Tree. Thus Geburah, on the Deity's right shoulder, is reflected back to our right shoulder, as we touch our right shoulder and vibrate "ve-Geburah." Chesed, also called Gedulah, is on the Deity's left side, which is reflected back to us as we touch our left shoulder and vibrate "ve-Gedulah." As magicians, we seek to bring the image of God inside our sphere of sensation to connect with Divinity.

The final Qabalistic Cross of the LRP further strengthens and seals the cross of light within the magician's aura. It also astrally transforms the Hexagram into the Banner of the East (chapter 6, Figure 56), which symbolizes divinity and the ultimate goal of the Great Work.

DIVINE HEBREW NAMES ASSOCIATED WITH THE LRP

All Hebrew godnames intoned in the Lesser Ritual of the Pentagram are composed of four letters; therefore, they are all considered tetragrams. The specific names used are attributed to the four sub-elements of Malkuth. The name of YHVH, the Tetragrammaton, is vibrated after the Pentagram is drawn in the east, the direction of elemental Air. Tradition tells us that YHVH is a symbol for the highest most divine name of God. Therefore, it is appropriate that this name is vibrated in the east, the place of the dawning of the light. YHVH is our sunrise, our source of life.

Adonai ("lord") is vibrated after the figure is traced in the south. This name is particularly associated with Malkuth, whose complete divine name is Adonai ha-Aretz. The title "lord" carries with it connotations of high rank, especially power, rulership, and dominion. Here the name is associated with Fire and the south, the direction of the Sun's greatest strength. This is a reminder that here in Malkuth, our immediate symbolic link with the lord of light and strength is through the life-giving rays of the Sun.

The godname of Kether, Eheieh, is vibrated after the western Pentagram. The west is the direction of sunset and the completion of the Sun's journey across the sky. It represents rest, peace, and the goal of spiritual attainment. To the ancient Egyptians, the Sun God Ra died each night when he entered Amentet—the west. Therefore, the west is an emblem of Kether, the goal that we seek throughout our incarnation on Earth and that we hope to reach at the end of life, when we, like Ra, journey to Amentet. The name Eheieh vibrated in the west suggests that the goal of all esoteric work is the magician's complete identification with the true and eternal Self of Kether.

In the north, the word "Agla" is vibrated. This is a notariqon formed from the initial letters of the phrase *Atah Gebur Le-Olam Adonai*, meaning "Thou art Great forever, my Lord." This is a powerful invocation, clearly calling upon all the might of Adonai to aid and guide us through the darkness of things unknown. Agla is vibrated in the north because that is the direction of the greatest symbolic cold, darkness, shadow, illusion, and the unfamiliar. It represents all the dormant and unmanifested forces of the Universe, as well as those that are hidden from us. These are forces we are largely ignorant of. However, all things, manifest or unmanifest, light or dark, exist then, now, and always under the rulership of Adonai. This we affirm by the phrase "Thou art Great forever, my Lord!"

Tracing the Pentagrams creates a cleansing, protective circle of force that is further empowered by the invocation of the four tetragrams of power around the boundary of the student's magical sphere. The archangels provide the ritual with a huge amount of stability and support.

The importance of the Golden Dawn's Lesser Ritual of the Pentagram cannot be overstated. Those who dismiss it as a simplistic rite of worth only to Neophytes are sadly mistaken. The LRP is one of the most potent, succinct, and perfectly constructed tools for all manner of magical work.

A Banishing with a Bang!

We once knew of a magician who wanted to rev up the power in his practice of the Lesser Banishing Ritual of the Pentagram. His performance was fairly standard, except for the fact that his chosen magical implement was a .38 special. He did the Qabalistic Cross and traced his Pentagrams in the air, vibrated the divine names . . . and charged the Pentagram by firing the gun through the center of the figure. He did this in all four quarters of his Temple space and ended up with bullet holes in all four walls. We're not sure if he attained his magical objective, but his banishing was effective. He banished his roommates, his family, and his landlord!

There may have been several reasons for this stunning display of poor judgment. One culprit may have been the classic "lust for results," wherein the magician focuses on the ends justifying the means. This throws the magician off balance, drives him or her to make poor choices, and diminishes the success of the ceremony. One way to make sure your ritual work is safe and effective is to use your common sense. You will be a better magician for it.

MAGICAL GESTURES

Ritualized gestures are used in the Order system as symbols of one's rank or grade. However, these same gestures are also used in the magician's personal practice for attracting, invoking, projecting, or curtailing specific energies. They are extensions of the magician's own auric energy field. Combined with visualization and intention, these physical gestures become living sigils in the astral light and are recognized as such by spiritual entities that are in affinity with them.

Two signs are ascribed to the Neophyte Grade: the Projection Sign and the Sign of Silence (Figure 41).

The Projection Sign

The Projection Sign is also called "the Saluting Sign," "the Sign of the Enterer," "the Attacking Sign," and "the Sign of Horus." First, bring the arms up as if touching Kether, then bring the hands down to either side of the head at eye level, fingers extended, hands held flat with palms down. Then step forward with the left foot, and at the same time thrust the arms directly forward, and sink the head till the eyes look exactly between the thumbs.

This sign is a forceful gesture for projecting energy at or through a symbol such as the Pentagram.

The Sign of Silence

The Sign of Silence is also called "the Sign of Protection" and "the Sign of Harpocrates." After giving the Projection Sign, bring the left foot back sharply, both heels together, stamping the ground once with the left foot as it is placed beside the right. At the same time, bring the left hand to the mouth and touch the center of the lower lip with the left forefinger. Close the other fingers and thumb and drop the right hand to the side.

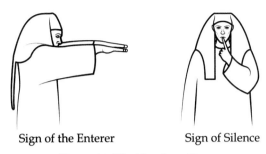

Sign of the Enterer   Sign of Silence

Figure 41: The Neophyte Signs

The Sign of Silence is used to stop the flow of energy from rebounding or to mark the end of a cycle.

The next four signs (Figure 42) are the symbolic gestures of the elemental grades, but they are also used to attract and acknowledge the powers of the elements.

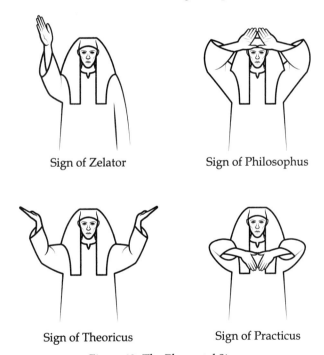

Sign of Zelator   Sign of Philosophus

Sign of Theoricus   Sign of Practicus

Figure 42: The Elemental Signs

The Sign of Earth

The Sign of Earth is called the Zelator Sign in the Order system. Raise the right arm straight up in a forty-five degree angle from the body, hand held flat with the thumb facing toward the ceiling. This sign is given after tracing an Earth Pentagram.

The Sign of Air

The Sign of Air is referred to as the Theoricus Sign in the Order system. Bend both arms at the elbow. Keep the hands at the level of the head, palms upward as if supporting a great weight. The sign is usually given after the tracing of an Air Pentagram.

The Sign of Water

The Sign of Water is the Practicus Sign. Form a Triangle apex downward over the chest with both hands. Keep the elbows level with the shoulders. This sign is given after tracing a Water Pentagram.

The Sign of Fire

The Sign of Fire is also referred to as the Philosophus Sign. Form a Triangle apex upwards on the forehead with both hands, palms outward. This sign is usually given after tracing a Fire Pentagram.

The Portal Signs

Like the grade of Neophyte, the Portal grade has two signs: the Opening of the Veil and the Closing of the Veil (Figure 43). Both are assigned to the element of Spirit: the first sign invokes Spirit and the second sign banishes it.

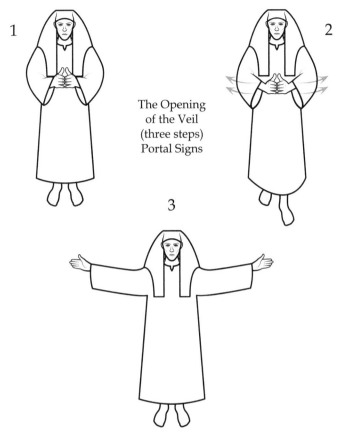

The Opening
of the Veil
(three steps)
Portal Signs

Figure 43: The Portal Signs

The Opening of the Veil

The Opening of the Veil is also called the Rending of the Veil. Clasp the hands together as if praying, then thrust them forward. Take a step forward with the left foot and separate the hands as if opening a curtain. Bring the right foot even with the left and extend your arms in the Tau Cross. This sign is used to invoke Spirit and is often given after tracing an Invoking Spirit Pentagram.

The Closing of the Veil

The Closing of the Veil is performed by following the steps in reverse order of the Opening sign. It is used to banish Spirit and is often given after tracing a Banishing Spirit Pentagram.

All of the Pentagrams described here are explained in chapter 7.

The LVX Signs

Collectively, the LVX Signs belong to the Adeptus Minor grade. Refer to the description of these signs in the section on the "Analysis of the Keyword" in chapter 8.

Magical gestures should not be simply rushed through in order to get to the next point in a ceremony. Each of them can be the subject of a separate meditation. Frequent meditation on each gesture can help the magician empower these living sigils in ritual. Meditate on one particular gesture per day or per week.

REVIEW QUESTIONS

1. What was the model for the athame?

2. What does a wand represent in magic?

3. What does LIRP stand for?

4. Why is the Pentagram called a pentalpha?

5. What Greek philosopher used the Pentagram as a holy symbol?

6. What Hebrew letter is assigned to the Pentagram?

7. What letters make up the Pentagrammaton?

8. How does the Pentagrammaton relate to the Tetragrammaton?

9. Why doesn't the Lesser Pentagram Ritual use all four Elemental Pentagrams?

10. Name some of the uses of the LRP.

11. What is your experience of the Lesser Ritual of the Pentagram? How often do you practice the invoking and banishing versions?

chapter 5

THE TAROT:
INTERPRETING MAGICAL IMAGES

Much of the material covered in chapter 2 concerning the "ABCs" of magic—the elements, Hebrew letters, Qabalistic Sephiroth, Four Worlds, planets, and zodiacal signs—all correlate with various cards of the tarot (the tarot's Universe card is shown in Figure 44). Not only is the tarot an important metasystem of magical images, it is a powerful tool for developing the magician's faculties of intuition and psychic awareness.

The tarot, or "Book T" as it is sometimes called, is a pictorial book of ageless, esoteric wisdom. For centuries, magicians, occultists, and mystics have used it for the purposes of divination and meditation. Like the Qabalah, the tarot is a complete and elaborate system for describing the hidden forces behind the manifest Universe. It is a key to all occult science and a map for uncovering the various parts of the human psyche. The cards of the tarot are the hieroglyphs of the Western Mystery Tradition.

The Golden Dawn considers the tarot primarily as a tool for meditation, for developing a connection with the Divine, and for training the magician's intuitive abilities. Divination, the principal reason most people buy a tarot deck, is also important, but secondary. Tarot cards express truths about the essence of the Universe and our relationship to it.

The original tarot used by the Golden Dawn was based upon W. Wynn Westcott's and S. L. MacGregor Mathers's work and research. Moina Mathers made subsequent drawings of the cards. Advanced students were required to copy all the cards by hand and use them in their personal practice. Many of the most popular tarot decks of today, including the Rider-Waite tarot deck and Aleister Crowley's Thoth tarot deck, are based upon Mathers's originals.

Figure 44: The Universe Card

QABALISTIC ASSOCIATIONS OF THE TAROT

The two systems of Qabalah and tarot are so strikingly similar that they easily comple-ment each other. The traditional tarot deck consists of seventy-eight cards made up of four suits of fourteen cards each, together with twenty-two Trumps. The Trumps are collectively called the Major Arcana or "greater mysteries" and tell the story of the Soul. The Trumps are each referred to as one of the twenty-two paths that connect the Sephi-roth on the Tree of Life. They also correspond to the twenty-two letters of the Hebrew alphabet.

The Minor Arcana or "lesser mysteries" has fifty-six cards. Each tarot suit of the Minor Arcana consists of ten numbered (or "pip") cards, as in modern playing cards, but there are four instead of three royal cards: the King, Queen, Prince, and Princess, resulting in a total of sixteen court cards.

The four suits are:

1. **Wands** (or Scepters) comparable to clubs

2. **Cups** (or Chalices) comparable to hearts

3. **Swords** comparable to spades

4. **Pentacles** (or Coins) comparable to diamonds

The ten numbered cards of each suit correspond to the ten Sephiroth. The four suits refer to the letters of Tetragrammaton and to the Four Qabalistic Worlds thus: Wands to Yod (Atziluth), Cups to Heh (Briah), Swords to Vav (Yetzirah), Pentacles to Heh Final (Assiah).

The sixteen court cards, or *honors* as they are sometimes called, are the ambassadors of the great name YHVH in the Qabalistic World to which each suit is referred.

The Minor Arcana cards represent the Sephiroth as objective centers of energy emanating from the Divine. They are static and fixed points of force whose qualities are impartial and immobile. These cards allude to the inherent and unchangeable parts of the human psyche.

The twenty-two paths and their corresponding Trump cards, on the other hand, are active and moving. They are subjective conduits or energy channels that run between the Sephiroth, connecting the spheres. These cards represent our own mutable experiences as we travel the pathways on the Tree of Life, encountering the differences that occur between one Sephirah and the next.

MAJOR ARCANA: THE TRUMPS

In addition to their Hebrew letter attributions, the twenty-two Trump cards represent the energies of the planets, the signs of the zodiac, and the elements. These paths, numbered 11 through 32 on the Tree of Life diagram in Figure 9, are dynamic, subjective conduits of karmic energy. They symbolize forces in transit and allude to the powers of consciousness in illustrated form. Their position on the Tree is imaged by the winding path of the Serpent of Wisdom. Unlike the cards of the Minor Arcana, the Trump cards are considered true initiatory forces—having both an esoteric or spiritual meaning as well as an exoteric or mundane meaning used in divination.

Table 25 shows how the Trumps align with the Hebrew letters.

Table 25: Tarot Trumps and the Hebrew Letters

Card	Letter	Path	Attribution
0. Fool	Aleph	11	Air
1. Magician	Beth	12	Mercury
2. High Priestess	Gimel	13	Luna
3. Empress	Daleth	14	Venus
4. Emperor	Heh	15	Aries
5. Hierophant	Vav	16	Taurus
6. Lovers	Zayin	17	Gemini
7. Chariot	Cheth	18	Cancer
8. Strength	Teth	19	Leo
9. Hermit	Yod	20	Virgo
10. Wheel of Fortune	Kaph	21	Jupiter
11. Justice	Lamed	22	Libra
12. Hanged Man	Mem	23	Water
13. Death	Nun	24	Scorpio
14. Temperance	Samekh	25	Sagittarius
15. Devil	Ayin	26	Capricorn
16. Tower	Peh	27	Mars
17. Star	Tzaddi	28	Aquarius
18. Moon	Qoph	29	Pisces
19. Sun	Resh	30	Sol
20. Judgment	Shin	31	Fire (and Spirit)
21. Universe	Tau	32	Saturn (and Earth)

Below are brief interpretations of these cards in divination.

0. The Fool

Potentiality, possibility. The beginning point. Unity, idealism, innocence, spirituality. (In material matters: folly.)

1. The Magician

Invocation, skill, adaptation, knowledge, direction of energy, occult power. (Sometimes cunning and deception.)

2. The High Priestess

Consciousness, wisdom, change, alternation, fluctuation. Increase and decrease.

3. The Empress

Unity, Universal Mother. Divine feminine power. Manifestation, form-building, pleasure, success, pure emotion, beauty, happiness.

4. The Emperor

Energy, authority, ambition. Universal Father. Divine masculine power. Realization, development, achievement, conquest, victory. (Sometimes strife and warfare.)

5. The Hierophant

Illumination, teaching, spiritual instruction. Divine wisdom, manifestation, mercy.

6. The Lovers

Inspiration, impulse. Divine love, liberation, integration, bonding. Freedom through unity.

7. The Chariot

Triumph, victory, success. Overcoming obstacles. Movement, journey, spiritual guidance. (Sometimes temporary victory.)

8. Strength

Control, courage, fortitude, might, resolve, harnessed force. (Sometimes obstinacy and abuse of power.)

9. The Hermit

Divine help and intervention. Divine inspiration. Divine wisdom. Vibration. Words of power. Also prudence and deliberation.

10. The Wheel of Fortune

Destiny, karma, time, good fortune, happiness, fluctuation, perpetual motion. Human incarnation. (Sometimes ill-fortune.)

11. Justice

Equilibration, balance, necessary adjustment, equilibrating action, compensation. Forward movement. Law and truth. Court proceedings. (Sometimes severity and bias.)

12. The Hanged Man

Sacrifice, suspension. Crucifixion. Self-sacrifice, self-denial. Suspended animation, trance-state. A period of withdrawal. Reversal. Baptism of Water. Sometimes involuntary sacrifice, punishment, loss. (Suffering generally.)

13. Death

Transformation, change, transmutation, transition. Cycle of death and rebirth. Purification. Time, ages, alteration. Involuntary change.

14. Temperance

Reconciliation, fusion. Tempering of opposites. Combination of forces. Mediation, arbitration, realization. Uniting. Material action (for good or ill).

15. The Devil

Materiality, material force, material temptation. Natural generative force. The powers of nature. Sexual force and natural reproduction. Also illusion and distorted perceptions. Mirth. (Sometimes obsession.)

16. The Tower

Ambition, fighting, strife, war, courage. Restructuring. Sudden involuntary illumination. Dramatic realization. Demolition of obsolete or outdated ideas. (Sometimes ruin.)

17. The Star

Meditation, contemplation. The Inner Voice. Hope, faith, imagination. Unexpected help. Pure consciousness.

18. The Moon

Voluntary change. Subconscious mind, illusion, unconscious impulses. Repressed ideas and desires. Personal demons. Evolution, progression. (Sometimes error, lying, falsity, deception.)

19. The Sun

Glory, gain, riches, happiness, joy. Conscious mind, the intellectual mind. The power of knowledge. Increased perception. (Sometimes vanity, arrogance, and display.)

20. Judgment

Final decision, verdict, sentence, result. Determination of a matter. Initiation. Baptism of Fire. Energy infusion. Awareness of the Divine. (Sometimes postponement.)

21. The Universe

Completion, synthesis, conclusion. The beginning and the end. Reward. The keys to the Universe. The world. Exploration, inquiry into the unconscious. A journey into the Underworld.

Yetziratic Attributions: A Magical Code

Table 25 shows the Yetziratic or formative attributions of the tarot Trumps. Since these cards correspond to the Hebrew letters, they can also be used to write names of power in a magical code or cypher.

The Yetziratic attributions of the Hebrew alphabet make it possible to signify certain Hebrew names and words by employing their elemental, planetary, or zodiacal symbols. This can result in some curious hieroglyphic symbolism. For example, the letters of the name YHVH can be written from left to right (or right to left if you prefer) using the symbolic counterpart of each letter: Virgo Aries Taurus Aries or ♍︎♈︎♉︎♈︎. The name Eheieh, spelled Aleph Heh Yod Heh (AHIH), can be transliterated as Air Aries Virgo Aries or △♈︎♍︎♈︎. Elohim, spelled Aleph Lamed Heh Yod Mem, can be encoded as Air Libra Aries Virgo Water or △♎︎♈︎♍︎▽.

You can use this symbol system to encode any magical name or motto on talismans, magical tools, and other items employed in your personal magical work.

THE MINOR ARCANA

To recap, the Minor Arcana is composed of forty small cards and sixteen court cards. It is divided into four suits that include Wands, Cups, Swords, and Pentacles. These four suits refer to the letters of Tetragrammaton (YHVH), which further correspond to the four elements and the Four Worlds of the Qabalah.

The Suit of Wands

The first suit of the tarot represents the force of Yod-Fire-Atziluth. Wands in general indicate great energy and dynamic power. They represent the great masculine power as the first stimulating spark of energy that begins life and sets things in motion.

The Suit of Cups

This suit symbolizes the force of Heh-Water-Briah. As a whole, Cups denote creativity, fecundity, and pleasure. They refer to the form-building capacity of the great feminine power.

The Suit of Swords

This suit is attributed to Vav-Air-Yetzirah. Swords indicate intellect, communication, mental faculties, and sometimes trouble.

The Suit of Pentacles

The fourth and final suit represents Heh Final-Earth-Assiah. For the most part, Pentacles (or Disks) suggest material or worldly affairs, business, or money matters.

THE PIPS

The cards Aces through Tens are naturally affiliated through number with the ten Sephiroth. All Aces represent Kether, all Twos are assigned to Chokmah, etc. Because the numbered cards are static, occupying fixed centers of energy on the Tree, they represent unvarying forces. This is why some of the small cards seem to be very beneficial and others are somewhat harsh and undesirable. Their functions are predetermined. They often indicate a progression of the human experience, but can also point out specific situations.

THE DECANATES

Inherent to the pip cards are the *decans* or *decanates* of the zodiac. The wheel of the zodiac is divided into twelve signs that also represent the houses. A house is a 30-degree section of the total 360-degree zodiac wheel, while a decanate is a 10-degree section. Thus there are thirty-six decanates in the zodiac. Each house has three decanates. Each decanate is ruled by a different planet and is represented by one of the pip cards—Twos through Tens. The thirty-six small cards depict the operation of the planets moving through the various zodiacal signs. Table 26 lists their attributes and keywords.

Table 26: The Pips and the Decanates

Card	Sephirah	Element	Decanate	Keyword
Ace of Wands	Kether	Fire	–	Energy
Two of Wands	Chokmah	Fire	Mars in Aries	Dominion
Three of Wands	Binah	Fire	Sun in Aries	Established Strength
Four of Wands	Chesed	Fire	Venus in Aries	Perfected Work
Five of Wands	Geburah	Fire	Saturn in Leo	Strife
Six of Wands	Tiphareth	Fire	Jupiter in Leo	Victory
Seven of Wands	Netzach	Fire	Mars in Leo	Valor
Eight of Wands	Hod	Fire	Mercury in Sagittarius	Swiftness
Nine of Wands	Yesod	Fire	Moon in Sagittarius	Great Strength
Ten of Wands	Malkuth	Fire	Saturn in Sagittarius	Oppression
Ace of Cups	Kether	Water	–	Pleasure
Two of Cups	Chokmah	Water	Venus in Cancer	Love
Three of Cups	Binah	Water	Mercury in Cancer	Abundance
Four of Cups	Chesed	Water	Moon in Cancer	Mixed Blessings
Five of Cups	Geburah	Water	Mars in Scorpio	Loss in Pleasure
Six of Cups	Tiphareth	Water	Sun in Scorpio	Pleasure
Seven of Cups	Netzach	Water	Venus in Scorpio	Illusionary Success
Eight of Cups	Hod	Water	Saturn in Pisces	Abandoned Success
Ninc of Cups	Yesod	Water	Jupiter in Pisces	Material Happiness
Ten of Cups	Malkuth	Water	Mars in Pisces	Perfect Success

Table 26: The Pips and the Decanates (continued)

Card	Sephirah	Element	Decanate	Keyword
Ace of Swords	Kether	Air	–	Invoked Force
Two of Swords	Chokmah	Air	Moon in Libra	Peace Restored
Three of Swords	Binah	Air	Saturn in Libra	Sorrow
Four of Swords	Chesed	Air	Jupiter in Libra	Rest from Strife
Five of Swords	Geburah	Air	Venus in Aquarius	Defeat
Six of Swords	Tiphareth	Air	Mercury in Aquarius	Earned Success
Seven of Swords	Netzach	Air	Moon in Aquarius	Unstable Effort
Eight of Swords	Hod	Air	Jupiter in Gemini	Shortened Force
Nine of Swords	Yesod	Air	Mars in Gemini	Despair & Cruelty
Ten of Swords	Malkuth	Air	Sun in Gemini	Ruin
Ace of Pentacles	Kether	Earth	–	Materiality
Two of Pentacles	Chokmah	Earth	Jupiter in Capricorn	Harmonious Change
Three of Pentacles	Binah	Earth	Mars in Capricorn	Material Works
Four of Pentacles	Chesed	Earth	Sun in Capricorn	Earthly Power
Five of Pentacles	Geburah	Earth	Mercury in Taurus	Material Trouble
Six of Pentacles	Tiphareth	Earth	Moon in Taurus	Material Success
Seven of Pentacles	Netzach	Earth	Saturn in Taurus	Success Unfulfilled
Eight of Pentacles	Hod	Earth	Sun in Virgo	Prudence
Nine of Pentacles	Yesod	Earth	Venus in Virgo	Material Gain
Ten of Pentacles	Malkuth	Earth	Mercury in Virgo	Wealth

THE COURT CARDS

The court cards are the final section of the Minor Arcana. Here the four suits of the tarot further are divided into four persons or "faces" of royalty: the King, Queen, Prince, and Princess. In most decks these are called King, Queen, Knight, and Page; however, the Golden Dawn titles stress the balance of gender within the royal "family." The sixteen court cards again point to the fourfold model of the Universe and the Tetragrammaton, YHVH. These cards symbolize the elemental forces of the divine four-lettered name in each of the Four Qabalistic Worlds: Yod-Fire, Heh-Water, Vav-Air, and Heh Final-Earth. They also symbolize the following:

1. King—Fire, Father, Birth

2. Queen—Water, Mother, Life

3. Prince—Air, Son, Death

4. Princess—Earth, Daughter, Resurrection

The four "royals" of a given suit embody the characteristics of a specific element in all four planes of existence. Each court card thus represents a sub-element, such as Fire of Water, Air of Earth, Water of Air, etc.

For example, the King of Wands represents the sub-element Fire of Fire. This means he personifies the Yod-Fire force in the Atziluthic world of Wands (Fire). The King epitomizes the most active, dynamic element in the highest divine world. In another example, the Princess of Cups alludes to the sub-element Earth of Water. She illustrates the qualities of Heh Final-Earth in the Watery world of Briah (Cups). This Princess symbolizes the creative, archangelic world in the stage of manifestation.

In a divination, the court cards can represent real persons, events, or a human factor influential to the nature of the reading. But they can also represent psychological states.

One way to interpret the court cards is to examine their sub-elemental correspondences. Another is to combine the qualities of their rank or position with that of their elemental suit, while disregarding archaic considerations of gender.

Kings

Kings are aligned with Chokmah on the Tree of Life, but they also display qualities of the Emperor. They are paternal, assertive, in charge, protective, and governing.

Queens

Queens are aligned with Binah, but also show qualities of the Empress. They are maternal, nurturing, emotive, and supportive.

Princes

Princes are assigned to Tiphareth, but also demonstrate traits of the Chariot. These cards display the qualities of a young adult. They are journeying, questing, zealous, enthusiastic, and heroic.

Princesses

Princesses are assigned to Malkuth, but also display traits of the Fool. These cards portray childlike qualities: playful, curious, developing, innocent, naive, and exploring.

In general, Kings and Queens are outgoing and extroverted while Princes and Princesses are more self-centered and introverted. Table 27 provides a breakdown of court card attributions and keywords.

Table 27: The Court Cards

Card	Sub-Element	Keyword
King of Wands	Fire of Fire	Dynamic Force
Queen of Wands	Water of Fire	Steady Force
Prince of Wands	Air of Fire	Swift Force
Princess of Wands	Earth of Fire	Enduring Force
King of Cups	Fire of Water	Creative Force
Queen of Cups	Water of Water	Reflective Force
Prince of Cups	Air of Water	Intense Force
Princess of Cups	Earth of Water	Imaginative Force
King of Swords	Fire of Air	Unstable Force
Queen of Swords	Water of Air	Severe Force
Prince of Swords	Air of Air	Intellectual Force
Princess of Swords	Earth of Air	Avenging Force
King of Pentacles	Fire of Earth	Stimulating Force
Queen of Pentacles	Water of Earth	Regenerating Force
Prince of Pentacles	Air of Earth	Resolute Force
Princess of Pentacles	Earth of Earth	Manifesting Force

TAROT CONSECRATION RITUAL

Once you have memorized the meanings of the cards and have meditated on them, you are ready to begin practical work with the tarot. The first step is to consecrate a newly purchased deck of cards, such as The Golden Dawn Magical Tarot. In addition to focusing your mind and will on the desired results, consecrating the deck helps draw the proper energies to the cards so that they will give true and undistorted readings. The time spent on these introductory procedures is well worth taking, for the prepared magician is many times more likely to get positive results.

For this ritual you will need the Outer Wand of Double Power, a tarot bag or white silk for wrapping the cards, and a new tarot deck that you intend to use for meditation and readings. If the deck has been previously opened and used, you should wipe each card with a clean white cloth that has been charged for that purpose.

1. Begin with your personal Pre-Ritual Meditation Practice.

2. Perform the LIRP.

3. Maintain the vision from the Qabalistic Cross—see the shaft of Divine Light blending Spirit and matter within you. The strongest point of this light is at your Tiphareth center. Will and visualize the light going down your arm and out the white end of your wand as you continue.

4. Place the new tarot deck on a table or Altar. Pointing with the black end of the wand, trace a circle and a Lesser Banishing Pentagram over the un-opened deck of cards. This begins the process of cleansing the cards. Pause and imagine the cards as completely cleansed from all mundane influences.

5. Then, pointing with the white end of the wand, strike the deck three times and vibrate: **"EHEIEH. YAH. YHVH ELOHIM."** With each stroke of the wand, intone one of these Supernal names. As you intone "Eheieh," imagine a brilliant sphere of light at the top of your head. As you vibrate "Yah," picture a sphere of light at your left Temple. As you intone "YHVH Elohim," imagine a sphere of light at your right Temple. See this Divine Trinity clearly as it causes more light to descend into your Kether center, to your Tiphareth center, and down your arm into the wand.

6. Then say: **"Unto the Highest do I, (state your magical name), consecrate these cards of Art, that they may become true reflected images of Thy manifestation and splendor. Not to *my* name but to Thine be the Power and the Glory."**

7. Trace a cross over the deck and say: **"In the Divine Name IAO I invoke the great angel HRU, who art set over the operations of this Secret Wisdom. Lay thine hand invisibly on these cards of Art and give them life. Anoint them with the Divine Science so that through their use I may obtain true knowledge of hidden things, to the glory of the Ineffable Name. Amen."**

8. Visualize the hand of a mighty angel held over the deck, which glows with a bright halo of white light. Take time to visualize this strongly.

9. Strike the card deck again three times with the wand. Above you, feel the white brilliance from the infinite Kether of the Universe as it sends the Sacred Light into your own Kether center. Fill yourself with its divine power that is grounded and balanced by the light of the Qabalistic Cross within you. Then propel this energy directly at the deck using the Projection Sign, three times in succession before giving the Sign of Silence. If properly performed, you should feel a bit drained at this point, so take a moment to catch your breath. Repeat the projections if necessary.

10. Now open the deck and take out the cards.

11. Fan the cards out in a circle on the Altar. Take the wand and trace a white cross in the air above them and say: **"By Names and Images are all Powers awakened and re-awakened."** Thrust the wand head through the center of the cross. Visualize the cross clearly.

12. Gather up the cards and wrap them in white silk or a specially provided tarot bag.

13. Say: **"I now release any beings that have attended this ceremony. Depart in peace with the blessings of YHVH. But be ready to come when ye are called."**

14. Perform the LBRP.

15. Finally say: **"The rite is ended. So mote it be."**

A Simple Tarot Meditation

This exercise is designed to enhance your memory with regard to the important symbolism of the various tarot images. The more these Sacred images become embedded within your psyche, the easier it will be to improve your intuitive card reading skills.

1. Begin with your Pre-Ritual Meditation Practice.

2. Perform the LBRP.

3. Shuffle the cards of the Major Arcana and pick one at random. Put the rest of the cards aside. Pause for a few moments to silence the mind before continuing.

4. Look at the card in front of you. Take time to carefully observe the symbolism and colors of the card. Simply take mental note of every detail in the card itself.

5. Now close your eyes and try to reproduce the card in your mind's eye. Try to recall every detail to the best of your ability. Take your time with the visualization.

6. After about five minutes of building the card's image in your imagination, begin to dismantle it, piece by piece like a jigsaw puzzle, until nothing of it remains in your mind.

7. After you have dissolved the image, try to hold on to this state of mental silence for as long as you can. If your mental chatter has really been silenced, some important spiritual information may now be transmitted to you.

8. Take your time to come out of the meditation. Don't get up abruptly.

Tarot Divination

Divination is a spiritual process through which we try to uncover what specific unseen forces are active in our lives. Properly done, a divination can determine which underlying energies are at work in our personal Universe, but this information is to be used as a guidance, not as a script for a drama that we are forced by fate to act out. A divination is like a map that we are given in order to choose what road we would like to take to arrive at a certain destination. Nothing compels us to take any one road over another, but certain routes are better than others. We are the ones with our hands on the steering wheel.

There are many forms of divination. One form depends entirely upon psychic information, using a mirror, crystal, or bowl of Water to aid vision. Other forms use a pendulum or the figures of geomancy. But the tarot is far and away the best and most comprehensive method of divination. It utilizes all the practitioner's Qabalistic knowledge, together with his or her own psychic abilities and creative powers. In addition, shuffling the deck ensures that the powers of chance and synchronicity also play a part in the divination.

It takes more than book knowledge alone to perform a proper tarot reading. It is also pointless to coerce a divination. The symbolism of the tarot is gradually built up as a related system of ideas in the reader's mind. But all the symbolism in the Universe will not avail one who is under strain or too tired to activate their psychic strengths. If a reading is forced, it will probably contain more untruth than truth.

The first step in learning to read the cards is to familiarize yourself with the principles of the Qabalah and the symbolism of all the tarot cards. This information is regularly contemplated and absorbed until there is a gradual alignment between the operation of the higher consciousness and the normal consciousness. The powers of perception regarding inner truths eventually become more acute.

The next step is to memorize the various interpretations of the cards and study the relationships that can occur between certain cards in an actual reading.

Finally, chose one or two specific card reading methods or tarot spreads for regular and consistent use in divination.

A card is often described as well-dignified or ill-dignified (strong or weak), according to the cards that are next to it. A card of the same suit placed next to the card in question strengthens it greatly either for good or ill, according to its nature. Cards of a suit that oppose the elemental nature of the card in question weaken it for good or ill. Air and Earth are contraries, as are Fire and Water. Therefore, an Air card placed next to an Earth card will weaken it, just as a Water card will weaken a Fire card. Air is friendly with Water and Fire, and Fire is friendly with Air and Earth.

The General Meanings of Several Similar Cards
After laying out the cards, the reader should look for a grouping of cards.

- **A Majority of Trumps:** Higher forces at work and spiritual matters

- **A Majority of Court Cards:** Influence of many people, meetings, society

- **A Majority of Wands:** Energy and vitality, possible opposition
- **A Majority of Cups:** Love, pleasure, merriment, and creativity
- **A Majority of Swords:** Intellectual matters or trouble and sickness
- **A Majority of Pentacles:** Money, business, or material success
- **A Majority of Aces:** Tremendous energy and new beginnings, strength
- **Four Aces:** Great power and force
- **Three Aces:** Riches and success
- **Four Kings:** Swiftness and rapidity
- **Three Kings:** Surprise meetings, news
- **Four Queens:** Authority, influence
- **Three Queens:** Powerful, influential friends
- **Four Princes:** Meetings with the great
- **Three Princes:** Honor, rank
- **Four Princesses:** New ideas, plans
- **Three Princesses:** Young society
- **Four Tens:** General anxiety, responsibility
- **Three Tens:** Generally, buying, selling, commercial transactions
- **Four Nines:** Added responsibility
- **Three Nines:** Much correspondence
- **Four Eights:** Much news
- **Three Eights:** Much journeying
- **Four Sevens:** Disappointments
- **Three Sevens:** Treaties and contracts
- **Four Sixes:** Pleasure
- **Three Sixes:** Gain and success

- **Four Fives:** Order, regularity

- **Three Fives:** Quarrels, fights

- **Four Fours:** Rest and peace

- **Three Fours:** Industry

- **Four Threes:** Resolution

- **Three Threes:** Deceit

- **Four Twos:** Conference and conversations

- **Three Twos:** Reorganization, restructuring, recommencement

When Two Suits Rule the Spread (Possible Influences)

- **Swords and Cups:** Strong opposing feelings are key to the problem. Friends and enemies will both take part. Health matters.

- **Wands and Pentacles:** Money and business issues must be resolved.

- **Wands and Swords:** Strong masculine influence. Father. Opposition to business.

- **Wands and Cups:** Balance of masculine and feminine energies. Dynamic energy plus intuition and creativity.

- **Cups and Pentacles:** Strong feminine influence. Mother. Strong emotional need for financial and material security. Home issues.

- **Swords and Pentacles:** Opposition to business. Financial disputes. Constant worry about money and finances.

In learning to read the cards, it is helpful to begin with your personal Pre-Ritual Meditation Practice. Formulate your question clearly and state it out loud. Keep your mind as clear and still as possible when shuffling the cards. Try to put any personal bias out of your mind. (In this respect, it is easier to read for someone you don't know since you can be more objective about the matter.)

We recommend that you invoke the great Angel HRU as in step 7 from the Tarot Consecration Ritual given earlier. This will help connect you with the Divine during the course of the reading.

In any reading, always look for relationships between the cards to aid in unveiling the story that the cards are pointing to.

THE CELTIC CROSS SPREAD

Traditionally, beginning students were taught simple card spreads such as the Celtic Cross. This spread was made popular by Golden Dawn adept A. E. Waite in his book *The Pictorial Key to the Tarot.* The deck designed by Waite and painted by artist Pamela Colman Smith, commonly known as the Rider-Waite tarot deck or the Waite-Smith tarot deck, is the single most popular tarot deck in the world, while the Celtic Cross Spread (Figure 45) is probably the most widely used card spread.

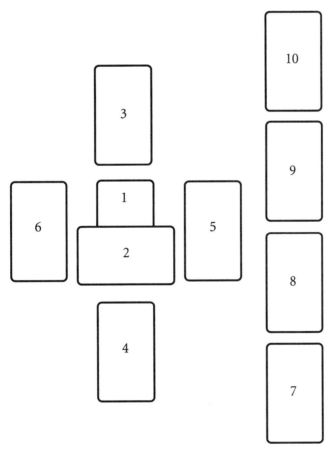

Figure 45: The Celtic Cross Spread

1. **The Significator.** This card represents the present, the matter at hand, or the questioner's state of mind. It is the situation that the *querent,* the person asking a question, currently finds him- or herself in.

2. **The Crossing Card.** An immediate conflict, challenge, or obstacle to the querent. A beneficial card may still represent a challenge.

3. **Above.** The querent's goal or aspiration. The best possible outcome.

4. **Below.** Subconscious motivations of the querent. The hidden core or driving force of the situation. Underlying feelings. Surprise messages.

5. **Past.** Events that have led up to the current situation. Something that is passing out of the querent's life. Something that the querent must let go of.

6. **Future.** Not the long term or final outcome, but what is likely to happen in the next few weeks or months.

7. **Guidance.** The Significator's power or attitude in the present situation. What needs to be developed. Advice and a recommendation for how to address the present situation.

8. **Outside Influences.** External influences, people, or events that the querent has no control over.

9. **Hopes and Fears.** What the querent hopes will happen and fears will not.

10. **Outcome.** How the situation may be resolved. It represents where the situation is headed based on current circumstances. If this outcome is not wanted, the querent will have to make necessary changes.

Be sure to consider various card relationships in your reading:

- Cards 1 and 2 represent the heart of the matter.

- Cards 3 and 4 represent the conscious and unconscious mind.

- Cards 5 and 6 represent the movement of time.

- Cards 3 to 6 represent immediate influences on the matter.

- Cards 7 to 10 represent the broader influences.

Pay attention to the relationships between:

- Cards 3 and 4

- Cards 3 and 10

- Cards 6 and 10

- Cards 4 and 9

- Cards 7 and 10

The YHVH Spread

The YHVH Spread (Figure 46) is the first part of a much longer Golden Dawn tarot reading method known as the Opening of the Key. But the YHVH Spread by itself is an excellent technique for learning the basics of interpretation in a uniquely Golden Dawn tarot reading.

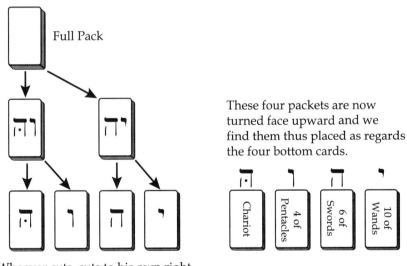

Full Pack

These four packets are now turned face upward and we find them thus placed as regards the four bottom cards.

Chariot — 4 of Pentacles — 6 of Swords — 10 of Wands

Whoever cuts, cuts to his own right

Figure 46: The YHVH Spread

At first you should simply concentrate on learning the tarot spread without a lot of ritual preparation. That can come later. At this point, it is more important that you commit the basic symbolism, attributions, and keywords of the cards to memory and allow the mechanics of the procedure to become second nature to your practice.

1. **Choose the Significator.** Before you begin, choose one of the cards to represent yourself or the querent. This card is the Significator. Traditionally, magicians choose one of the court cards for this purpose, but you could also choose a card that you identify with, be it a Trump card or a pip card that carries a meaningful astrological correspondence.

2. **Formulate the question.** Shuffle the entire deck of seventy-eight cards while thinking about the question you want answered.

3. **Cut the deck.** Cut the deck in half. Place the top half to the right.

4. **Cut the two piles.** Cut each of the two piles in half to the right, so that you end up with four roughly even piles corresponding to the name YHVH and the four elements. The far right pile refers to Yod-Fire, while the far left pile is that of Heh Final-Earth.

5. **Interpret.** Turn the four piles faceup and interpret the bottom (now the top) card of each pile. This will give a general indication of the matter at hand. Take note of the basic interpretations of these four cards as they relate to each other in order from right to left (Table 28).

   a. If a card is on its elemental pile (such as: Ace of Wands in the Yod pile), its strength is increased.

   b. If a card is on a pile that is unfriendly to its elemental suit (example: Ace of Wands in the Heh-Water pile), its strength is decreased.

You should also look to see if there is a predominance or deficit of any particular element and interpret accordingly.

Table 28: The YHVH Spread Interpretation

HEH Final: Earth	VAV: Air	HEH: Water	YOD: Fire
Business	Health	Pleasure	Energy
Money	Trouble	Creativity	Leadership
Stability	Communication	Fertility	Beginnings
Environment	Reconciliation	Emotional life	Transformation

6. **Find the Significator.** Find which pile has the Significator in it. Is it in the pile that relates to the question? This should give you a general direction for the reading.

7. **Horseshoe.** Work with the pile containing the Significator. Put the other piles aside. Without altering the cards' order at all, spread them out to form a horseshoe (Figure 47). Starting with and moving in the direction the Significator is looking, use the counting method described below.

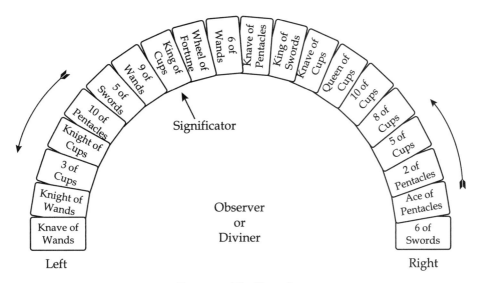

Figure 47: The Horseshoe

Note: In the Golden Dawn Magical Tarot, the directions that the court cards are facing are not always apparent. So as a general rule, Kings turn left, Queens face right, Princes turn left, and Princesses face right. (These directions are from the perspective of the reader who is looking at the card.) The reason for this is because the masculine (White Pillar) cards face their feminine (Black Pillar) counterparts and vice versa.

If you use a deck that shows the court cards looking to the left or right, count cards in the direction that the Significator is facing.

8. **Similar cards.** First, check to see if there is a majority of several similar cards and interpret your findings.

9. Card counting. Proceed by counting over certain cards in the directions described above, from and including the Significator, which is the first card of the count:

- **From every Ace:** count five cards (for Spirit and the four elements)

- **From every Princess:** count seven cards (for seven palaces of Malkuth)

- **From Kings, Queens, Princes:** count four cards (for YHVH)

- **From Twos through Tens:** count its own number (the Sephirah number)

- **From Trumps 0, 12, and 20:** count three cards (for the Mother Letters)

- **From planetary Trumps:** count nine cards (planets plus lunar nodes)

- **From zodiacal sign Trumps:** count twelve cards

For every instance that you count and land on a new card, interpret that triad of cards—the card you land on and the two cards on either side of it. You can refer to these as the central card and the side cards. Count from one central card to the next, creating a narrative as you progress. If you land on a card at either end of the horseshoe, consider that the line of cards is actually circular and includes the card on the other end as one of the side cards. Keep counting until you land on the same card twice, which ends the counting.

Card counting and reading in triads allows the reader to weave a sequential story together like threads in a tapestry, uncovering layer upon layer of subtlety that allows for rich detail. Each triad of cards is woven together into a chronology that indicates the matter's development over time, providing mini stories within a larger framework.

Some threads are simple and uncomplicated while others can become intricate and winding. It is often helpful to record the reading. The nature of the weaving often mirrors the simplicity or complexity of the matter. A short thread can indicate the essential information of the reading, or that one's options are limited. A long thread can sometimes become convoluted and confusing, so concentrate on the cards that draw your attention the most. A thread that seems to go round and round in an endless or meaningless circle may indicate a negative behavior pattern that is difficult to break. In this case, the cards may signify an important lesson that the querent continues to miss.

Take time to get acquainted with this method. Practice is the key to proficiency here.

10. **Card pairing.** Starting at the bottom ends of the horseshoe, pair the cards from opposite sides and interpret them together. When interpreting card pairs, it is often helpful to focus on one or two key words that encapsulate the meaning of each card, then combine them to make a meaningful narrative.

11. **The tarot journal.** Keep a journal of all your tarot readings. Having a written record will help you enormously. Being able to review and compare readings at various stages of your practice is an invaluable learning tool.

Review Questions

1. How many different sections of the tarot can you assign to the name YHVH?

2. How many cards are in the Minor Arcana?

3. How are the cards of the Major Arcana attributed to the Tree of Life?

4. What tarot Trump corresponds to Sagittarius?

5. What tarot Trump corresponds to Cancer?

6. What tarot Trump corresponds to Venus?

7. What tarot Trumps correspond to the three Mother Letters?

8. What method uses the elemental and astrological symbols of Hebrew letters to write in code?

9. The Minor Arcana is divided into what two subgroups?

10. What is a decanate?

11. Which court card is aligned with Binah?

12. Which court card is aligned with Tiphareth?

13. A majority of which card indicates new beginnings?

14. What does a majority of Trumps indicate?

15. What do four Eights indicate?

16. What do three Fives indicate?

17. What do Wands and Pentacles indicate?

18. What do Wands and Cups indicate?

chapter 6

SACRED SPACE AND
MAGICAL TOOLS

After committing the rudiments of occult knowledge to memory, you may feel it is time to begin to build a dedicated Temple space in which to pursue magic. Many Golden Dawn magicians have a Temple within their own living space, regardless of whether or not they are members of an Order or Temple group. Much of the practical magic of the Inner Order is intended to be worked at the personal level outside of group work. While the Great Work does not require all the furnishings and trappings of a full-blown initiating Temple, there is no question that creating a Sacred Space in which you can practice in security and privacy will be of great benefit.

Keep in mind that there is no such thing as an essential piece of magical paraphernalia. The most important tool in magic is the human mind. Nevertheless, the regalia, Elemental Tools, Altars, and other implements used in magic can greatly enhance your ritual experience and provide focus for your willpower and imagination. The lack of a robe, wand, or any other ritual item should never stop you from going ahead with the work at hand. These items are meant to be supports, not crutches.

Other books provide instruction on how to make Temple implements and regalia, so there is no need for us to do so here. Students who want more information on the items presented here are advised to consult our texts on *Secrets of a Golden Dawn Temple* and *Creating Magical Tools*.

---

watch out for the cat!

One magician we know painstakingly carved a gorgeous *Sigillum de Emeth* (the Enochian Seal of Truth) out of a beeswax disk. It took him two weeks to create and before he could even use it, his cat knocked it off the dresser, shattering it completely.

While it is admirable to create magical tools exactly as they were made centuries ago, it is also good to remember that magicians of old used materials that were commonplace for their day. Use what works and try to create things as durable as possible. At some point, you *will* drop something in the middle of a ritual. Practicality often wins out over flamboyance when it comes to ritual preparation. Most magicians who have practiced their art for a while have stories about someone who tripped over their sash, accidently stabbed a painting, or set their robe on Fire. Our advice: use common sense and, above all, don't panic if the unexpected happens!

RITUAL CLOTHING

Ceremonial attire can be an important tool for enhancing one's magical practice. Clothing yourself in ceremonial garb, like taking on a magical motto, is a means of shifting consciousness, of separating yourself from the mundane, secular world. Putting on a ritual robe and other regalia for Temple work is a statement of the magician's intent—making even the clothing worn a part of one's total magical environment. Ritual clothing helps focus the mind on the work at hand, putting the magician into a more mystical state of consciousness, and providing a psychological lift that can increase the quality, intensity, and effectiveness of any ritual.

The Tau Robe

The Tau robe (Figure 48) is standard dress for Golden Dawn magicians. In an Order setting, Outer Order members wear black robes while Inner Order members don white robes. The Tau Cross, which looks like the letter "T" when the arms are raised, is the preferred form of this robe. This also refers to the Hebrew Tau, the last letter of the Hebrew alphabet. One theory states that this symbol originated among the Egyptians from the image of the wide rack of a bull's horns and the vertical line of the animal's face.

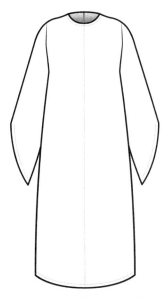

Figure 48: The Tau Robe

The Nemyss

The nemyss or Egyptian headdress (Figure 49) is part of the traditional ceremonial garb of a Golden Dawn magician. It is shown in many ancient papyri as either flowing down the back of the neck or gathered at the back to end in a "tail." We have chosen the gathered-style of nemyss as more truly representing the symbolism of eternal life, the ankh, which the nemyss is partly based upon.

Figure 49: The Nemyss

The ankh cross is a Sacred symbol that indicates the manifestation of the divine life force. It signifies the divine union of opposites; active and passive, male and female. The ankh combines the masculine Tau shape with the feminine oval, alluding to the powers of generation. The circle of the ankh refers to the Sun, the horizontal line to the sky, and the vertical line to the earth. As a Microcosmic sign, the circle represents the human head or reasoning powers, the horizontal line implies arms, and the upright line is the body.

The ankh can also be interpreted as an early form of the emblem of Venus (Figure 50), the only planet whose sigil touches all the Sephiroth when superimposed over the diagram of the Tree of Life. This, too, is very significant to the symbolic makeup of the nemyss. To wear an ankh (Figure 51) in the form of a headdress signifies the striving for eternal life that only spiritual attainment can bring. In Hebrew tradition, the back of the head (Qoph) is covered during worship. It is a symbol that one is in the presence of God. By covering one's head with the sacred emblem of the ankh, the Golden Dawn magician puts him-

or herself in a magical state of mind and calls upon the forces of eternal life and light for protection against all outside influences, including ones that might otherwise enter the subconscious through "the back of the head."

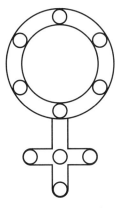

Figure 50: Venus Symbol on the Tree of Life

Head

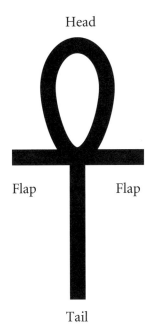

Flap   Flap

Tail

Figure 51: The Ankh

By wearing the Tau robe and the nemyss, the magician becomes a complete, living symbol of the ankh.

Sashes

In an Order setting, Golden Dawn magicians wear a long band of cloth over one shoulder as a symbol of their grade. Outer Order members wear a black sash, embellished with the insignia of their rank from the left shoulder to the right hip. Inner Order members wear the same, but with the addition of a similarly adorned white sash running from the right shoulder to the left hip. Solitary students generally do not need to concern themselves with sashes, however.

Cloaks, Mantles, Tabards, and Stoles

One final item we need to mention is an outer garment worn over the robe by officers in a Temple setting as an emblem of their authority, adorned with symbolism in the proper colors. The original form was a cloak or mantle that was well suited to a cold northern clime. Many Temples today, especially those in tropical or subtropical climates, prefer lighter garb such as tabards and stoles. But as with the sash, solo students generally don't need to worry about these items, unless they wish to design personalized versions of them to enhance their ritual work.

THE TEMPLE

A personal Temple is a space where the magician can control the various components of all magical work, especially when it involves ceremonial operations. The Temple space is a physical embodiment of the magician's most important tool—the mind. Like the magician's own psyche, the Temple should be kept clear of all outside influences and astral contaminants.

It is preferable for any Golden Dawn student to have a private space for Temple work. Ideally, the Temple should be set up in a spare room, although if this is not feasible magicians will often move aside furniture in their living room to create a temporary Sacred Space that can be created and dissolved at will. It is important that there be enough space to move around comfortably.

One's personal Temple space can be as elaborate or sparse as desired, but at the minimum, the student should make or acquire the following items.

- An Altar

- Cross and Triangle

- A white pillar candle and a black pillar candle

- A chalice of Water

- A censer for incense or stick incense holder

- A Banishing Dagger

- The Outer Wand of Double Power

A chalice, incense holder, and pillar candles should be easy to obtain. We've discussed the Banishing Dagger and the Outer Wand of Double Power in chapter 4. Other items are described below.

The Altar

The Altar is a primary point of focus, the heart and core of the Temple. Any convenient table, nightstand, or similar piece of furniture can be substituted, so long as it is covered with a black cloth. Another option is a plastic storage tower or cart complete with wheels and drawers. These are inexpensive to purchase and can be covered with an Altar cloth. They also provide an excellent container for ritual tools, candles, robes, and other implements. However, nothing is better than a traditional Golden Dawn Altar (Figure 52).

Figure 52: Double Cubical Altar

The Altar is painted black to symbolize the physical world in which we live—a world sometimes dark and obscure. It is constructed in the shape of a double cube. This alludes to a passage taken from the Emerald Tablet of Hermes which states, "Whatever is below is like that which is above, and whatever is above is like that which is below." In the Neophyte ritual, this restatement of the Hermetic Axiom is paraphrased as "the things that are below are a reflection of the things that are above."

The Altar is positioned in the center of the Temple. The pillar candles should be placed on the eastern side of the Altar with the white candle on the right and the black candle on the left. Place the chalice in the northern side of the Altar and the incense on the southern side (Figure 53).

Figure 53: The Altar Top

When working in Temple, the magician stands west of the Altar, facing east, the direction of the shining Sun of the Golden Dawn.

Cross and Triangle

The symbol of the Golden Dawn is a red Cross above a white Triangle (Figure 54). These can be made out of paper and laminated, or they can be made from wood, resin, or any other convenient material.

Figure 54: Cross and Triangle

These emblems represent the forces of the Divine Light centered in the white Triangle of the Supernal Sephiroth—Kether, Chokmah, and Binah.

The red Cross is symbolically composed of six equal units, aligning it with Tiphareth. It is placed above the white Triangle, not to dominate it, but to cause it to descend and manifest into the outer world. The Cross and Triangle together represent life and light.

In preparation for personal magical work, the Cross and Triangle should always be placed upon the Altar, acting as a nucleus for the ceremony and attracting the divine forces into manifestation.

Quarter Altars

The four quarters or cardinal directions are important factors in any Golden Dawn Temple. All Temples are oriented to face east, the place of the rising of Sun from which the Golden Dawn takes its name. As the four elements are each attributed to one of these directions, it is advantageous to place four small side Altars in each quarter. Small tables, nightstands, or similar items can be draped in elemental-colored Altar cloths: yellow for Air in the east, red for Fire in the south, blue for Water in the west, and black for Earth in the north. These hold Enochian Tablets, elemental-colored candles, and other appropriate symbolism.

The Pillars

The two pillars are among the most noticeable features of a Golden Dawn Temple. They represent the two columns in the Temple of King Solomon and the two great contending forces of the Cosmos. Symbolic of the outer pillars on the Tree of Life, these are the epic polarities of male and female, day and night, hot and cold, active and passive, positive and negative, etc. Remember that the terms "positive" and "negative" are not meant as value judgments. They are more in keeping with the positive protons and negative electrons of an atom: both are needed in order for the atom to function. They express the reconciliation of opposing forces and the eternal balance of light and darkness that gives rise to the visible Universe.

The White Pillar on the south side of the Temple is called *Jachin*, and represents the male or Yang principle. It is known as the Pillar of Light and Fire and the positive polarity. The Black Pillar on the left or north side of the Temple is called *Boaz*, and symbolizes the female or Yin principle. It is also known as the Pillar of Cloud and the negative polarity. These columns are referred to as the Pillar of Force and the Pillar of Form.

In Egyptian symbolism, the pillars represent the Sacred gateway to the Underworld. The two pillars of the Neophyte Hall are ornamented with symbolism consisting of Egyptian vignettes or drawings. The archaic drawings on the Jachin Pillar are painted in black upon a white ground, and those on the Boaz Pillar in white upon a black ground.

The bases of the pillars are black to represent the darkness of matter into which the quintessence of Spirit descends to implement Light and Life. Just above each base is the image of a lotus flower to represent regeneration.

The two columns are topped with red triangular capitals emblematic of the triune manifestation of the Divine Spirit of Life. And while only two pillars are physically present in the Temple, the threefold aspect of divinity is emphasized through the implied existence of the Middle Pillar of Mildness, for as the Hierophant tells the Neophyte: "There are two contending forces and one always uniting them."

In the previous section, we recommended that black and white pillar candles be placed atop the Altar to represent these energies. But for readers who want the more traditional pillars, there are a variety of ways to make them. They should be large but not overly so. For a basic set of functional black and white pillars, it is not absolutely necessary that they include the Egyptian vignettes. If desired, you can simply paint the letter Yod (for Jachin) at the top of the white pillar and the letter Beth (for Boaz) at the summit of the black one (Figure 55). Here are some suggestions for creating the pillars:

- Heavy cardboard tubes found inside rolls of carpeting. Two square wooden boxes can be utilized for the bases. Simply cut a circle into the top of the box and slide the tube down into the base.

- Architectural salvage might provide wooden pillars from old houses.

- Long, thick lengths of PVC pipe can be made into pillars and set into wooden bases.

- Use stovepipe bought from a home-builders supply store.

- Round, interlocking plastic trash cans, when placed one on top of the other, can make perfectly smooth, slender pillars.

- Portable pillars can be constructed from cloth and polystyrene or Styrofoam rings (used to make wreathes) purchased from a craft store.

The Triangles composing the pyramid capitals can be cut out of poster board and painted red.

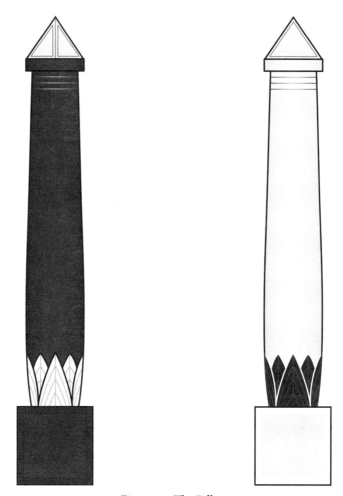

Figure 55: The Pillars

The Banners

Pillars and Banners (Figure 56) are among the lodge furnishings that the Golden Dawn adapted from Freemasonry. Both groups use these items to symbolize esoteric ideas. But in the case of the Golden Dawn these items are also considered reservoirs of magical power. Not only do they act as barriers and signposts for the eastern and western axis of the Temple, they are also battery points along which the Divine Light can travel from one end of the Temple and back again.

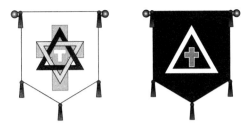

Figure 56: The Banners of the East and West

The white Banner of the East is also referred to as the Banner of Light. It is placed in the eastern part of the Temple to mark the place of the emerging light of morning—otherwise known as the Golden Dawn!

The black Banner of the West is also called the Banner of the Evening Twilight and is placed in the western part of the Temple for obvious reasons.

Ideally, the Banners should be made out of cloth and hung from gold-colored bars on Banner poles painted black and white, respectively. But for the purpose of this book, they can be photocopied and laminated or framed to hang on the walls of the Temple room. The Banners should contain the following symbolism:

Banner of the East

- Field of white

- A golden-yellow Calvary Cross

- A Hexagram formed from a red upright Triangle and a blue inverted Triangle

- A white Tau Cross (T-shaped Cross) in the center

- Red tassels hanging from each of the five corners

Banner of the West

- Field of black

- White upright Triangle

- Red Calvary Cross with gold trim on all edges

- Red tassels hanging from each of the five corners

The white Banner is a symbol of light and purity. It is used as a conduit for bringing the Divine Light-force into the Temple. It can be employed as a protective shield as well as a vehicle for Purification and Consecration within the Temple.

The black Banner is a symbol of restriction and containment used to bar negative energies from the Temple.

TOOLS OF THE ADEPT

The implements described below are traditionally the tools of the Second Order. Many of them are implements belonging to the grade of Zelator Adeptus Minor (ZAM) and above. Like other material presented in this text, we assume that some readers will want to stick to the bare-bones basics while others will use this book as the beginning point of a lifelong magical practice in the Golden Dawn tradition. Therefore, we provide options for both.

THE ENOCHIAN (OR ELEMENTAL) TABLETS

The Enochian Tablets of the Golden Dawn (also known as the Elemental Tablets) (Figure 57) originated from a system of magic that was developed from the ceremonial skrying of Dr. John Dee and Edward Kelley. Beginning in 1582, the Elizabethan magician and his seer continued to uncover the Enochian system over a period of seven years. The two men accumulated a great quantity of work, including an entire language with its own unique alphabet and syntax. This language, known as the "Secret Angelic Language," became known as Enochian because it was said to have been the angelic language revealed to Enoch by the angel Ave.

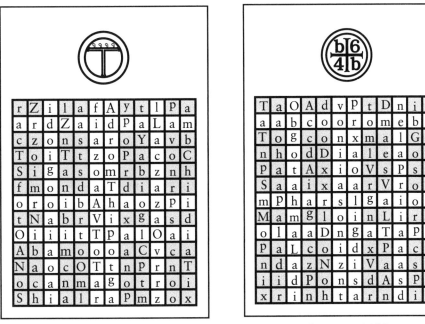

The Air Tablet

The Water Tablet

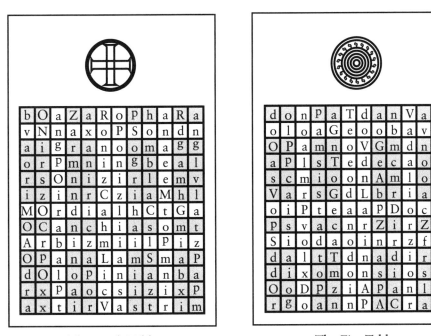

The Earth Tablet

The Fire Tablet

Figure 57: The Enochian (or Elemental) Tablets

The Enochian Tablets are also called the "Watchtower Tablets" because they represent four elemental portals for great angels known as the *Chaioth ha-Qadesh* or "Holy Living Creatures" depicted as great pillars that support the firmament of heaven. These angels keep watch over all things under their dominion.

Enochian is the unifying system of magic that underlies much of the practical work of the Golden Dawn within the higher grades. It combines Qabalah, tarot, geomancy, and astrology as well as elemental, planetary, and astral work into a unified and comprehensive scheme.

The structure of the Enochian system is based upon a cipher of numerological permutations of elements, arranged on grids of letters such as the four Elemental Tablets. From these Tablets were derived the names of various elemental powers, angels, beings, and spiritual dominions known as aethyrs.

The four Elemental Tablets are assigned respectively to Air, Water, Earth, and Fire. Our tradition teaches that each of the elements also contains the other elements within them as well. Therefore, each Tablet is divided into four quarters that represent the sub-elements of that particular Tablet. For example, on the Fire Tablet these include: Earth of Fire, Air of Fire, Water of Fire, and Fire of Fire.

Each of the four Elemental Tablets contains four types of squares (Figure 58):

- **The Great Cross** of thirty-six squares, lettered in black on white, stretching through the entire Tablet.

- **The Sephirotic Calvary Crosses**, lettered also in black on white, in the four corners of each Tablet.

- **The Kerubic Squares**, which are usually painted in the elemental color of the Tablet, and are the four squares immediately above each Sephirotic Cross.

- **The Servient Squares**, usually painted in the elemental color of the Tablet, consist of the sixteen squares of each lesser sub-element beneath each Sephirotic Cross.

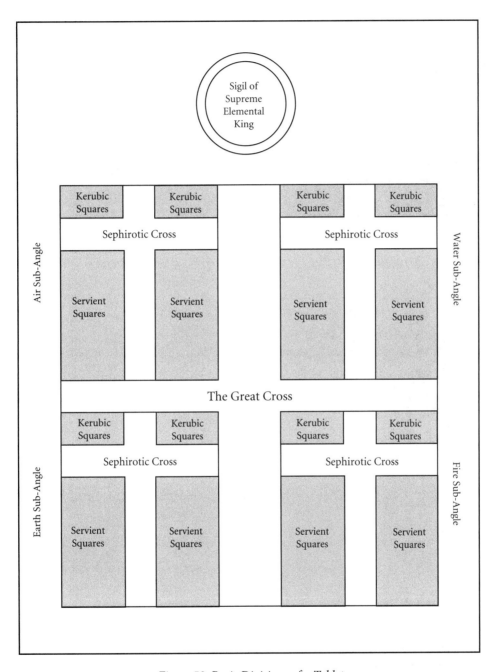

Figure 58: Basic Divisions of a Tablet

The most important section on each Angelic Tablet is the central Great Cross whose shaft descends from top to bottom and whose Crossbar divides the Tablet from left to right. The Great Cross is the mechanism that partitions the Tablet: it separates and binds together the sub-elements (also called sub-angles) of the Tablet.

From this Great Cross of letters, various angelic and divine names are produced, which are of supreme importance. First are the "Three Great Secret Holy Names of God," which are found on the horizontal Crossbar of the Great Cross. This line is composed of twelve letters divided into names of three, four, and five letters each, read from left to right:

- **Oro Ibah Aozpi,** on the Air Tablet

- **Mph Arsl Gaiol**, on the Water Tablet

- **Mor Dial Hctga**, on the earth Tablet

- **Oip Teaa Pdoce**, on the Fire Tablet

The Three Great Secret Holy Names of God are the major names of the Tablets and are used to open the elemental forces of the four Watchtowers. These names are conceived to be borne as ensigns upon the Banners of very powerful Kings who rule each quarter. The name of the Great King is found in a spiral or whirl of letters at the center of each Tablet. The Kings are:

- **Bataivah,** the Great King of Air

- **Raagiosel**, the Great King of Water

- **Ic Zod Heh Hal**, the Great King of Earth

- **Edelperna**, the Great King of Fire

These Enochian names of power are commonly called upon in advanced rituals to invoke the elements. Collectively, the Enochian Tablets contain the names of angelic forces that are far too numerous for us to list here.

In addition to the Elemental Tablets, there is a smaller Tablet called the Tablet of Union (Figure 59), referring to the fifth element of Spirit. The four lines on the Tablet of Union are:

- **EXARP**, attributed to Air

- **HCOMA**, attributed to Water

- **NANTA**, attributed to Earth

- **BITOM**, attributed to Fire

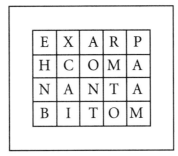

Figure 59: The Tablet of Union

The function of the Tablet of Union, as its name implies, is to unite and bind together the energies of the four Elemental Tablets. Figure 60 shows how the order of the names on the Tablet of Union follows the lines of the Pentagram as well as the four sub-elemental divisions on the larger Tablets.

In an Order setting, students are introduced to the Tablets in the elemental grades, one Tablet per grade. The Tablet of Union is introduced in the Portal grade, which corresponds to the element of Spirit. However, students may frame photocopied or laminated versions of all the Tablets to hang on the walls of their Temple or place on the quarter Altars.

Fully consecrated Enochian Tablets are highly potent talismans and reservoirs of energy. They serve as portals that allow elemental energy to flow into the Temple.

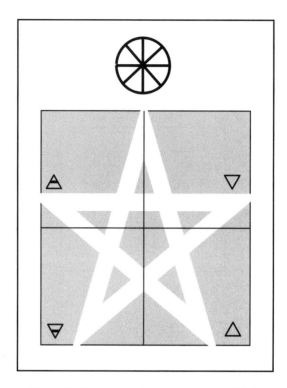

Figure 60: Pentagram Arrangement on a Tablet

THE LOTUS WAND

The Lotus Wand is the single most useful tool in Golden Dawn magic. This general-purpose wand can be used for all magical situations and rituals. It is especially useful for fine-tuning the invocation and banishment of any and all elemental, Sephirotic, planetary, and zodiacal energies.

In ancient Egypt, the lotus was a symbol of purity and regeneration. For this reason, the Golden Dawn's Lotus Wand is dedicated to the Goddess Isis. The wand head is a twenty-six-petaled lotus flower made from three layers of petals (Figure 61). The outer two layers each have eight petals that are white on the inside and olive with black veins on the outside. The central interior layer has ten petals that are white on both sides. At the base of the flower is an orange four-sepaled outer calyx.

Figure 61: The Lotus Wand

The shaft of the wand is divided into the King Scale colors of the twelve zodiacal signs. Above and below these are two longer sections of white at the top and black at the bottom, with the white section above the red (Aries) band. The white section is always slightly longer than the black. The magician's motto is usually painted on the white band.

As a general rule, point with the white lotus flower to invoke and with the black end to banish.

The various colored bands are grasped by holding the wand between the thumb and two fingers when invoking or banishing specific energies (Table 29). If the bands on your wand are too narrow, just make sure that your thumb (the digit assigned to Spirit) is firmly pressed on the appropriate band.

Table 29: How to Use the Lotus Wand

Energy Force	Band	Reason for band choice
All ten Sephiroth	White	Spirit; the Divine
Fire	Yellow (Leo)	Kerubic Fire
Water	Blue-green (Scorpio)	Kerubic Water
Air	Violet (Aquarius)	Kerubic Air
Earth	Red-orange (Taurus)	Kerubic Earth
12 zodiacal signs	Each in accordance with its attributed band	
Saturn	Violet (Aquarius) for day, Blue-violet (Capricorn) at night	
Jupiter	Blue (Sagittarius) for day, Red-violet (Pisces) at night	
Mars	Red (Aries) for day, Red-violet (Scorpio) at night	
Sol	Yellow (Leo) for either day or night	
Venus	Green (Libra) for day, Red-orange (Taurus) at night	
Mercury	Orange (Gemini) for day, Yellow-green (Virgo) at night	
Luna	Yellow-orange (Cancer) for either day or night	

For planetary workings, it is also acceptable to hold the wand by the band of the sign that the planet is in at the time of the ritual.

Hold the black band only for material and mundane matters.

The lotus flower is not to be touched during ritual, but in Sephirotic and spiritual workings, the flower should be directed toward the forehead.

For those readers who might not wish to create a full-fledged Lotus Wand, there are two perfectly good alternatives: the Outer Wand of Double Power, which is a good all-purpose wand, or the Rainbow Wand from Donald Michael Kraig's *Modern Magick*. The Rainbow Wand is a Lotus Wand without the lotus flower on top.

THE MAGIC SWORD

The Magic Sword (Figure 62) is to be used in all cases where great force and strength are required, but principally for banishing and for defense against evil forces. For this reason, it is attributed to Sephirah Geburah and of the planet Mars. The sword is to be used with great respect only for banishings, protection, and certain rituals where the force of Geburah is needed to bar and threaten.

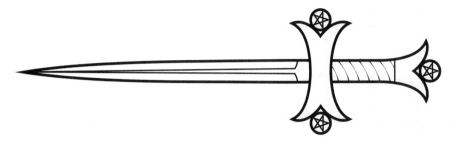

Figure 62: The Magic Sword

Any convenient sword of medium length and weight may be adapted to this use, but the handle, hilt, and guard should be wide enough to write the necessary inscriptions on. Every part of the handle is to be painted red, although a strip of leather can be wrapped around the grip for added comfort. In addition to divine names and sigils of Geburah and Mars, protective Pentagrams are added in green to the hilt:

- Godname: **Elohim Gibor**
- Sephirotic archangel: **Kamael**
- Sephirotic angels: **Seraphim**
- Planet: **Madim** (Mars)
- Planetary angel: **Zamael**
- Planetary intelligence: **Graphiel**
- Planetary Spirit: **Bartzabel**
- Magical motto: add your own

For a more basic Magic Sword, simply paint the handle red.

THE ELEMENTAL WEAPONS

The four Elemental Weapons or tools are the Earth Pentacle, the Air Dagger, the Water Cup, and the Fire Wand (Figure 63). These are the tarot symbols equating to the divine name YHVH. They have a certain bond and sympathy between them, so that even if only one is to be used, the others should also be present, just as each of the four Elemental Tablets is divided into four quarters representing the other three elements bound together within the same Tablet.

Figure 63: The Elemental Weapons

The Fire Wand

The Fire Wand is used in all magical workings that involve elemental Fire. This wand falls under the Hebrew letter Yod of the Tetragrammaton and is a potent symbol of the magician's willpower. It should not be used in anything other than a ritual that involves the elements.

The shape of the wand is phallic: it is a cone mounted on a shaft. The symbolism of the cone may be derived from the association of the circle with the Triangle or pyramid, and may also be a form of the solar glyph. In any event, the flaming Yods painted around the cone firmly establish its masculine Fire energy.

The Fire Wand is the most challenging of all the Elemental Weapons to construct. The problem it presents is that a magnetic wire must run through its center, end to end. The Golden Dawn manuscripts suggest making the wand out of bamboo cane, which has a natural hollow running through it, but this is not the most satisfactory way to create it.

The wand is traditionally painted red with three yellow Yods on the cone and four yellow rings on the shaft. One recent innovation is to paint the wand completely in the flashing Fire colors of red and green without any yellow. Divine and angelic names and sigils are painted in green on the red portions of the wand:

- Divine Name: **Elohim**
- Archangel: **Michael**
- Angel: **Ariel**
- Ruler: **Seraph**
- River of Paradise: **Pison** (River of Fire)
- Cardinal Point: **Darom** (South)
- Element: **Ash** (Fire)
- Magical motto: add your own

Options: In addition to using bamboo, a simplified but functional way to get a magnetized wire into the Fire Wand is to create it out of PVC or copper tubing instead of wood. Readers who simply wish to create a basic wooden wand without all the bells and whistles can forgo the magnetic wire and the Hebrew writing.

The Water Cup

The Water Cup is used in all magical workings relating to the nature of elemental Water, under the presidency of the Hebrew letter Heh of YHVH. The Cup is to be marked with eight raised, etched, or painted lotus petals.

This is one implement whose construction seems to vary with the ingenuity of the magician making it. The Golden Dawn instructions suggest that any glass cup with a stem can be used, and paper petals attached. Although this method is the least satisfying and easiest to break, it appears to have been the most common method used to create the Cup in the early days of the Order.

Many magicians have a way of finding a metal, ceramic, or wooden cup that will work nicely for the Water Cup and has the added advantage of sturdiness and durability. Metal cups or goblets made out of brass or pewter are easy to find in many department stores or flea markets. Eight petals can be cut out of leather or card stock and glued to the cup for the required design.

The Water Cup should be painted blue with the outlines of the petals and the Hebrew names and sigils in orange:

- Divine Name: **EL**

- Archangel: **Gabriel**

- Angel: **Taliahad**

- Ruler: **Tharsis**

- River of Paradise: **Gihon** (River of Water)

- Cardinal Point: **Maarab** (West)

- Element: **Mayim** (Water)

- Magical motto: add your own

If a simpler design is more to your liking, you can leave off the Hebrew writing and sigils.

The Air Dagger

The Air Dagger is to be used in all magical workings of the element of Air, and falls under the Hebrew letter Vav of YHVH. It is to be used with the three other Elemental

Tools. In symbolism, the dagger can be likened to the tip of the spear, cast through the Air to hit its target.

There should be no confusion between the Magic Sword and the Air Dagger. The Magic Sword is under Geburah and is for strength and defense. These two implements belong to different planes and any substitution of one for the other will serve to undermine your magical efforts.

In a similar vein, the Air Dagger is not to be used in rituals that call for a plain dagger, such as the Lesser Banishing Ritual of the Pentagram. For the LBRP, a black-handled dagger of no special design should suffice.

The blade of the dagger should be between four and six inches. The handle of the Air Dagger is yellow, the color assigned to elemental Air. The handle should be wide enough to add the appropriate divine names and sigils, painted in violet.

- Divine Name: **YHVH**

- Archangel: **Raphael**

- Angel: **Chassan**

- Ruler: **Arel**

- River of Paradise: **Hiddikel** (River of Air)

- Cardinal Point: **Mizrach** (East)

- Element: **Ruach** (Air)

- Magical motto: add your own

If a simple Air Dagger is all you require, then paint the handle yellow and leave off all writing.

The Earth Pentacle

A pentacle is a circular disk that serves as a container for the magical forces inscribed on it. The Earth Pentacle of the Golden Dawn is used in all workings pertaining to the nature of Earth, and is under the presidency of the Hebrew letter Heh Final of the Tetragrammaton.

One or both sides of the pentacle are inscribed with a white Hexagram superimposed over a circle that is divided into the colors of Malkuth. A white border along the edge contains the divine names and sigils of elemental Earth.

The four quarters of the pentacle are painted in the Queen Scale colors of Malkuth to indicate the sub-elements that exist within the makeup of the tenth Sephirah. The citrine quarter is the airy part of Earth, formed from the mixture of orange and green (Hod and Netzach). Russet is the fiery part of Earth, formed from the mixture of orange and violet (Hod and Yesod). Olive is the Watery part of Earth, created from combining green and violet (Netzach and Yesod). Black is Earth of Earth, a combination of all the colors grounding in Malkuth.

The white Hexagram is a symbol of the divine union of opposites, the marriage of Fire and Water. It represents perfect harmony and reconciliation. The white border symbolizes the Divine Spirit surrounding and binding together all four sub-elements of Malkuth.

Circular disks around five inches in diameter and between half and three-fourths of an inch in thickness can be purchased at craft stores and inscribed with the necessary symbolism on both sides including the divine names of Earth:

- Godname: **Adonai**

- Archangel: **Uriel**

- Angel: **Phorlakh**

- Ruler: **Kerub**

- River of Paradise: **Phrath** (River of Earth)

- Cardinal Point: **Tzaphon** (North)

- Element: **Aretz** (Earth)

- Magical motto: add your own

Other than the magician's magical motto, the writing on all four tools is traditionally painted in Hebrew letters with black paint.

To create the simplest form of the Earth Pentacle, inscribe the Hexagram and Malkuth quarters on one side only. You can leave off the Hebrew and sigils. Paint the bottom side black.

THE ROSE CROSS LAMEN

The word "Lamen" comes from the Latin word for "plate" and indicates a symbolic breastplate that generally signifies the magician's rank, authority, or power. A Lamen is a magical pendant worn by the magician in ritual. It is suspended from a cord, ribbon, chain, or collar so that it hangs over the heart center of Tiphareth.

Lamens come in an endless variety of shapes and symbolism. Golden Dawn officers wear Lamens to indicate their specific station and duties within the Hall. Another type of Lamen is talismanic in nature; it functions as a storehouse for the particular energy that the magician wishes to attract. Some Lamens contain the sigils of angels or Spirits that the magician wears only when working with those particular beings.

The Rose Cross Lamen (Figure 64) can be described as the key symbol or a magical coat of arms for the adept of the Second Order. Based on the Rosicrucian symbolism of the red rose united to the golden Cross, it combines a vast amalgam of ideas and forces that lie at the heart of Hermetic magic, including the elements, planets, zodiacal signs, Sephiroth, Hebrew alphabet, Pentagrams, Hexagrams, alchemical principles, etc. The Lamen is a complete synthesis of the masculine, positive, or King Scale of color attributions. This single emblem is described as "the Key of Sigils and Rituals" and it represents the Great Work itself, balanced and completed.

Figure 64: The Rose Cross Lamen

The four arms of the cross are attributed to the four elements in their proper colors. The white portion belongs to Spirit and the planets are embodied in the Hexagram. The floriated ends of the arms show the symbols of the three alchemical principles.

The central rose is a symbol of the entire manifest Universe. It contains twenty-two petals assigned to the letters of the Hebrew alphabet and the twenty-two Navitoth on the Tree of Life. The petals of the rose are arranged in three rows that divide the Hebrew alphabet into the three Mother Letters (elements), the seven Double Letters (planets), and the twelve Simple Letters (signs). When properly painted, the rows of petals should resemble a perfect artists' color wheel. At the very center of the rose is a white glory containing a five-petaled red rose with four green rays and a six-squared golden Cross.

Large white rays springing from behind the rose at the intersecting arms of the cross are waves of the Divine Light issuing forth, and the letters and symbols on them refer to the Analysis of the Keyword described in chapter 8.

In addition to alchemical symbols, the back of the cross is ornamented with the following inscriptions in Latin: "The Master Jesus Christ, God and Man," and "Blessed be the Lord our God who hath given us the Symbol Signum." These serve to emphasize the Rosicrucian origins of the symbol. Below these sentences is the magical motto of the magician.

Many practitioners make this Lamen out of heavy cardboard that is then painted in the appropriate colors. For a sturdier Lamen, use wood.

If you wish to make your own Rose Cross Lamen, paint it as follows:

The Arms

- *Right Arm:* Blue with orange symbols

- *Left Arm:* Red with green symbols

- *Top Arm:* Yellow with violet symbols

- *Bottom Arm:* Upper half: white with black symbols. Lower half: citrine, olive, russet, and black with white symbols.

The Center of the Rose

- Gold Cross with green glories and a red rose of five petals in the center

- Background circle of white

The Petals of the Rose

Aleph	yellow petal, violet letter
Beth	yellow petal, violet letter
Gimel	blue petal, orange letter
Daleth	green petal, red letter
Heh	red petal, green letter
Vav	red-orange petal, blue-green letter
Zayin	orange petal, blue letter
Cheth	yellow-orange petal, blue-violet letter
Teth	yellow petal, violet letter
Yod	yellow-green petal, red-violet letter
Kaph	violet petal, yellow letter
Lamed	green petal, red letter
Mem	blue petal, orange letter
Nun	blue-green petal, red-orange letter
Samekh	blue petal, orange letter
Ayin	blue-violet petal, yellow-orange letter
Peh	red petal, green letter
Tzaddi	violet petal, yellow letter
Qoph	red-violet petal, yellow-green letter
Resh	orange petal, blue letter
Shin	red petal, green letter
Tau	blue-violet petal, yellow-orange letter

The back of the cross is completely white with black lettering. The Lamen is suspended from a yellow collar or chain and wrapped in white silk when not in use.

The Rose Cross Lamen can be used for:

- Meditation on various symbols it contains.

- Memorization of the King Scale colors assigned to the Hebrew letters.

- Divine protection during magical work.

- Creating sigils drawn from the Hebrew letters on the rose.

- Healing rituals that draw upon the various energies and their symbols as depicted on the Lamen.

- Projecting energy from the magician's Tiphareth center through a symbol on the Lamen.

- Use in the Supreme Rituals of the Pentagram and Hexagram.

- Use in magical work with the three alchemical principles.

- A mandala of all the magical forces the magician works with.

- A talisman to attract the Higher and Divine Genius.

- Consecrating the magician's aura with divine symbols through frequent use in magical work.

The Rose Cross Lamen is traditionally worn by advanced magicians. Some readers might wish to gain more proficiency in the work before creating this intricate Lamen. For a basic, less complicated version, simply paint a gold Cross with a red rose. The back of the Lamen can be all white with just your magical motto and protective Pentagrams in black.

TEMPLE CONSECRATION RITUAL

The following ritual is a simple rite you can use to consecrate your Temple space and all magical paraphernalia and tools within it. Keep in mind that some of the items described in this chapter, specifically the Tools of the Adept, have their own traditional consecration rituals that can be found in Israel Regardie's book *The Golden Dawn*. Nevertheless, you can use the ritual given here for a general-purpose consecration of any implement in your Temple.

1. Begin with your personal Pre-Ritual Meditation Practice.

2. Perform the LIRP.

3. Retain the vision from the Qabalistic Cross of the shaft of Divine Light blending Spirit and matter within you. The strongest point of this light

is at your Tiphareth center. Will and visualize the light going down your arm as needed when tracing figures, purifying, or consecrating.

4. Trace a Cross over the chalice of Water and say: **"Unto the Highest do I, (state your magical name), consecrate this chalice of Water that it may be rendered pure and holy, like unto the Celestial rivers of paradise."**

5. Trace a Cross over the censer of incense and say: **"Unto the Highest do I, (state your magical name), consecrate this censer of incense that it may be rendered pure and holy, like unto the sweet fragrance of the Celestial Temple of which this Temple is a reflection."**

6. Take up the cup and purify the room with Water, starting in the east and moving clockwise around the room. Trace a Cross followed by the Invoking Water Triangle in all four quarters (Figure 65). (The three lines of the Triangle may be traced, or the magician may simply mark the three points of the Triangle by sprinkling Water thrice toward the quarter.) As you do so, say: **"So therefore, first, the Priest who governeth the works of Fire, must sprinkle with the lustral Waters of the loud resounding sea."** Visualize the pure, clear Water cleansing your Sacred Space. Return the cup.

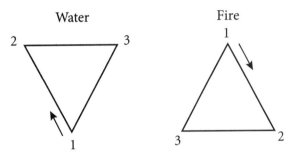

Figure 65: Triangles for Purification and Consecration

7. Take up the incense and consecrate the room with Fire, starting in the east and moving clockwise around the room. Trace a Cross followed by the Invoking Fire Triangle in all four quarters. (The three lines of the Triangle may be traced, or the magician may simply mark the three points of the Triangle.) As you do so, say: **"And when after all the Phantoms are banished, thou shalt see that Holy and Formless Fire, that Fire which darts**

and flashes through the hidden depths of the Universe, hear thou the voice of Fire!" Visualize the Holy Fire of the Divine Spirit sanctifying your Temple space. Return the incense.

8. Start by consecrating the (*Altar*) thus: With the cup of Water, trace a Cross followed by the Invoking Water Triangle over the (*Altar*). Raise the cup and say: "In the name of the Lord of the Universe, who works in Silence and whom naught but Silence can express. I purify this (*Altar*) with Water."

9. With the incense, trace a Cross followed by the Invoking Fire Triangle over the (*Altar*). Raise the incense and say: "In the name of the Lord of the Universe, who works in Silence and whom naught but Silence can express. I consecrate this (*Altar*) with Fire."

10. Visualize the two Triangles and the cross you have traced on the (*Altar*) in white light. Combined, the traced figures form an image of the Banner of the East in flaming brilliance, marking the (*Altar*) with the Sacred protection and power of the Divine Light-force. Concentrate strongly on this vision.

11. For every item or implement in your Temple that you wish to consecrate, repeat steps 8 through 10 above, replacing the word (*Altar*) with the name of whatever item you are consecrating.

12. When finished, say: "Most holy and Source of all things, Source of Love, Source of Life! The Vast and the Mighty One! Bless this Sacred Space with your Divine Power! Help me, a true seeker of Wisdom, to establish this Temple as a fit dwelling place for the Holy Light Divine, so that I may advance in the Great Work. To Thy Name be the glory! Amen!"

13. Say: "I now release any Spirits who have aided this ceremony. Depart in peace. Go with the blessings of Yeheshuah Yehovahshah."

14. Perform the LBRP.

15. Finally say: "The rite is ended. So mote it be."

PURIFICATION AND CONSECRATION

Purifying the Temple with Water acts to ritually cleanse the Temple in a passive way, not unlike a blessing. It is a gentler way of cleansing as opposed to the Banishing Ritual. Consecrating the Temple with Fire sanctifies it. This action charges and vitalizes the Temple, dedicating it as a Sacred Space. Both actions together have a balancing effect that equilibrates and calms the area after banishing.

The following is a standard Golden Dawn formula for cleaning and sanctifying the Temple space with Water and Fire. It is often added to a magical working after the appropriate banishing rituals have been performed. In this mode, the Purification and Consecration are always performed one right after the other.

Purification

1. Take up the cup of Water. Go to the east.

2. Stand at the eastern edge of the Hall facing east. Hold up the cup of Water and trace the figure of a Cross (up, down, left, right). Then sprinkle some Water thrice in the form of an Invoking Water Triangle.

3. Purify the Temple in the same manner in the south, west, and north, while saying the following: **"So therefore, first, the Priest who governeth the works of Fire, must sprinkle with the lustral Water of the loud resounding sea."**

4. When returning to the east, hold up the cup and say: **"I purify with Water!"** Replace the cup.

Ritual Note: The above speech can be broken up as the magician circumambulates the Temple and traces the figures thus: *East:* ✠ ▽ **"So therefore first …"** *South:* ✠ ▽ **"the Priest who governeth the works of Fire …"** *West:* ✠ ▽ **"must sprinkle with the lustral Waters …"** *North:* ✠ ▽ **"of the loud resounding sea."** *Returning to east,* holds up the cup and says: **"I purify with Water!"**

Consecration

1. Take up the incense. Go to the east.

2. Stand at the eastern edge of the Hall facing east. Hold up the incense and trace the figure of a Cross (up, down, left, right). Then wave the incense thrice in the form of an Invoking Fire Triangle.

3. Consecrate the Temple in the same manner in the south, west, and north, while saying the following: **"And when after all the Phantoms are banished, thou shalt see that Holy and Formless Fire, that Fire which darts and flashes through the hidden depths of the Universe, hear thou the voice of Fire!"**

4. When returning to the east, hold up the incense and say: **"I consecrate with Fire!"** Replace the incense.

Ritual Note: The above speech can be broken up as the magician circumambulates the Temple and traces the figures thus: *East:* ✚ △ **"And when after all the Phantoms are banished…"** *South:* ✚ △ **"thou shalt see that Holy and Formless Fire…"** *West:* ✚ △ **"that Fire which darts and flashes through the hidden depths of the Universe…"** *North:* ✚ △ **"hear thou the voice of Fire!"** *Returning to east*, holds up the incense and says: **"I consecrate with Fire!"**

REVIEW QUESTIONS

1. What is the most important magical tool?

2. What is the name of the Golden Dawn's headdress?

3. What symbol is the headdress derived from?

4. What is the symbol of the Golden Dawn?

5. What shape is the Altar?

6. What is Jachin?

7. What is another name for the Banner of the East?

8. What is another name for the Banner of the West?

9. Where did the Enochian Tablets come from?

10. What is the fifth Enochian Tablet called? What does it do?

11. What is found on the horizontal Crossbar of the Great Cross on each Elemental Tablet?

12. Where is the name of the Great King found on each Elemental Tablet?

13. What can the Lotus Wand be used for?

14. Who is the Lotus Wand dedicated to?

15. What do the bands of the Lotus Wand signify?

16. What implement is attributed to Geburah?

17. What are the four Elemental Weapons? How do they relate to the Tetragrammaton?

18. Where does the word "Lamen" come from?

19. What is the Rose Cross Lamen based on?

20. How are the rose petals arranged on the Rose Cross Lamen?

chapter 7

PENTAGRAM RITUALS

The focus of this chapter and the next is on the basic rituals that make up the Golden Dawn practitioner's magical tool kit, the building blocks of ritual magic in our tradition. These are the basic rites of invocation for every force that has been described in previous chapters: elemental, Qabalistic, planetary, and zodiacal. In short, they are the Rituals of the Pentagram and Hexagram, which play an integral role in practical workings and are among the key features of Golden Dawn magic.

Advanced students are given these rites for their own personal magical work. They should be memorized, which is actually easier than it may seem, because the individual rituals are not that long. Committing the Pentagrams and Hexagrams to memory is essential. These short, separate rituals are often used in more complex ceremonies, strung together back-to-back, or adapted for specific energy workings as we will later show.

Most of the rituals given in these chapters have the following characteristics in common. They can be used to:

- Set up the theurgist's magic circle of protection

- Consecrate the Sacred Space with specific energies

- Balance and harmonize the energies invoked

- Align the magician with the guiding energy of Spirit

- Pinpoint a single energy force for extra emphasis in a working

- Center the magician at a balanced cross point of the invoked energies

- Imprint the magician's psyche with the balanced energies invoked

- Increase spiritual attainment and awareness

- Create more complex rituals such as talisman consecrations, invocations, evocations, divination rituals, spiritual development, Spirit Vision Work, etc.

Using these standard rituals by themselves or as part of a longer magical working, Golden Dawn practitioners are able to invoke or banish virtually every spiritual force that we have covered in this book thus far. Table 30 lists the rituals found in this chapter along with their abbreviated titles.

Table 30: SRP Abbreviations

SRP	Supreme Ritual of the Pentagram
SBRP	Supreme Banishing Ritual of the Pentagram *(a form of the SRP)*
SIRP	Supreme Invoking Ritual of the Pentagram *(a form of the SRP)*

AN INTRODUCTION TO THE SUPREME RITUAL OF THE PENTAGRAM

The Supreme Ritual is a more advanced version of the Pentagram Ritual and was originally taught only to Second Order students. Whereas the Lesser Ritual of the Pentagram is used for general invokings and banishings in the sub-elemental sphere of Malkuth in the material world of Assiah, the SRP is used to summon and dismiss the forces of the four elements in a direct, fine-tuned, and more potent way. Properly performed, the influence of this ritual can be felt in the Yetziratic realm—the World of Formation that exists immediately above our world.

This rite also invokes or banishes the fifth element of Spirit in combination with the four elements, each in its assigned direction. Spirit is an important addition to the elemental energies, because it rules over and controls the balance of energies in this rite. Spirit is the divine force that grants the magician authority in any magical working.

This versatile ritual can be fine-tuned for a single element. And it is also regularly adapted for invoking and banishing energies of the twelve zodiacal signs, which correlate to the Pentagram through their elemental triplicities.

Like the Lesser Ritual of the Pentagram, the elements of the Supreme Ritual are assigned to the directions in accordance with the "four winds" attributions of the ancients: Air-east, Fire-south, Water-west, and Earth-north.

There are two versions of this ritual: the Supreme *Invoking* Ritual of the Pentagram (SIRP) and the Supreme *Banishing* Ritual of the Pentagram (SBRP). Each version employs six forms of the Pentagram: one for the four elements, and two for Spirit, which is divided into *Active Spirit* and *Passive Spirit*.

Instead of using the four alchemical Triangles, this rite employs the emblems of the Kerubic Signs to represent the elemental points of the Pentagram. To the Air, Earth, Fire, and Water points are allotted the symbols of Aquarius, Taurus, Leo, and the eagle's head, a symbol of Scorpio (Figure 66).

Figure 66: Pentagram with Kerubic Signs

why the eagle's head for scorpio?

The sign of Scorpio has traditionally been assigned at least two different animal emblems: the scorpion and the eagle (and sometimes the phoenix). This alludes to the spiritually transformative nature of the sign—from a creature that crawls to one that soars.

Many astrologers refer to Aquarius, Taurus, Leo, and Scorpio as the fixed signs because they fall in the middle of their respective seasons, anchoring the four parts of the year. Golden Dawn magicians usually refer to them as the Kerubic Signs to signify that they represent the strongest, most stable essence of the four elements. For centuries, the fixed signs have been used as symbols of powerful angels known as the Kerubim who preside over the four elements and who were immortalized in the biblical prophet Ezekiel's vision, which was believed to have been based on Babylonian astrology: *"As for the likeness of their faces, they four had the face of a man* [Aquarius], *and the face of a lion* [Leo], *on the right side: and they four had the face of an ox* [Taurus] *on the left side; they four also had the face of an eagle* [Scorpio] (Ezekiel 1, verse 10). These mighty Kerubic figures are shown in their respective Pentagram positions in the four corners of the Universe card in many traditional tarot decks.

By tracing the Kerubic emblems in the center of a Pentagram, magicians call upon the great angelic forces who govern the elements under their control.

THE ELEMENTAL PENTAGRAMS

There are a total of eight Elemental Pentagrams: four of them invoke the elements and four of them banish the same. The difference between them is this:

- To invoke an element, trace a line *toward* its point.

- To banish an element, trace a line *away from* its point.

In both cases, the Kerubic symbol of the element is traced in the center of the completed Pentagram.

Invoking Air

Invoking Water

Invoking Earth

Invoking Fire

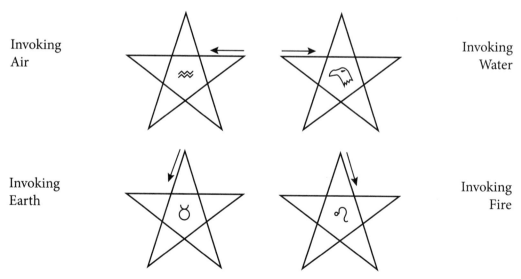

Figure 67: Invoking Elemental Pentagrams

Figure 67 shows the tracing for invoking the Elemental Pentagrams, and Figure 68 for banishing the Elemental Pentagrams. Notice that the Pentagrams for Invoking Air and Banishing Water are drawn in an identical way. The same is true for Banishing Air and Invoking Water. What distinguishes them in practice are the divine names that are vibrated in accompaniment, as well as the emblems traced in the center.

Banishing
Air

Banishing
Water

Banishing
Earth

Banishing
Fire

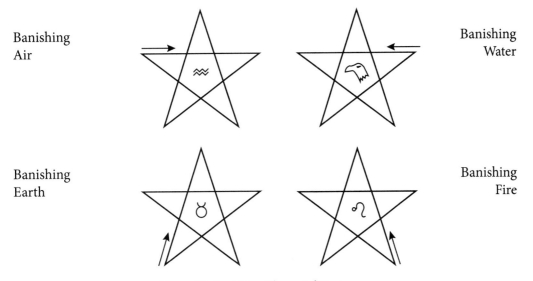

Figure 68: Banishing Elemental Pentagrams

Below are the words of power vibrated with the Elemental Pentagrams:

- For Air: **ORO IBAH AOZPI** and **YHVH**

- For Fire: **OIP TEAA PEDOCE** and **ELOHIM**

- For Water: **EMP ARSEL GAIOL** and **AL**

- For Earth: **MOR DIAL HECTEGA** and **ADONAI**

The first words vibrated while tracing the Pentagrams are Enochian: they are the "Three Great Secret Names of God" found on the Elemental Tablets described in chapter 6.

The second words vibrated are Hebrew godnames taken from four Sephiroth and their corresponding elements. These words are vibrated while tracing the central symbols:

- **YHVH**: from Tiphareth's *YHVH Eloah Ve-Daath*, assigned to Air

- **ELOHIM**: from Geburah's *Elohim Gibor*, assigned to Fire

- **AL** (or **EL**): from Chesed's *El*, assigned to Water

- **ADONAI**: from Malkuth's *Adonai ha-Aretz*, assigned to Earth

Israel Regardie suggested that students vibrate the letters of the divine name *AL* for Water, to make for a longer vibration: "*Aleph Lamed, AL.*"

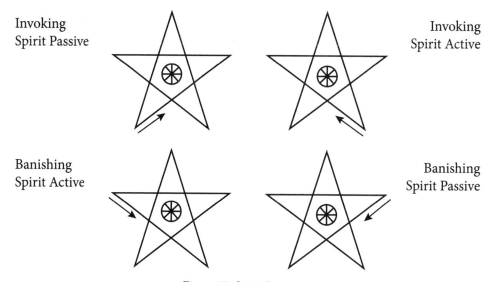

Figure 69: Spirit Pentagrams

THE SPIRIT PENTAGRAMS

There are a total of four Spirit Pentagrams: two control the active elements of Fire and Air, and two control the passive elements of Water and Earth (Figure 69).

Unlike the Elemental Pentagrams, Spirit Pentagrams don't start or end at the Spirit point of the Pentagram. Instead, the Spirit Active Pentagrams link the elements of Fire and Air, while the Spirit Passive Pentagrams connect the Earth and Water points. The invoking lines that lead from Fire to Air and from Earth to Water are mediating currents that provide equilibrium and harmony between the masculine and feminine energies.

The words vibrated with the Spirit Pentagrams are given below. The first word comes from the Enochian Tablet of Union and is vibrated while tracing the Pentagram.

The second word is a Hebrew name of power vibrated while tracing the central Spirit Wheel:

Actives

- For Air: **EXARP, EHEIEH**
- For Fire: **BITOM, EHEIEH**

Passives

- For Water: **HCOMA, AGLA**
- For Earth: **NANTA, AGLA**

Because they don't touch the Spirit point directly, students often have a hard time memorizing the four Spirit Pentagrams. Here are a couple of ideas that can help:

- Picture the Pentagram as an "X" with a circle above it (Figure 70). The circle is the Spirit point. One line is masculine, connecting Air and Fire. The other line is feminine, linking Water and Earth.

Figure 70: "X" Formation

- In the Invoking form for Spirit Actives, the starting point is Fire, the most active element.

- In the Invoking form for Spirit Passives, the starting point is Earth, the most passive element.

- The starting point for invoking either Actives or Passives is at the bottom point of their respective lines.

- The starting point for banishing either Actives or Passives is at the top point of their respective lines.

- Another aid to memory is to imagine the right and left sides of the Pentagram as the right and left pillars on the Tree of Life. To invoke the Actives, you start at the base of the White Pillar; to invoke the Passives, you start at the base of the Black Pillar. To banish the Actives, *return to the base of the White Pillar*; to banish the Passives, *return to the base of the Black Pillar.* Up to invoke, down to banish.

In the Supreme Ritual of the Pentagram, the Spirit Pentagrams always precede and close the other four Elemental Pentagrams: a Spirit Active Pentagram is always used in conjunction with a Pentagram of Air or of Fire, just as a Spirit Passive Pentagram is used in conjunction with a Pentagram of Water or of Earth.

After tracing any Spirit Pentagram, the sigil of the Spirit Wheel is drawn in the center of the figure. Like all sigils, the Spirit Wheel should be traced clockwise from left to right (Figure 71).

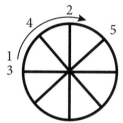

Figure 71: Tracing the Spirit Wheel

Ritual Note: If the Enochian Tablets are placed in the four quarters of your Temple, you should trace a large circle in front of each Tablet before tracing the Pentagram (a clockwise circle for invoking, an anticlockwise circle for banishing). This has the effect of focusing your efforts and drawing forth or closing down the elemental forces represented by the Tablets. When using the four Tablets, place the Tablet of Union on the central Altar.

There are four parts to the SRP:

1. Opening: The Qabalistic Cross

2. Tracing the Pentagrams, either invoking or Banishing forms (two in each quarter)

3. Conjuration of the Four Archangels

4. Closing: The Qabalistic Cross

THE SUPREME INVOKING RITUAL OF THE PENTAGRAM

This ritual is a powerful rite for invoking the forces of the elements. For tracing the Pentagrams, you can use your index finger, the Outer Wand of Double Power, the Rainbow Wand, or the Lotus Wand, pointing with the white end throughout.

Ritual Note: If you use the Lotus Wand or the Rainbow Wand, grasp the white band for the Spirit Pentagrams, and the Kerubic bands for the Elemental Pentagrams: *Air,* the violet band of Aquarius; *Fire,* the yellow band of Leo; *Water,* the blue-green band of Scorpio; *Earth,* the red-orange band of Taurus.

Also, when vibrating a divine name in conjunction with tracing a Pentagram, you can either 1) begin the vibration simultaneously with the tracing of the first line and end with the last syllable as you thrust through the center of the figure, or 2) vibrate the names after tracing the figure, while you are thrusting through the center. We prefer the former.

Opening: The QC

1. Stand and face east. Perform the Qabalistic Cross. (You can start in the east or at the center of your Temple space just west of the Altar facing east. From there, walk to the east, south, west, and north to trace the Pentagrams.)

Tracing the Invoking Pentagrams

EAST

2. Trace a large white Invoking Pentagram of Spirit Active. Thrust through the center of the Pentagram and vibrate **"EXARP."** Trace the Spirit Wheel in the center and intone, **"EHEIEH."** Give the Sign of the Opening of the Veil, followed by the LVX Signs.

3. Trace the Invoking Pentagram of Air and vibrate, **"ORO IBAH AOZPI."** Draw the sigil of Aquarius in the center and intone, **"YHVH."** Give the Sign of Air.

SOUTH

4. Turn to the south and trace a large Invoking Pentagram of Spirit Active. Thrust through the center of the Pentagram and vibrate **"BITOM."** Trace

the Spirit sigil in the center and intone, **"EHEIEH."** Give the Sign of the Opening of the Veil, followed by the LVX Signs.

5. Trace the Invoking Pentagram of Fire and vibrate, **"OIP TEAA PEDOCE."** Draw the sigil of Leo in the center and intone, **"ELOHIM."** Give the Sign of Fire.

WEST

6. Turn to the west and trace a large Invoking Pentagram of Spirit Passive. Thrust through the center of the Pentagram and vibrate **"HCOMA."** Trace the Spirit sigil in the center and intone **"AGLA."** Give the Sign of the Opening of the Veil, followed by the LVX Signs.

7. Trace the Invoking Pentagram of Water and vibrate **"EMPEH ARSEL GAI-OL."** Draw the sigil of the eagle in the center and intone, **"Aleph Lamed, AL."** Give the Sign of Water.

NORTH

8. Turn to the north and trace a large Invoking Pentagram of Spirit Passive. Thrust through the center of the Pentagram and vibrate **"NANTA."** Trace the Spirit sigil in the center and intone, **"AGLA."** Give the Sign of the Opening of the Veil, followed by the LVX Signs.

9. Trace the Invoking Pentagram of Earth and vibrate, **"EMOR DIAL HECTEGA."** Draw the sigil of Taurus in the center and intone, **"ADO-NAI."** Give the Sign of Earth.

Conjuration of the Four Archangels

10. Return to the east (or center of the Temple facing east). Keep the arm extended. Extend both arms out in the form of a cross and say, **"Before me, RAPHAEL. Behind me, GABRIEL. On my right hand, MICHAEL. On my left hand, URIEL. For about me flames the Pentagram, and in the column shines the Six-Rayed Star."** Visualize the archangels as you did in the LRP.

Closing: The QC

11. Repeat the Qabalistic Cross as in the beginning.

Ritual Note: The Sign of the Opening of the Veil is attributed to Spirit, which is why we suggest giving it after opening the Spirit Pentagrams in this ritual. Traditionally, magicians gave only the LVX Signs at this point as a sign of their rank, since this ritual was traditionally taught in the Adeptus Minor grade. Students can use either the Opening of the Veil or the LVX Signs, or both, as we suggest here.

When giving the Sign of the Opening of the Veil, clearly visualize the opening of a curtain, allowing the white brilliance of Spirit to stream into the Temple.

EXPANDED VISUALIZATION OF THE SUPREME PENTAGRAM RITUAL

Whether using either the Invoking form or the Banishing form of this ritual, imagine the Divine Light obtained during the preliminary Qabalistic Cross as completely filling your auric sphere for the duration of the rite.

In tracing the Pentagrams, picture the shaft of light at your Kether center receiving more energy from the Macrocosmic Kether above, and welling up from your grounded Malkuth to gather at your Tiphareth center, where the light is at its strongest. Will and visualize the light going down your arm and out your hand or implement to inscribe the Pentagrams.

You can either visualize the line of all the Pentagrams in brilliant white light or you can image them in lines of their elemental colors: Spirit-white, Air-yellow, Fire-red, Water-blue, and Earth-black. The same with the symbols traced in the center.

Will and imagine the energies of the four elements, balanced and governed by Spirit, entering the Temple through the Pentagram portals you have created.

THE SUPREME BANISHING RITUAL OF THE PENTAGRAM

The SBRP mirrors the SIRP in many ways. It is a robust and effective method for closing down the elemental forces invoked during a magical working. The more powerful the force invoked, the more powerful the force used to banish it. This rite is designed to restore balance and calm back to the place of working, especially if that space is used for another mundane purpose such as a family room, bedroom, etc.

For this ritual, you can use your index finger, the Outer Wand of Double Power, the Rainbow Wand, or the Lotus Wand, pointing with the white end for the QC and the black end for tracing the banishing Pentagrams.

Opening: The QC

1. Stand and face east. Perform the Qabalistic Cross. (If you began the SIRP at the center of your Temple, do the same for the SBRP.)

Tracing the Banishing Pentagrams

EAST

2. Facing east, trace a large Banishing Pentagram of Air and vibrate, **"ORO IBAH AOZPI."** Draw the sigil of Aquarius in the center of the Pentagram and intone, **"YHVH."** Give the Sign of Air.

3. Trace the Banishing Pentagram of Spirit Active. Thrust through the center of the Pentagram and vibrate, **"EXARP."** Trace the Spirit sigil in the center and intone, **"EHEIEH."** Give the Sign of the Closing of the Veil, followed by the LVX Signs.

SOUTH

4. Turn to the south and trace a large Banishing Pentagram of Fire while vibrating **"OIP TEAA PEDOCE."** Draw the sigil of Leo in the center of the Pentagram and intone, **"ELOHIM."** Give the Sign of Fire.

5. Trace the Banishing Pentagram of Spirit Active while vibrating **"BITOM."** Trace the Spirit sigil in the center and intone, **"EHEIEH."** Give the Sign of the Closing of the Veil, followed by the LVX Signs.

WEST

6. Turn to the west and trace the Banishing Pentagram of Water while vibrating **"EMPEH ARSEL GAIOL."** Draw the sigil of the eagle in the center of the Pentagram and intone, **"Aleph Lamed, AL."** Give the Sign of Water.

7. Trace the Banishing Pentagram of Spirit Passive while vibrating **"HCOMA."** Trace the Spirit sigil in the center and intone **"AGLA."** Give the Sign of the Closing of the Veil, followed by the LVX Signs.

NORTH

    8. Turn to the north and trace the Banishing Pentagram of Earth while vibrating **"EMOR DIAL HECTEGA."** Draw the sigil of Taurus in the center of the Pentagram and intone, **"ADONAI."** Give the Sign of Earth.

    9. Trace a Banishing Pentagram of Spirit Passive while vibrating **"NANTA."** Trace the Spirit sigil in the center and intone, **"AGLA."** Give the Sign of the Opening of the Veil, followed by the LVX Signs.

Conjuration of the Four Archangels

    10. Keep the arm extended. Turn to face the east. Extend both arms out in the form of a cross and say, **"Before me, RAPHAEL. Behind me, GABRIEL. On my right hand, MICHAEL. On my left hand, URIEL. For about me flames the Pentagram, and in the column shines the Six-Rayed Star."** Visualize the archangels as you did in the LRP.

Closing: The QC

    11. Repeat the Qabalistic Cross.

Ritual Note 1: In the SIRP, the Spirit Pentagrams are traced before the Elemental Pentagrams because Spirit is the force that guides and rules the elements: it establishes a controlling influence or Sacred Space in which the element can be safely invoked.

Conversely, if Spirit is the first element to be invoked, it should also be the last to leave. We recommend that the banishing Elemental Pentagram is traced before the banishing Spirit Pentagram. This ensures that Spirit always maintains control over the elemental force.

Ritual Note 2: The Sign of the Closing of the Veil is also attributed to Spirit, which is why it is given after closing down the Spirit Pentagrams in this ritual. In similar fashion to the SIRP, students can use either the Closing of the Veil or the LVX Signs, or both. When performing the Closing of the Veil, image a curtain closing, as the Spirit gently leaves the Temple space.

Ritual Note 3: When performing an invoking ritual such as the SIRP, all circles as well as symbols drawn in the center of the Pentagrams are traced clockwise from left to right. When performing a banishing ritual such as the SBRP, all circles as well as symbols drawn in the center of the Pentagrams may be traced counterclockwise.

SINGLE ELEMENT PENTAGRAM RITUALS

The Golden Dawn teaches that within each of the four elements the other three elements are also present in balanced portion. This is why the Sephirah of Malkuth as well as the Enochian Watchtower Tablets are divided into four elemental quarters. In both cases, these internal elemental divisions are sub-elements.

Single Element Pentagram Rituals can be used whenever the magician wants to place special emphasis on a specific element in a particular working. One example of this would be the *Supreme Invoking Ritual of the Pentagram of Air*, called the *SIRP of Air* for short. The other three Single Element Rituals follow the same pattern.

Ritual Note: If you employ the Enochian Tablets for a Single Element Pentagram Ritual, trace a circle and the Pentagrams in front of the *sub-element* of the Tablet. For example: in the *SIRP of Air*, trace all the Pentagrams over the Air sub-element (the upper left-hand quarter) in each of the four Tablets. In the *SIRP of Fire*, trace all Pentagrams over the Fire sub-element (lower right quarter) in each of the four Tablets. In the *SIRP of Water*, trace all Pentagrams over the Water sub-element in all four Tablets. In the *SIRP of Earth,* trace all Pentagrams over the Earth sub-element in all four Tablets.

The SIRP of Air

1. Stand and face east. Perform the Qabalistic Cross.

2. Facing east, trace a large Invoking Pentagram of Spirit Active and vibrate, **"EXARP."** Trace the Spirit sigil in the center and vibrate, **"EHEIEH."** Give the Sign of the Opening of the Veil, followed by the LVX Signs.

3. Trace the Invoking Pentagram of Air and vibrate, **"ORO IBAH AOZPI."** Draw the sigil of Aquarius in the center and vibrate, **"YHVH."** Give the Sign of Air.

4. Turn to the south. Trace the exact same Pentagrams and vibrate the same words and give the same gestures as in step 2. Do the same in the west and north.

5. Return to the east. Extend both arms out in the form of a cross and say, **"Before me, RAPHAEL. Behind me, GABRIEL. On my right hand, MI-CHAEL. On my left hand, URIEL. For about me flames the Pentagram, and in the column shines the Six-Rayed Star."** Visualize the archangels as you did in the LRP.

6. Repeat the Qabalistic Cross.

The SIRP of Fire

1. Stand and face east. Perform the Qabalistic Cross.

2. Facing east, trace a large Invoking Pentagram of Spirit Active and vibrate, **"BITOM."** Trace the Spirit sigil in the center and intone, **"EHEIEH."** Give the Sign of the Opening of the Veil, followed by the LVX Signs.

3. Trace the Invoking Pentagram of Fire and vibrate, **"OIP TEAA PEDOCE."** Draw the sigil of Leo in the center and vibrate, **"ELOHIM."** Give the Sign of Fire.

4. Turn to the south. Trace the exact same Pentagrams and vibrate the same words and give the same gestures as in step 2 and 3. Do the same in the west and north.

5. Give the invocation of the archangels and the Qabalistic Cross.

The SIRP of Water

1. Stand and face east. Perform the Qabalistic Cross.

2. Facing east, trace a large Invoking Pentagram of Spirit Passive and vibrate, **"HCOMA."** Trace the Spirit sigil in the center and intone, **"AGLA."** Give the Sign of the Opening of the Veil, followed by the LVX Signs.

3. Trace the Invoking Pentagram of Water and vibrate, **"EMPEH ARSEL GAI-OL."** Draw the sigil of the eagle in the center and intone, **"Aleph Lamed, AL."** Give the Sign of Water.

4. Turn to the south. Trace the exact same Pentagrams and vibrate the same words and give the same gestures as in step 2 and 3. Do the same in the west and north.

5. Give the invocation of the archangels and the Qabalistic Cross.

The SIRP of Earth

1. Stand and face east. Perform the Qabalistic Cross.

2. Facing east, trace a large Invoking Pentagram of Spirit Passive and vibrate, **"NANTA."** Trace the Spirit sigil in the center and intone, **"AGLA."** Give the Sign of the Opening of the Veil, followed by the LVX Signs.

3. Then trace the Invoking Pentagram of Earth and vibrate, **"EMOR DIAL HECTEGA."** Draw the sigil of Taurus in the center and intone, **"ADONAI."** Give the Sign of Earth.

4. Turn to the south. Trace the exact same Pentagrams and vibrate the same words and give the same gestures as in step 2 and 3. Do the same in the west and north.

5. Give the invocation of the archangels and the Qabalistic Cross.

SINGLE ELEMENT BANISHING RITUALS

These four rituals follow a similar formula as their SIRP counterparts with these differences: 1) only the Banishing forms of the respective Pentagrams are used, 2) the Spirit Pentagram is traced *after* the Elemental Pentagram, and 3) the Sign of the Closing of the Veil is used. One example of a single element SBRP is given below.

The SBRP of Water

1. Stand and face east. Perform the Qabalistic Cross.

2. Facing east, trace a large Banishing Pentagram of Water and vibrate, **"EM-PEH ARSEL GAIOL."** Draw the sigil of the eagle in the center and intone, **"Aleph Lamed, AL."** Give the Sign of Water.

3. Trace a Banishing Pentagram of Spirit Passive and vibrate, **"HCOMA."** Trace the Spirit sigil in the center and intone, **"AGLA."** Give the Sign of the Closing of the Veil, followed by the LVX Signs.

4. Turn to the south. Trace the exact same Pentagrams and vibrate the same words and give the same gestures as in step 2 and 3. Do the same in the west and north.

5. Return to the east, extend both arms in the form of a cross and invoke the four archangels. End with the Qabalistic Cross.

Symbolism and Use of the SRP

The Supreme Ritual of the Pentagram is one of the most versatile of all Golden Dawn rituals for practical magic. Like all the standard Golden Dawn rituals given in this chapter, it can be used to set up the theurgist's magical circle in the astral light.

But as we've demonstrated, this single ritual can be used to fine-tune a specific elemental or zodiacal energy, by zeroing in on the divine powers and angelic forces that govern them. The basic ritual has two forms, the SIRP and the SBRP. Each form yields four single element variations and twelve basic zodiacal versions for a total of thirty-four different SRP rituals! And these are not the only forms possible.

Whereas the Lesser Ritual of the Pentagram is used for general invokings of Malkuth in the material world of Assiah, performance of the Supreme Ritual influences the higher Yetziratic World of Formation and reaches into the lower levels of the Briah, the Creative World.

Hebrew names vibrated in the Supreme Ritual reflect this. *YHVH* is affiliated with the Pentagram of Air through its connection with the godname of Tiphareth, an airy Sephirah. *Elohim* is assigned to the Fire Pentagram because of its link with the godname of fiery Geburah. *Al* (or *El*), the godname of Watery Chesed, is joined to the Pentagram of Water. *Adonai*, a godname of earthy Malkuth, correlates to the Earth Pentagram.

The Hebrew godnames *Eheieh* and *Agla* were discussed in the Lesser Pentagram Ritual in chapter 4. In the Supreme Ritual, they are vibrated with the Spirit Pentagrams: Eheieh for Spirit Actives, Agla for Spirit Passives. These are used to signify Spirit connecting polar opposites on the Tree of Life, Kether and Malkuth, respectively.

Enochian names vibrated in the Supreme Ritual include the "Three Holy Secret Names of God" found on the center of each Elemental Tablet, as well as the divine names of the Tablet of Union.

THE GREATER RITUAL OF THE PENTAGRAM

There is another Pentagram Ritual beside the Lesser and Supreme, known as the Greater Ritual of the Pentagram (or GRP) that includes both Invoking and Banishing forms. It is essentially the same as the Supreme Ritual, but instead of using both Hebrew and Enochian divine names in the tracing of the Pentagrams, it employs just one or the other. However, the Supreme Ritual is more commonly used because it aligns the magician with a broad range of Golden Dawn magic and expresses a more comprehensive practice.

ZODIACAL PENTAGRAMS

Pentagrams are also used to invoke and banish the energies of the twelve zodiacal signs, because the signs are attributed to the four elements through their triplicities.

For example, if you wanted to invoke the energy of Aries, you would use the Pentagram and divine names associated with the Invoking Fire Pentagram. But instead of tracing the usual symbol of Leo in the center, you would draw the symbol of Aries (Figure 72).

For banishing the energy of Pisces, use the Pentagram and divine names associated with the Banishing Water Pentagram. In the center, trace the sigil of Pisces.

For invoking the energies of Scorpio, use the Pentagram and divine names associated with the Invoking Water Pentagram. In the center, trace the sigil of Scorpio (the usual zodiacal emblem ♏, *not* the Kerubic emblem).

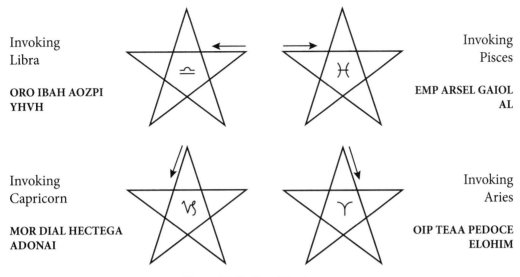

Invoking
Libra

**ORO IBAH AOZPI
YHVH**

Invoking
Pisces

**EMP ARSEL GAIOL
AL**

Invoking
Capricorn

**MOR DIAL HECTEGA
ADONAI**

Invoking
Aries

**OIP TEAA PEDOCE
ELOHIM**

Figure 72: Zodiacal Pentagrams

For whatever sign you are working with, find out what part of the sky the sign is in at the time of your practice, and face that quarter or direction when tracing the Pentagram of the sign. If you don't know where the sign is in the sky but still want to work with that zodiacal force, then treat the circle of your Sacred Space like a flat zodiacal wheel with Aries in the east, Cancer in the north, Libra in the west, and Capricorn in the south.

SINGLE ZODIACAL SIGN SRP

The Supreme Ritual of the Pentagram can be used to invoke or banish the energy of a single zodiacal sign whenever the magician wants to place special emphasis on that sign in a specific working, in similar fashion to the invocation of a single element. One example of this would be the Supreme Invoking Ritual of the Pentagram of Libra (called the *SIRP of Libra* for short). This would be exactly the same as the SIRP of Air described earlier, the only difference would be to replace the sigil of Kerubic Air with the symbol of Libra.

Ritual Note: If you use the Lotus Wand or the Rainbow Wand, grasp the white band for the Spirit Pentagrams, and the colored band assigned to the zodiacal sign you are working with for the zodiacal Pentagram: Libra—the green band, Aries—the red band, Sagittarius—the blue band, and so forth.

In Summary

Pentagrams:

- Are traced with a continuous line along five points.

- Are composed of five points attributed to the four elements, plus Spirit.

Pentagram Rituals:

- Invoke and banish elemental forces.

- Invoke and banish zodiacal forces.

- Open and close with the QC.

Invoking and Banishing:

- Invoking Pentagrams are traced *toward* the point of the desired element.

- Banishing Pentagrams are traced *away from* the point of the desired element.

Greater Pentagram Rituals:

- Use either Hebrew or Enochian words of power, not both.

Supreme Pentagram Rituals:

- Open and close with the Qabalistic Cross.

- Follow the "four winds" attribution of the elemental directions.

- Trace two separate Pentagrams in each quarter.

- Have two forms of the Pentagram that invoke Spirit.

- Have two forms of the Pentagram that banish Spirit.

- Can be used to invoke or banish elemental forces or a single element.

- Can be used to invoke or banish zodiacal forces or a single zodiacal sign.

- Invoke the four archangels of the elements.

- Use both Hebrew and Enochian words of power.

INTRODUCTION TO THE OPENING BY WATCHTOWER

The Opening by Watchtower, created by Israel Regardie, is a powerful rite that can be used to open any magical operation. The Watchtower Ritual as it is sometimes called, contains portions of other rituals, including the Consecration Ceremony of the Vault of the Adepti, the Supreme Invoking Ritual of the Pentagram, and the Portal Ceremony. It is solidly based on Golden Dawn ritual techniques.

The Watchtowers opened in this rite are the Enochian Watchtower Tablets of the elements. In order to perform this ritual, the magician will need the Enochian Tablets and the Elemental Weapons described in chapter 6. The inclusion of these items, along with additional invocations addressed to the elemental powers, helps secure the cooperation of these forces toward the success of the working.

Regular practice of the Opening by Watchtower imprints the equilibrated force of the five elements into the magician's aura, allowing for additional spiritual realignment. Regardie believed that continued and persistent repetition of the Opening by Watchtower Ceremony over a long period of time was a form of self-initiation that could result in the acceptance of the practitioner as an adept in the astral realms.

Some practitioners use the Opening by Watchtower in place of the more traditional (and shorter) Supreme Invoking Ritual of the Pentagram. Others prefer the SIRP because it doesn't require the Enochian Tablets. Both rituals can serve the same function of purifying Sacred Space, casting a magic circle, and invoking the elemental guardians of the four quarters. However, the Watchtower Ritual does so in a more potent and dramatic way.

One of the primary differences between the SIRP and the Watchtower Ritual is in the ordering of the invocations. In the Pentagram Ritual, the invocations follow the "four winds" formula, going clockwise around the room from east to south, to west, and north. In contrast, the Watchtower Ritual uses the YHVH formula in the ordering of the invocations going from Fire in the south, to Water in the west, to Air in the east, to Earth in the north. This has the effect of bringing the elemental energy down through the Four Qabalistic Worlds in order from the most ethereal to the most corporeal. In addition, the invocation of Spirit over the Tablet of Union results in a Pentagrammaton formation with the magician and the quintessence at a point of balance in the center of the divine forces.

Regardie created at least three different versions of this ritual, some more complex than others. Again, there is no "One True Way!" The version provided here is the one we use most often, just as Regardie taught us. There are four parts to the Opening by Watchtower:

1. Initial Banishings

2. Invoking the Elemental Watchtowers

3. Invoking Spirit: The Tablet of Union

4. Circumambulation and Adoration

OPENING BY WATCHTOWER RITUAL

Preparation of the Hall: The Temple is to be arranged in accordance with the Neophyte Hall. The Elemental Tablets should be placed in the appropriate quarters sitting on or placed above side Altars in front of each Tablet. On the center of the main Altar should be the Tablet of Union with the Elemental Weapons around it. (Air Dagger-east, Fire Wand-south, Water Cup-west, Earth Pentacle-north.) The magician should be relaxed and robed in full ceremonial regalia.

For this ritual you can also use the Outer Wand of Double Power, the Rainbow Wand, or the Lotus Wand, pointing with the white end for the QC and invoking figures, and the black end for tracing the banishing figures.

Initial Banishings

1. Commence the ritual with five knocks (4+1), to indicate the four elements crowed by Spirit. Go to the northeast and say in a loud voice, **"Hekas, Hekas Este Bebeloi!"**

2. Go to the east (or center to begin) and perform the LBRP.

3. Perform the LBRH (explained in chapter 8).

Invoking the Elemental Watchtowers

SOUTH

4. Go to the south side of the Altar and take up the Fire Wand. Turn to the Elemental Tablet of Fire in the south and wave the implement three times in front of the Tablet.

5. Then holding the wand high, slowly circumambulate the room clockwise while saying: **"And when, after all the phantoms are banished, thou shalt see that Holy and Formless Fire, that Fire which darts and flashes through the hidden depths of the Universe, hear thou the Voice of Fire."**

6. Upon reaching south, face the Fire Tablet and wave the wand in front of the Tablet again, three times. Trace a large white circle in the Air in front of the Tablet. Within this circle, draw a large white Invoking Spirit Active Pentagram and vibrate, **"BITOM."** In the center, draw the Spirit Wheel and vibrate, **"EHEIEH."** Give the Sign of the Opening of the Veil, followed by the LVX Signs.

7. Trace the Invoking Pentagram of Fire over the one just drawn while vibrating, **"OIP TEAA PEDOCE."** In the center, draw the sigil of Leo and vibrate, **"ELOHIM."** Give the Sign of Fire.

8. Remain in the sign of Fire and say, "**In the Names and Letters of the Great Southern Quadrangle, I invoke ye, ye Angels of the Watchtower of the South!**" Replace the wand.

WEST

9. Take up the Water Cup and go to the west. Wave the cup thrice before the Water Tablet. Hold the cup high while circumambulating slowly around the room and say, **"So therefore first the Priest who governeth the works of Fire must sprinkle with the Lustral Water of the Loud Resounding Sea."**

10. On reaching the west, wave the cup three times in front of the Tablet as before and trace a large white circle around the Tablet. Within the circle, draw a large Invoking Spirit Passive Pentagram with the cup while vibrating, **"HCOMA."** In the center, trace the Spirit Wheel and vibrate, **"AGLA."** Give the Sign of the Opening of the Veil, followed by the LVX Signs.

11. Draw the Invoking Pentagram of Water over the Spirit Pentagram while vibrating **"EMPEH ARSEL GAIOL."** Draw the sigil of the eagle in the center and vibrate, **"Aleph Lamed, AL."** Give the Sign of Water.

12. Remain in the Sign of Water and say: **"In the Names and Letters of the Great Western Quadrangle, I invoke ye, ye Angels of the Watchtower of the West."** Replace the cup.

EAST

13. Take up the Air Dagger and go to the east. Turn to the east and wave the dagger three times in front of the Air Tablet. Begin the slow Circumambulation while saying, **"Such a Fire existeth, extending through the rushings of Air, or even a Fire formless whence cometh the Image of a Voice, or even a flashing Light, abounding, revolving, whirling forth, crying aloud."**

14. Stop again in the east and wave the implement thrice before the Tablet. Trace the circle and the Invoking Spirit Active Pentagram while vibrating **"EXARP."** Draw the sigil of Spirit in the center and vibrate, **"EHEIEH."** Give the Sign of the Opening of the Veil, followed by the LVX Signs.

15. Trace the Invoking Pentagram of Air while intoning **"ORO IBAH AOZPI."** Draw the sigil of Aquarius in the center and vibrate, **"YHVH."** Give the Sign of Air.

16. Remain in the Sign of Air and say: **"In the Names and Letters of the Great Eastern Quadrangle, I invoke ye, ye Angels of the Watchtower of the East."** Replace the dagger.

NORTH

17. Go clockwise to the north of the Altar and take up the Earth Pentacle. Turn to the north and wave the implement thrice in front of the Earth Tablet. Begin the slow Circumambulation while saying, **"Stoop not down into the darkly splendid world wherein continually lieth a faithless depth, and Hades wrapped in gloom, delighting in unintelligible images, precipitous, winding a black, ever-rolling Abyss, ever espousing a body, unluminous, formless and void."**

18. Stop upon reaching the north and again wave the implement thrice in front of the Earth Tablet. With the Pentacle, trace the circle and the Invoking Spirit Passive Pentagram. Vibrate, **"NANTA."** Trace the Spirit sigil in the

center while intoning **"AGLA."** Give the Sign of the Opening of the Veil, followed by the LVX Signs.

19. Draw the Invoking Pentagram of Earth over the previous figure while vibrating **"EMOR DIAL HECTEGA."** Draw the sigil of Taurus in the center and intone, **"ADONAI."** Give the Earth Sign.

20. Remain in the Earth Sign and say, **"In the Names and Letters of the Great Northern Quadrangle, I invoke ye, ye Angels of the Watchtower of the North."** Replace the Pentacle.

Invoking Spirit: The Tablet of Union

21. Go clockwise to the west of the Altar and face east. Trace a circle over the Tablet of Union. Then draw each of the Invoking Spirit Pentagrams and vibrate the appropriate words: **"EXARP EHEIEH. HCOMA AGLA. NANTA AGLA. BITOM EHEIEH."**

22. Then say, **"In the Names and Letters of the mystical Tablet of Union, I invoke ye, ye Divine Forces of the Spirit of Life."** Make the Sign of the Rending of the Veil. Visualize the Veil opening as you step through it.

23. Say the following Enochian oration, **"OL SONUF VAORSAGI GOHO IAD BALATA. ELEXARPEH. CO-MANANU. TABITOM. ZODAKARA, EKA ZODAKARE OD ZODAMERANU. ODO KIKLE QAA PIAPE PIAMOEL OD VAOAN."**
    (Pronunciation: Oh-ell son-oof vay-oh-air-sah-jee go-ho ee-ah-dah bahl-tah. El-ex-ar-pay-hay. Co-mah-nah-noo. Tah-bee- toh-em. Zohd-ah-kah-rah eh-kah zohd-ah-kah-ray oh-dah zohd-ah-mehr-ah-noo. Oh-doh kee-klay kah-ah pee-ah-pay pee-ah-moh-el oh-dah vay-oh-ah-noo.) This oration is usually memorized, but have it ready on an index card if you need it.
    (This means: "I reign over you, saith the God of Justice [*three magical names that rule over the Tablet of Union*]. Move, therefore, move and appear. Open the mysteries of creation: balance, righteousness and truth.")

24. Say, **"I invoke ye, ye Angels of the Celestial spheres, whose dwelling is in the invisible. Ye are the guardians of the gates of the Universe, be ye also the guardians of this mystic sphere. Keep far removed the evil and the**

unbalanced. **Strengthen and inspire me so that I may preserve unsullied this abode of the mysteries of the eternal Gods. Let my sphere be pure and holy so that I may enter in and become a partaker of the secrets of the Light Divine.**" Give the LVX Signs (optional here).

Circumambulation and Adoration

25. Go clockwise to the northeast and say, **"The visible Sun is the dispenser of Light to the earth. Let me therefore form a vortex in this chamber that the Invisible Sun of the Spirit may shine therein from above."**

26. *Circumambulation.* The Mystic Circumambulation signifies the rising of the Light. Walk three times clockwise around the circumference of the Temple in a wide circle. This will build up the energy in a Temple, especially if the pace is quick. Give the Projection Sign and the Sign of Silence whenever passing the east.

    When performed during a Circumambulation, the Projection Sign has the effect of pushing the Light forward around the Temple, while the Sign of Silence keeps the energy from rebounding back to the magician. The Circumambulation is usually followed by the Adoration to the Lord of the Universe. After the third and final circuit in the Circumambulation, go to the west of the Altar, and face east.

27. *The Adoration.* The Adoration is a ritualized prayer that signifies the fourfold aspect of Divinity. It portrays the magician's deference to the Highest Source of All, with which the magician must always act in alignment and harmony—never against. This simple yet potent prayer to the Ultimate Unity is combined with magical gestures that orient the magician to the Divine. It is one of the first magical prayers that the student learns, and it emphasizes the transcendent and immanent nature of High Divinity. The Adoration is performed as follows while facing east.

    "Holy art Thou, Lord of the Universe." (Give the Projection Sign as you do this.)

    "Holy art Thou, whom Nature hath not formed." (Projection Sign as before.)

    "Holy art thou, the Vast and the Mighty One." (Projection Sign.)

    "Lord of the Light and of the Darkness." (Sign of Silence at the end.)

This marks the completion of the Opening by Watchtower and the beginning of the primary work or meditation at hand. At this point, clearly state your intention for performing the rite. Then the main ritual working can begin. This could be the consecration of a talisman, a specific invocation, Spirit Vision work, a ritual healing, etc. When the main working is completed, perform the Closing by Watchtower.

Ritual Note 1: Waving the implement three times in front of the Tablet can be done in a couple of different ways: 1) wave the implement three times directly in front of the circular sigil at the top of the Tablet, or 2) wave the implement three times over the whole Tablet to mark the points of the upright Triangle for Fire and Air, or the points of the inverted Triangle for Water and Earth.

Ritual Note 2: As an option, you can use the Lotus Wand for all the Pentagrams traced in front of the Tablets instead of the Elemental Tools. If you do this, grasp the white band for the Spirit Pentagrams, and the Kerubic bands (Aquarius, Leo, Scorpio, Taurus) for the Elemental Pentagrams. You can hold the Elemental Weapons in your other hand for added emphasis. Leave the Elemental Tools in front of their respective Tablets once the Tablet has been invoked. This forms a powerful link with the opened gateways of the Tablets. During the Closing of the Watchtower, bring the Elemental Tools back to the central Altar after their respective Tablets are closed.

Ritual Note 3: As we mentioned, there are several versions of this particular ritual. The version we learned from Regardie uses both Enochian and Hebrew words of power when tracing the Pentagrams. Some magicians prefer to use just the Enochian words.

CLOSING BY WATCHTOWER: VERSION 1

The long version of the Closing of the Watchtower is a complete reversal of the Opening. It uses the same Pentagrams as the SBRP. Use the same implements to banish as you used to invoke.

    1. *The Reverse Circumambulation:* The Reverse Circumambulation represents the fading or releasing of the Light. Walk three times anticlockwise (widdershins) around the circumference of the Temple in a wide circle, giving the Projection Sign and the Sign of Silence each time you pass the east,

slowing the pace gradually. This will act to naturally dissipate the energy in the Temple. Feel the energy that you have carefully built up throughout the ceremony begin to fade. Follow this with the Adoration.

Banishing Pentagrams. Dismiss all the powers with the banishing Pentagrams as follows:

SOUTH

2. Go clockwise to the south and trace a large Banishing Pentagram of Fire before the Tablet of Fire, while vibrating **"OIP TEAA PEDOCE."** Draw the sigil of Leo in the center and vibrate, **"ELOHIM."** Give the Sign of Fire.

3. Trace the Banishing Pentagram of Spirit Active and vibrate, **"BITOM."** Trace the Spirit sigil in the center and intone, **"EHEIEH."** Give the Sign of the Closing of the Veil, followed by the LVX Signs.

WEST

4. Go to the west and trace the Banishing Pentagram of Water before the Water Tablet and vibrate, **"EMPEH ARSEL GAIOL."** Draw the sigil of the eagle in the center and vibrate, **"Aleph Lamed, AL."** Give the Sign of Water.

5. Trace the Banishing Pentagram of Spirit Passive and vibrate, **"HCOMA."** Trace the Spirit sigil in the center and intone, **"AGLA."** Give the Sign of the Closing of the Veil, followed by the LVX Signs.

EAST

6. Go to the east and trace a large Banishing Pentagram of Air before the Air Tablet and vibrate, **"ORO IBAH AOZPI."** Draw the sigil of Aquarius in the center and vibrate **"YHVH."** Give the Sign of Air.

7. Trace the Banishing Pentagram of Spirit Active. Thrust through the center of the Pentagram and vibrate, **"EXARP."** Trace the Spirit sigil in the center and intone, **"EHEIEH."** Give the Sign of the Closing of the Veil, followed by the LVX Signs.

NORTH

8. Go to the north and trace the Banishing Pentagram of Earth in front of the Earth Tablet while vibrating **"EMOR DIAL HECTEGA."** Draw the sigil of Taurus in the center and vibrate, **"ADONAI."** Give the Sign of Earth.

9. Trace a Banishing Pentagram of Spirit Passive and vibrate, **"NANTA."** Trace the Spirit sigil in the center and intone, **"AGLA."** Give the Sign of the Opening of the Veil, followed by the LVX Signs.

10. *License to Depart:* The License to Depart grants all spiritual energies present permission to leave the Temple after the work of magic has been completed. One should always give the entities present the option of leaving on their own before banishing them. The License to Depart for the Closing by Watchtower is as follows: **"I now release any Spirits that may have been imprisoned by this ceremony. Depart in peace to your abodes and habitations. Go with the blessings of *Yeheshuah, Yehovashah."***

11. Knock five times (4+1) as in the beginning.

12. Say, **"I now declare this Temple duly closed. So mote it Be!"**

CLOSING BY WATCHTOWER: VERSION 2

This is the short version for closing:

1. Perform the Reverse Circumambulation followed by the Adoration.

2. Perform the LBRP.

3. Perform the LBRH (chapter 8).

4. Give the standard License to Depart.

5. Knock five times (4+1) as in the beginning.

6. Say, **"I now declare this Temple duly closed. So mote it Be!"**

SYMBOLISM AND USE OF THE OPENING BY WATCHTOWER

Like the Supreme Ritual of the Pentagram, the Opening by Watchtower is used to summon the powers of the elements in the Yetziratic World of Formation, which is home to the astral plane where everything is formulated prior to manifestation on the physical plane. However, there are considerable differences between the two rituals.

The SRP is far more adaptable; it can be used to invoke the four elements, a single element, four zodiacal quadruplicity signs (such as the four Cardinal Signs), or a single zodiacal sign. Unlike the SRP, the Watchtower Ritual was never designed to invoke a single element or the zodiacal signs. And you would not use the Opening by Watchtower for banishing. And yet you could easily do all those things and more in the main working after the Temple was opened by the Watchtower Ritual.

Far more than a simple ritual for invoking elements, the Watchtower Ritual also invokes the forces of Creation at the dawn of the Universe as epitomized in the powerful speeches included from *The Chaldean Oracles*. Summoning the elements in the YHVH formula only intensifies this—the energies come into the Temple following the structure of the Four Worlds, becoming more manifest from the spiritual to the physical with each invoked level.

Because of its power, beauty, and symmetry, the Opening by Watchtower is an extraordinary ceremony for opening any magical working and raising the power needed for a successful ritual.

REVIEW QUESTIONS

1. What is the difference between the LRP and the SRP?

2. How many Elemental Pentagrams are there?

3. What symbol is traced in the center of the Water Pentagram?

4. How many Spirit Pentagrams are there? What are they?

5. How is the order of invocation in the SRP different from that in the Opening by Watchtower?

6. What is the Opening by Watchtower used for?

7. How would you use the SIRP to invoke a single element?

8. How would you use the SIRP to invoke Pisces?

9. Where do the Enochian names vibrated in the SRP come from?

chapter 8

HEXAGRAM RITUALS

This chapter examines the remainder of the Golden Dawn's best-known rituals for practical magic. Table 31 lists the rituals found in this chapter along with their abbreviated titles.

Table 31: Ritual Abbreviations

LRH	Lesser Ritual of the Hexagram
LBRH	Lesser Banishing Ritual of the Hexagram (a form of the LRH)
LIRH	Lesser Invoking Ritual of the Hexagram (a form of the LRH)
GRH	Greater Ritual of the Hexagram
GBRH	Greater Banishing Ritual of the Hexagram (a form of the GRH)
GIRH	Greater Invoking Ritual of the Hexagram (a form of the GRH)
AK	Analysis of the Keyword
RCR	Rose Cross Ritual (also called the Ritual of the Rose Cross)

THE HEXAGRAM

The Hexagram is a geometric figure that has six points formed from two interlocking Triangles corresponding to the opposing forces of Fire and Water. The interlocking Triangles show these rival energies balanced and in harmony with each other. Also referred to as the "Six-Rayed Signet Star," the Hexagram is related by number to Tiphareth, but its importance in magic is far more encompassing than this. It is a very powerful symbol of protection that represents the seven planetary forces under the rule of the ten Sephiroth. This is an emblem of great spiritual might.

The Hexagram is the symbol of the *Ruach Elohim* or "Spirit of God." This Spirit has two essential principles—masculine and feminine—represented by the Triangles of Fire and Water in perfect equilibrium. It represents the Elohim, the Supernal Father and the Supernal Mother united as with One Mind and One Being. And when these two Triangles are combined within the figure of the Hexagram, the bifurcated Triangles of Air and Earth are formed.

Like the Pentagram, four elements are clearly indicated here. But unlike the Pentagram, which has a separate point for Spirit, the Spirit element in the Hexagram is *implied* as the fundamental force that binds the Triangles together. This is the invisible Breath of God that animates the Universe and is at the mystical center of the figure.

The penetration of one Triangle by another also represents the penetration of man's lower nature by the higher and divine forces. While the Pentagram is a symbol of man the Microcosm, the Hexagram is an emblem of the Macrocosm. Unlike the Pentagram, it cannot be reversed or inverted for evil; even when the Hexagram is turned so that two points are upright, the symbol is still perfectly symmetrical and balanced. It is a symbol of matter joined in perfect harmony with Spirit, and it is therefore an image of the perfected human being sublimated by the Great Work.

The usual form of the Hexagram is the well-known "Star of David" formation, showing the Sephirotic ordering of the planets. The six points of the figure are attributed to the Sephiroth on the Tree of Life and their planetary correspondences (Figure 73). Starting from the topmost point going clockwise around the figure we have Daath (and the planet Saturn, which is reflected from Binah); Chesed (Jupiter); Netzach (Venus); Yesod (Luna); Hod (Mercury); and Geburah (Mars). In the center of the figure is Tiphareth (Sol). In Hermetic symbolism this is the spiritual Sun at the center of our being. It is the seat of our connection with the Divine.

Unlike the Pentagram, the Hexagram is not traced in one continuous line, but by drawing each Triangle separately. When tracing a Hexagram to invoke or to banish, remember that there are two starting points—one for each of the two Triangles. Since the Hexagram is based on planetary energies with the Sun at its center, the rule is to trace the lines clockwise following the course of the Sun when invoking. When banishing, the lines are traced counterclockwise. This is true for all Hexagram Rituals.

Figure 73: The Hexagram of the Planets in the "Star of David" Formation

When tracing the Hexagram of a particular planet or Sephirah, the first Triangle starts at the point affiliated with the desired planet, the second Triangle is traced from the point that lies directly opposite that planet on Figure 73. Always clockwise to invoke, anticlockwise to banish.

"What about the Sun?" you might ask. The Sun has no point on the Hexagram but is found at the center. To invoke or banish the Sun, all six of the other planetary Hexagrams are drawn in their regular Sephirotic order.

Hexagrams are only used to invoke and banish Sephirotic and planetary energies. They are never used for elemental or zodiacal forces.

why not use the unicursal Hexagram?

Some magicians choose to replace the traditional forms of the Hexagram with the unicursal or "single-line" Hexagram, also called the pseudohexagram (Figure 74). There are several problems with this. The unicursal Hexagram violates the basic dynamic principle of the Hexagram, which is to trace sunwise to invoke and antisunwise to banish. Tracing the unicursal Hexagram requires the magician to draw clockwise and counterclockwise simultaneously, thus invoking and banishing at the same time and canceling each other out. And because two of the points of the unicursal Hexagram are larger than the others, the energies are not in balance, which risks an overload of some energies and a shortage of others. There is a specific, limited use for the unicursal Hexagram in the Golden Dawn system that involves the alchemical energies of Sol, Luna, and the four elements, but that is a topic for another time.

Figure 74: Unicursal Hexagram

HEXAGRAM EXERCISES

The following exercises are designed to familiarize students with tracing the figure of a Hexagram combined with the various magical techniques that will enliven and empower this symbol on the astral plane.

A: Visualization Exercise

1. Begin with your personal Pre-Ritual Meditation Practice.

2. When ready, stand and extend your arm straight out in front of you, pointing with your index finger. Bring your hand up higher and visualize a point of white light there. This is your starting point.

3. Trace the three lines of a large upright Triangle in brilliant white light, proceeding clockwise (Figure 75). Strongly visualize this figure.

Figure 75: First Hexagram

4. Now begin the starting point of an inverted Triangle about three feet down from the starting point of the first Triangle.

5. Trace the three lines of a large inverted Triangle in brilliant white light, proceeding clockwise. Strongly visualize the figure.

6. Visualize the overlapping Triangles forming the complete figure of the Hexagram. See it clearly.

7. When finished, trace the lines of the two Triangles in reverse (Figure 76). Begin with the upright Triangle. Trace both Triangles going anticlockwise from their original starting points. Mentally dissolve the entire figure. Take note of how you feel and any insights that you may have experienced during the exercise.

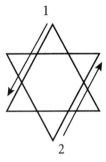

Figure 76: Second Hexagram

B: Vibration Exercise

1. Perform steps 1 and 2 as in the previous exercise.

2. In tracing the first Triangle, vibrate: **"ARA …"** In tracing the second Triangle, vibrate: **"… RITA."** The tracing of the Triangles and the vibration of the two halves of the word *Ararita* should flow into one another. While intoning the final syllable, charge the center of the figure with your index finger or wand.

3. Repeat the process with the second Hexagram, vibrating **"ARA …"** and **"… RITA"** as you trace the Triangles.

C: Color Visualization Exercise

1. Perform steps 1 through 4 as in exercise A on Hexagram visualization, but change the following:

2. As you trace the first Triangle, visualize it in red lines, instead of white. As you trace the second Triangle, visualize it in blue lines, instead of white.

D: Color Visualization Exercise

1. Perform steps 1 through 4 as in exercise A, but change the following:

2. As you trace both Triangles, visualize them in flaming golden lines.

E: Intention Exercise

1. Perform steps 1 through 4 as in exercise A, but add the following:

2. While tracing the first Hexagram, imagine that the figure is like a key that opens a door. After the figure is complete, state the following magical intention: **"To all that is Sacred, balanced, harmonious, and beneficial to me at this time; be welcomed."** Pause for a few moments to take in any images, thoughts, or feelings before allowing the figure to fade.

3. When tracing the second Hexagram, imagine that the figure is like a key that closes a door. Once the figure is complete, state the following magical intention: **"To all entities present at this time, go with peace and blessings back to your abodes and habitations."** Allow the image to fade.

F: Divine Light Exercise

1. Perform steps 1 through 4 as in exercise A, but add the following:

2. After your personal Pre-Ritual Meditation Practice, perform the Qabalistic Cross with the Expanded Visualization given in chapter 4.

3. In tracing the Hexagram, picture the shaft of light at your Kether center receiving more energy from the Macrocosmic Kether above and welling up from your grounded Malkuth to gather at your Tiphareth center, where the light is at its strongest. Will and visualize the light going down your arm and out your hand or implement to inscribe the Hexagram.

4. Add the QC to any of the previous exercises listed above.

5. After you have completed an exercise, take note of any feelings or insights.

THE LESSER RITUAL OF THE HEXAGRAM

The Lesser Ritual of the Hexagram is similar to the Lesser Ritual of the Pentagram in that both are used for general-purpose invocations and banishings. The Hexagram Ritual can be used in conjunction with, or instead of, that of the Pentagram, depending on the circumstances of the working. However, the Hexagram Ritual affects a higher plane: it is used to establish a protective magical circle of planetary energies in the Temple. Pentagram Rituals are terrestrial; Hexagram Rituals are Celestial.

The name "Lesser Ritual of the Hexagram" seems a bit misleading to students because it is actually more complicated than the Greater Ritual of the Hexagram. The LRH is "lesser" because it is not used to accomplish the main purpose of a planetary or Sephirotic working. Instead, it is employed solely to establish the planetary or Sephirotic magic circle in which the energy of the Greater Hexagram is invoked.

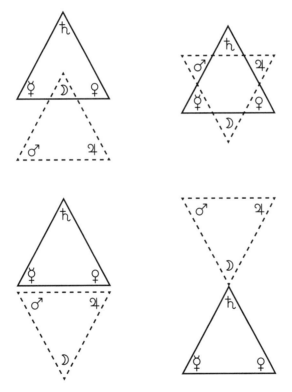

Figure 77: The Four Forms of the LRH

The LRH is unique in its makeup because it employs four different variations on the basic form of the Hexagram (Figure 77). These four forms are based on the symbolic images of the elements: the Hexagram of Fire resembles flames; that of Earth looks like the pentacle; that of Air bears a likeness to a diamond or spearhead; and that of Water resembles a cup. Although they are referred to as the Hexagrams of Fire, Water, Air, and Earth, they are *not* used to invoke these elements. Instead, they reflect the presence of the planetary forces in the realm of the elements on the astral plane.

While these four forms are unique to the rituals of the Golden Dawn and its off-shoots, there is evidence of them in the medieval grimoire known as the *Greater Key of Solomon* where they appear in the diagram of the magic circle and are described as "hexagonal pentacles" (Figure 96 in chapter 10).

The Hexagrams of the LRH represent a Celestial plane of working, so the four elemental forms are placed in an astrological order rather than that of the four winds attribution. They are assigned to the four quarters in accordance with the Cardinal Signs of the zodiacal wheel thus: Fire (Aries) to the east, Earth (Capricorn) to the south, Air (Libra) to the west, and Water (Cancer) to the north.

Figure 78: Hexagram with ARARITA

The symbolism of Tiphareth plays a primary role in the Hexagram Ritual. The sixth Sephirah is often imaged by Gods of death and resurrection, such as Osiris, Attis, Dionysus, and Christ, who mediate between the worlds of matter and Spirit, human and divine, lower and higher. This is emphasized by the major invocation at the end of this ritual, called the Analysis of the Keyword, examined later in this chapter.

There is only one word of power vibrated when tracing the four forms of the Lesser Hexagrams, *Ararita*, which has been described earlier as a notariqon formed from the first letters of the sentence: *Achad Rosh Achdotho Rosh Ichudo Temurahzo Achad* ("One is His beginning, One is His individuality, His permutation is One"). This affirms that the Ultimate Divinity is unitary in nature. Ararita is a word of seven letters, each of which is attributed to one of the seven points of the Hexagram (counting the central solar point) (Figure 78).

Figure 79 shows the tracings for the Invoking and Banishing Hexagrams of the LRH.

INVOKE   **BANISH**

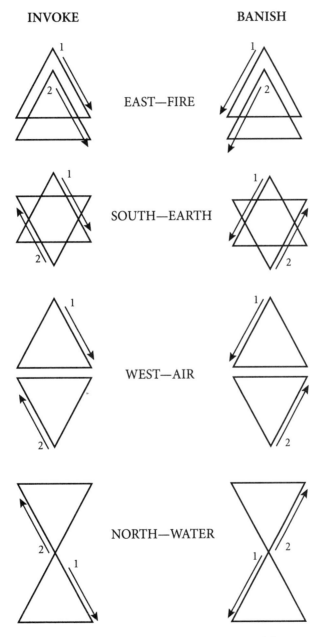

EAST—FIRE

SOUTH—EARTH

WEST—AIR

NORTH—WATER

Figure 79: Invoking and Banishing Hexagrams of the LRH

THE KEYWORD

Within the context of the Hexagram Ritual, the *Keyword* refers to the letters I.N.R.I., an important acronym in both orthodox religion and in magic. These letters were placed above the head of Christ on the cross, and stand for *Jesus Nazarenus Rex Judecorum*, or "Jesus of Nazareth, King of the Jews." The Keyword I.N.R.I is used in the Golden Dawn's Inner Order to describe the sequence of the seasons, the equinoxes and solstices, as well as the cycles of birth, death, and rebirth.

The Analysis of the Keyword (AK) is an invocation of related names and images. Within the invocation, the Latin letters I.N.R.I are followed by their Hebrew equivalents, Yod Nun Resh Yod. From the Yetziratic attributions of these letters are derived Virgo (Yod), Scorpio (Nun), Sol (Resh), and Virgo (Yod). These correspond to a trio of deities—Isis, Apophis, and Osiris—who embody the Egyptian legend of the dying and resurrected god. The initial letters of these Deity names form the name IAO, the Gnostic name of God. Added to these letters are gestures made to form the Latin word *lux*, (LVX) meaning "light."

This entire cycle of revolving words, ideas, and gestures represents the death and rebirth of the Sun and the self, all of which embody the regenerative essence of Tiphareth in the world of human experience.

The Keyword also symbolizes the grades and work of the Second Order, which we need not address here. But it basically invokes the sacrifice and redemption of the magician's imbalances and destructive impulses in order to facilitate the complete embrace of the Light Divine.

After the figures were traced in the Pentagram Ritual, four archangels were called upon to lend their power and protection to the magician's circle. At this point in the Hexagram Ritual, however, it is the magician who briefly takes on the godforms associated with rebirth and redemption in order to invoke a personal transmutation of the self, transforming the Pentagram of the aspiring but imperfect human to the Hexagram of the perfected and balanced human being.

Like the Qabalistic Cross, the Analysis of the Keyword is an invocation rite in and of itself that is often placed at the middle or end of more complex rituals.

THE ANALYSIS OF THE KEYWORD (AK)

1. Extend your arms out in the shape of the Tau Cross, palms facing forward. Say with feeling, **"I.N.R.I."** (Pronounce each letter.) **"Yod Nun Resh Yod"**

(Yode-noon-raysh-yode). As the names of the Hebrew letters are pronounced, trace them in the Air before you, from right to left.

2. Return to the Tau Cross position and say, **"Virgo, Isis, Mighty Mother! Scorpio, Apophis, Destroyer! Sol, Osiris, Slain and Risen! Isis, Apophis, Osiris!"**

3. Through the previous oration, gradually raise the arms and lift the head upward. Vibrate strongly and slowly, **"IAO."**

The LVX Signs (Figure 80)

4. Return to the stance of the Tau Cross saying, **"The Sign of Osiris Slain."**

The Sign of
Osiris Slain

L. The Sign of the
Mourning of Isis

V. The Sign of
Typhon and Apophis

X. The Sign of
Osiris Risen

Figure 80: The LVX Signs

5. Put your right arm straight up in the Air from the shoulder. The left arm should be straight out from the left shoulder so that the position of the two arms together resemble the letter "L". Hands are to be open flat with palms forward. Turn your head so that you are looking over your left arm. Say, **"L, the Sign of the Mourning of Isis."**

6. Raise the arms overhead to an angle of sixty degrees so that they form the letter "V". Keep the arms straight and the palms facing forward. Throw the head back and say, **"V, the Sign of Typhon and Apophis."**

7. Cross the arms on the chest, right arm over left, to form the letter "X". Bow your head and say, **"X, the Sign of Osiris Risen."**

8. Say slowly and powerfully, **"L.V.X."** (Spell out each letter separately and give the sign of each as you do so.) Say **"LUX"** [lukes].

9. Remain in the Sign of Osiris Slain and say, **"The Light…"** (hold arms out in the Tau Cross position for a moment then recross them again on the chest) **"… of the Cross."**

Ritual Note: This is the end of the Analysis of the Keyword as performed in the Hexagram Ritual. However, the AK is performed in a slightly different manner in the Rose Cross Ritual, given later in this chapter.

THE LESSER BANISHING RITUAL OF THE HEXAGRAM

This is the general-purpose Lesser Banishing Ritual of the Hexagram. It can be used in conjunction with or instead of the Lesser Banishing Ritual of the Pentagram for certain rites. For example, if you have previously worked with the elements or the zodiacal signs, a LBRP should be done before you continue on to a planetary working, because the energies are different and might not be harmonious with your next working. You can then ward the place of working with the LBRH.

There are three parts to the LBRH:

1. Opening: The Qabalistic Cross

2. Tracing the Hexagrams

3. Closing: The Analysis of the Keyword

Use any of the following implements: your index finger, a Banishing Dagger, the Magic Sword, the Outer Wand of Double Power, or the Lotus Wand. If using one of the wands, point with the white end for the QC and the AK, but point with the black end to trace the Hexagrams.

Opening: The QC

1. Go to the east (or center) of the Temple and perform the Qabalistic Cross.

Tracing the Hexagrams

2. Go to the eastern edge of the Temple. Trace the Lesser Banishing Hexagram of Fire toward the east. Thrust through the center of the figure and vibrate the word **"ARARITA."**

3. Walk to the southern boundary of the Temple and trace the Lesser Banishing Hexagram of Earth toward the south. Charge the center of the figure as before and vibrate, **"ARARITA."**

4. Go to the western edge of the Temple and draw the Lesser Banishing Hexagram of Air toward the west. Energize it by thrusting through the center of the figure and vibrate as before, **"ARARITA."**

5. Walk to the northern boundary of the Temple and draw the Lesser Banishing Hexagram of Water toward the north. Thrust and intone as before, **"ARARITA."**

Closing: The AK

6. Return to the east (or center) and perform the Analysis of the Keyword.

Ritual Note: Remember, as an alternative to vibrating "Ararita" at the end of each tracing of the Hexagram, you can vibrate the word in halves: intone "Ara..." while tracing the first Triangle and "...rita" while tracing the second Triangle, making sure to vibrate the last syllable at the end for the final thrust through the center of the figure.

THE LESSER INVOKING RITUAL OF THE HEXAGRAM

This is the general-purpose Lesser Invoking Ritual of the Hexagram. It is not differentiated for any planet or force. This is an appropriate ritual for creating a magic circle wherein a balance of all planetary or Sephirotic forces is desired.

Implement: Use your index finger, the white end of the Outer Wand of Double Power, or the Lotus Wand to trace the Hexagrams.

Opening: The QC

1. Go to the east (or center) of the Temple and perform the Qabalistic Cross.

Tracing the Hexagrams

2. Trace the Lesser Invoking Hexagram of Fire toward the east. Thrust through the center of the figure and vibrate the word "**ARARITA.**"

3. Turn to the south and trace the Lesser Invoking Hexagram of Earth. Charge the center of the figure as before and vibrate, "**ARARITA.**"

4. Turn to the west and draw the Lesser Invoking Hexagram of Air. Energize it by thrusting through the center of the figure and vibrate as before, "**ARARITA.**"

5. Go to the north and draw the Lesser Invoking Hexagram of Water. Thrust and intone as before, "**ARARITA.**"

Closing: The AK

6. Go to the east (or center) of the Temple and perform the Analysis of the Keyword.

SINGLE PLANET LESSER HEXAGRAM RITUALS

There are many variations of the Lesser Hexagram Ritual. All are designed with one purpose in mind: to set up a magical circle that is in total alignment with a specific planetary or Sephirotic working.

Single Planet Lesser Hexagram Rituals are performed exactly the same as the general Lesser Ritual of the Hexagram with one exception: the starting points on the two Triangles vary with the planet involved.

These rituals use the same four forms of the Hexagram shown in Figure 77. When working the ritual for a single planet, the first Triangle is traced starting from the point of the desired planet. The second Triangle is traced starting from the point opposite from that planet (in accordance with the Sephirotic ordering of the planets on the basic Star of David formation). This can get a little tricky, especially on the Fire Hexagram in the east, since the inverted Triangle is flipped upwards. You can see this in the Lesser Mercury Hexagrams (Figures 81 and 82). The starting point for the first Triangle is always Mercury, while the starting point for the second Triangle is always Jupiter. It's just that the Jupiter point has moved around in the various configurations.

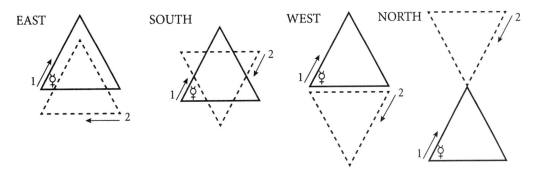

Figure 81: Lesser Invoking Hexagrams of Mercury

Here is a list of Lesser Hexagram Rituals for the planets. Remember that each of them has two forms, invoking and banishing.

- The Lesser Hexagram Ritual of Saturn

- The Lesser Hexagram Ritual of Jupiter

- The Lesser Hexagram Ritual of Mars

- The Lesser Hexagram Ritual of Sol

- The Lesser Hexagram Ritual of Venus

- The Lesser Hexagram Ritual of Mercury

- The Lesser Hexagram Ritual of Luna

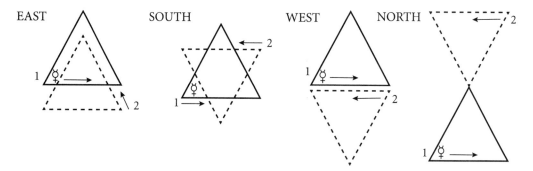

Figure 82: Lesser Banishing Hexagrams of Mercury

Sol doesn't have a point but is located at the center of each Hexagram, just as the Sun lies at the center of our solar system with the planets orbiting it. So for the Lesser Hexagram Ritual of Sol, all six Hexagrams must be traced in their proper Sephirotic order in the four configurations, resulting in a total of twenty-four Hexagrams. This makes the Lesser Hexagram Ritual of Sol the most complicated Hexagram Ritual of all!

Ritual Note: A planet's symbol can be traced in the center of each of the four Hexagrams in the LRH of a single planet, but it is not necessary to do so. However, the figures traced for the general Lesser Ritual of the Hexagram and the Lesser Hexagram Ritual of Saturn look identical. One way to tell them apart is to trace the symbol of Saturn in the center of the four Hexagrams in the latter ritual.

SEPHIROTIC LESSER HEXAGRAM RITUALS

The Lesser Hexagram Ritual can also be used to set up a magical circle that is in total alignment and harmony with a specific Sephirotic working.

Sephirotic Lesser Hexagram Rituals are performed exactly the same as the Single Planet Lesser Hexagram Rituals with a couple of exceptions:

1. The three Supernal Sephiroth (Kether, Chokmah, and Binah) all utilize the four Hexagram configurations of Saturn just as in the Lesser Hexagram Ritual of Saturn. The symbol of Saturn would be traced in the center of all four forms.

2. Yesod and Malkuth both utilize the four Hexagram configurations of Luna as in the Lesser Hexagram Ritual of Luna. The symbol of Luna would be traced in the center of all four forms.

   The remaining Sephiroth all make use of their planetary counterparts: for Chesed, use the four Hexagrams of Jupiter; for Geburah, the four Hexagrams of Mars; for Tiphareth, the twenty-four Hexagrams of Sol; for Netzach, the four figures of Venus; and for Hod, the four Hexagrams of Mercury.

The Greater Ritual of the Hexagram

While the primary purpose of the Lesser Ritual of the Hexagram is to create a magic circle appropriate to the main working, the Greater Ritual of the Hexagram (GRH) is intended as part of the main working, which involves the invocation or banishing of the force itself. The Greater Ritual is almost never done without first establishing the magic circle with the Lesser Ritual.

The Greater Ritual uses only one form of the Hexagram, the classic Star of David formation. And only one Hexagram is actually traced, that of the desired planet or Sephirah (Figure 83). This is because the Greater Ritual is designed to open a passageway between the desired force and the magician's Temple.

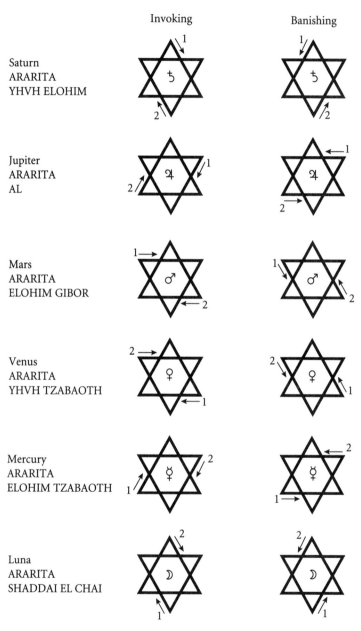

Figure 83: Greater Hexagrams of the Planets

If the force is planetary, the magician will need to determine which area of the sky the planet is located in during the time of the ritual. The specific Hexagram assigned to that planet is then traced toward the force in order to draw its energy into the Temple.

Six of the planets whose symbols are located along the points of the Hexagram each have two Hexagrams associated with them; one for invoking and one for banishing.

For Sol, which has no point, all six Hexagrams must be traced in their proper Sephirotic order. The divine name associated with Sol is not vibrated and the symbol of the Sun is not traced until *after* the sixth Hexagram is completed (Figure 84).

Sol
ARARITA

YHVH ELOAH
VE-DAATH

Invoking

Banishing

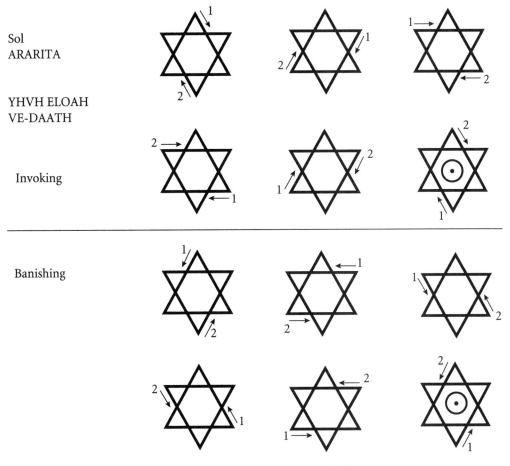

Figure 84: Greater Hexagrams of Sol

DIVINE NAMES OF THE GREATER HEXAGRAM RITUAL

In addition to ARARITA, the godname of the Sephirah corresponding with the specific planet is vibrated to charge the Hexagram (Table 32). When tracing the Triangles that compose a greater Hexagram, the word "ARARITA" is vibrated. Then the magician vibrates the associated Hebrew godname while tracing and charging the planetary symbol in the center. Finally, the letter of ARARITA corresponding to the planet is vibrated and traced in the center. This is followed by the LVX Signs and invocations to the appropriate planetary angels.

Table 32: Divine Names of the Greater Hexagrams

Planet	Vibrate	Godname	Planet Symbol	Ararita Letter
Saturn	ARARITA	YHVH Elohim	♄	Aleph א
Jupiter	ARARITA	El	♃	Resh ר
Mars	ARARITA	Elohim Gebur	♂	Aleph א
Sol	ARARITA	YHVH Eloah Ve-Daath	☉	Resh ר
Venus	ARARITA	YHVH Tzabaoth	♀	Yod י
Mercury	ARARITA	Elohim Tzabaoth	☿	Tau ת
Luna	ARARITA	Shaddai El Chai	☽	Aleph א

SEPHIROTIC GREATER HEXAGRAM RITUALS

Sephirotic Greater Hexagram Rituals are performed exactly the same as the planetary Hexagram Rituals with a couple of exceptions:

1. The three Supernal Sephiroth all utilize the Greater Hexagram of Saturn and the symbol of Saturn is traced in the center. However, the godnames of Kether (Eheieh), Chokmah (Yah), and Binah (YHVH Elohim) are vibrated for their own respective Hexagrams.

2. Yesod and Malkuth both utilize the Greater Hexagram of Luna and the symbol of Luna is traced in the center. However, the godnames of Yesod (Shaddai El Chai), and Malkuth (Adonai ha-Aretz) are vibrated for their own respective Hexagrams.

The remaining Sephiroth all make use of their planetary counterparts: for Chesed, use the Hexagram of Jupiter; for Geburah, the Hexagram of Mars; for Tiphareth, the Hexagram of Sol; for Netzach, the Hexagram of Venus; and for Hod, the Hexagram of Mercury.

How the Lesser and Greater Hexagram Rituals Work Together

This section shows how to use both rites in a single working. Our example will be for a planetary talisman consecration. When using the Greater Hexagram Ritual to consecrate a planetary talisman of Mercury, for instance, the magician would do the following:

1. Find the location of Mercury in the sky beforehand.

2. Start with any appropriate banishings to cleanse the space.

3. Perform the Lesser Invoking Ritual of Mercury to set up the magic circle suitable to the working.

4. Trace the Greater Invoking Hexagram of Mercury in the direction of the planet, vibrating the appropriate names, summoning the force into the Temple.

5. Trace a circle over the talisman. Then trace the Greater Invoking Hexagram of Mercury over the talisman, vibrating the appropriate names, and charging it with the summoned force. Visualize the force invoked through your Kether center, descending to Tiphareth and down through your implement into the talisman.

6. Wrap or cover the consecrated talisman in a protective cloth.

7. Trace the Greater Banishing Hexagram of Mercury in the direction of the planet, vibrating the appropriate names, dismissing the force.

8. Perform the Lesser Banishing Ritual of Mercury to close down the working.

Ritual Note: When tracing a Greater Hexagram toward a planetary force, there is no need to trace a confining circle around the Hexagram. If consecrating a talisman with that planetary force, then trace a circle around the talisman to focus and contain the force into the talisman prior to tracing the Hexagram over it.

IN SUMMARY

Hexagrams:

- Are always traced in two separate Triangles.

- The starting points for both Triangles lie opposite each other in accordance with the basic Sephirotic ordering of the planets.

Hexagram Rituals:

- Invoke and banish planetary forces.

- Invoke and banish Sephirotic forces.

- Open with the Qabalistic Cross.

- Close with the Analysis of the Keyword.

Invoking and Banishing:

- Invoking Hexagrams are traced sunwise (clockwise) from the point of the desired planet and the point of the opposite planet.

- Banishing Hexagrams are traced antisunwise from the point of the desired planet and the point of the opposite planet.

Lesser Hexagram Rituals:

- Are used as general-purpose rites to establish a magic circle for a planetary or Sephirotic working.

- Are assigned to the Celestial elements in accordance with the Cardinal Signs of the zodiac (Aries-Fire-east), and so on.

- Trace Hexagrams in all four quarters of the Temple.

- Use four distinct forms of the Hexagram.

- Can be used to set up a magical circle for a single planet.

- Can be used to set up a magic circle for single Sephirah.

- Are more complex than Greater Hexagram Rituals.

Greater Hexagram Rituals:

- Are used as part of the main planetary or Sephirotic working.

- Use only one form of the Hexagram, not four.

- Are not traced in the four quarters of the Temple.

- Are traced in the direction of the desired planet.

- Are traced over talismans to charge them with planetary or Sephirotic energies.

ROSE CROSS EXERCISE

The following exercise focuses on the visualization of the Rose Cross and the vibration of the divine name of the Pentagrammaton, Yeheshuah.

1. Begin with your personal Pre-Ritual Meditation Practice.

2. Trace a large cross and circle in the Air (Figure 85). As you draw the cross, visualize it in a golden light. The circle should be imagined as flaming red. While tracing this symbol, vibrate the name **"YEHESHUAH"** broken up in syllables as follows: For the shaft **"Yeh."** For the crossbar **"heh."** For the circle **"shu."** On the last syllable, **"ah,"** thrust through the center of the circled cross, charging it.

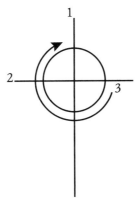

Figure 85: Tracing the Rose Cross

3. When finished, slowly dissolve the figure. Take note of any feelings or insights.

INTRODUCTION TO THE RITUAL OF THE ROSE CROSS

The Ritual of the Rose Cross (RCR), more than any other rite, is the epitome of the Rosicrucian nature of the Golden Dawn's Inner Order. Like the other rituals in this chapter, the Rose Cross Ritual was originally intended for use by advanced members within the Order setting.

Rosicrucianism takes its name from the symbol of the golden cross with a red rose at its center. Readers have been previously introduced to some of this symbolism in chapter 6 regarding the Rose Cross Lamen.

The symbol of the cross is first and foremost an emblem of conjunction, a joining of opposites. It also represents eternal life. The rose is a symbol of completion and perfection that embodies the mystic center and the heart. Together, the rose and the cross present a multitude of ideas: the union of the divine masculine and the divine feminine, regeneration and redemption, the blessings of the Christ impulse and consciousness, and strength through sacrifice. Additionally, it depicts the four points in space on a flat plane with a fifth at the center. Like the Pentagram, the Rose Cross is indicative of Spirit ruling over matter, but while the Pentagram depicts Spirit as the *head* ruling over matter, the Rose Cross portrays Spirit permeating the very *heart* of matter. The Pentagram and the Rose Cross are both symbols of protection, but while the Pentagram is well suited for summoning and dismissing specific energies, the Rose Cross is particularly suited for meditation, protection, balancing, blessing, and healing.

In all the Pentagram Rituals, the figures are traced at the four cardinal points. In the RCR, the Rose Crosses are traced at six points: in the Cross Quarters as well as zenith and nadir, above and below. A seventh, central point is formed by the magician, standing in the center of the crosses. After the crosses are traced, the ritual closes with the Analysis of the Keyword.

The primary godname invoked in this ritual is the Pentagrammaton, *Yeheshuah*, the name associated with the Christos, pointing to another association with the mediating Sephirah of Tiphareth.

There are seven parts to the Rose Cross Ritual:

1. Opening: The Qabalistic Cross

2. Tracing the Rose Crosses: The Four Cross Quarters

3. Tracing the Rose Crosses: Above and Below

4. Creating the cross within Sacred Space

5. Sealing the Cross Quarters

6. The Analysis of the Keyword, Rose Cross Version

7. Closing: The Descent of the Light

The Ritual of the Rose Cross

The room should be clear of any obstructions and the Altar should be moved aside. The only implement needed will be a stick of incense. A number of other options are also available, including the Outer Wand of Double Power, the Lotus Wand, the Rainbow Wand, or a Rose Cross Wand.

Opening: The QC

1. Perform the Qabalistic Cross (or a full LRP if desired).

Tracing the Rose Crosses: The Four Cross Quarters

2. Go to the southeast (SE) corner of the room and face outward. Trace a large Cross and circle there with the incense or wand (Figure 86). As you draw the cross, visualize it in a golden light. The circle should be imagined as flaming red. While tracing this symbol, vibrate the name **"YEHESHUAH."** On the last syllable, thrust through the center of the circled cross, charging it.

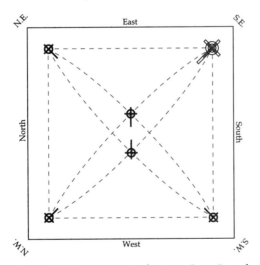

Figure 86: Movements in the Rose Cross Ritual

3. Keep the tip of the implement at the level of the center of the cross and walk to the southwest (SW) corner of the room. Draw the cross and circle (rose) as before and thrust the implement through the center of the figure intoning, **"YEHESHUAH."**

4. Move to the northwest (NW). Trace the figure and intone, **"YEHESHUAH."**

5. Move to the northeast (NE). Trace the figure and intone, **"YEHESHUAH."**

6. Return to the SE and complete the circle. Touch the head of the implement to the cross already drawn there, but do *not* retrace or intone the name.

Tracing the Rose Crosses: Above and Below

7. Now move diagonally across the room toward the NW, holding the implement high, but stop in the center of the Temple and make the Rose Cross directly above your head. Vibrate the name **"YEHESHUAH"** as before.

8. With the implement held straight up in the Air, walk to the NW corner of the room. Touch the tip of the implement to the center of the cross already formulated there. Do *not* retrace the cross or intone the name.

9. Move diagonally across the room again toward the SE, but lower your implement and stop in the center of the Temple. Trace the Rose Cross below you and vibrate the name **"YEHESHUAH."**

10. Bring the tip of the implement up and continue to walk to the SE corner. Touch the tip of the implement to the center of the Rose Cross already traced there. Do *not* retrace or intone.

11. Move clockwise to the SW and touch the head of the implement to the cross already traced there.

Creating the Cross within Sacred Space

12. Walk diagonally toward the NE but stop in the middle of the room to touch the center of the cross above your head. Intone the name **"YEHESHUAH."**

13. Continue on to the NE and simply touch the implement to the center of the cross already formulated there.

14. Move diagonally across the room toward the SW but stop in the middle of the Temple to touch the cross below you. Vibrate the name **"YEHESH-UAH."**

15. Continue on to the SW corner and simply touch the center of the cross already formulated there.

16. Move clockwise and link up with all the crosses by simply touching their centers with the wand (NW, NE, and SE). No need to intone as you do so.

Sealing the Cross Quarters

17. Upon returning to the SE, the site of the first cross, touch the center and pause. Then retrace the golden cross over the original, only much larger (Figure 87). Trace a large circle and vibrate, **"YEHESHUAH"** while tracing the lower half of the red circle. Vibrate, **"YEHOVASHAH"** while tracing the upper half of the red circle.

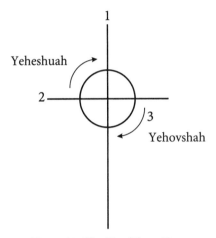

Figure 87: The Final Rose Cross

18. Walk clockwise to the center of the room. Observe all six Rose Crosses surrounding you, all connected by ribbons of light.

The AK, Rose Cross Version

19. Return to center of the Temple and perform the Analysis of the Keyword as follows. Extend your arms out in the shape of the Tau Cross. Say with feeling, **"I.N.R.I."** (Pronounce each letter.) **"YOD NUN RESH YOD"** (Yode-noon-raysh-yode). As the names of the Hebrew letters are pronounced, trace them in the Air before you, from right to left.

20. Return to the stance of the Tau Cross saying, **"The Sign of Osiris Slain."**

21. Put your right arm straight up in the Air from the shoulder. The left arm should be straight out from the left shoulder so that the position of the two arms together resembles the letter "L". Hands are to be open flat with palms forward. Turn your head so that you are looking over your left arm. Say, **"L, the Sign of the Mourning of Isis."**

22. Raise the arms overhead to an angle of sixty degrees so that they form the letter "V". Keep the arms straight and the palms facing forward. Throw the head back and say, **"V, the Sign of Typhon and Apophis."**

23. Cross the arms on the chest to form the letter "X". Bow your head and say, **"X, the Sign of Osiris Risen."**

24. Say slowly and powerfully, **"L.V.X."** (Spell out each letter separately and give the sign of each as you do so.) Say **"LUX"** [lukes].

25. Remain in the Sign of Osiris Slain and say, **"The Light…"** (hold arms out in the Tau Cross position for a moment then recross them on the chest) **"…of the Cross."**

26. Return to the Osiris Slain position and say, **"Virgo, Isis, Mighty Mother! Scorpio, Apophis, Destroyer! Sol, Osiris, Slain and Risen! Isis, Apophis, Osiris."**

27. Through the previous oration, gradually raise the arms and lift the head upward. Vibrate strongly, **"IAO."**

Closing: The Descent of the Light

28. End the Analysis by vibrating the four Tablet of Union names to equilibrate the Light: **"EXARP. HCOMA. NANTA. BITOM."**

29. Then aspire to the Light and draw it down over your head to your feet. Say, **"Let the Divine Light Descend!"**

USES OF THE ROSE CROSS RITUAL

The Ritual of the Rose Cross is a straightforward rite for soothing disruptive forces, both external and internal. The Cross Quarters—southeast, southwest, northeast, and northwest—are areas where the elemental forces meet, blend, and sometimes clash with each other. Tracing the crosses in conjunction with the vibration of the Pentagrammaton at these points helps to calm and settle these energies, invoking balance and equilibrium wherever and whenever it is needed.

Rather than a banishing, the Rose Cross Ritual is a rite of blessing and healing. It is like a cloak, enclosing the magician's aura with a protective veil against outside influences. Whereas the Pentagrams of the LRP protect, they also tend to light up on the astral plane and make entities aware of you. Use the Pentagrams to invoke or banish and the Rose Cross to calm disturbed energies and maintain peace.

The RCR is a call to another mode of consciousness. It is a good preparation for meditation, and when followed with the Middle Pillar exercise, is an invocation of Higher Wisdom that is helpful when solving problems or trying to maintain inner peace.

Because of the ritual's natural affiliation with Tiphareth, it is a wonderful means of aligning the magician with the Higher and Divine Self.

When you are quite familiar with the ritual, it can be done in the imagination while sitting or lying down. Used with rhythmic breathing, it will withdraw the mind from pain and release you for sleep.

The ritual can be done to help others in pain or difficulty. For this purpose, build up an astral image of the person in the center of the room, and, after surrounding the person with six crosses, call down the light upon him or her.

The RCR can be used as protection against psychic attack from the angry or melancholy thoughts of others or from disturbed psychic conditions.

REVIEW QUESTIONS

1. What does the Hexagram represent?

2. What is the Sephirotic ordering of the planets?

3. What is the difference between the Lesser Ritual of the Hexagram and the Greater Ritual of the Hexagram?

4. What are the problems with the unicursal Hexagram?

5. How did the Greater Key of Solomon describe the Hexagrams of the LRH?

6. How are the Hexagrams of the LRH assigned to the four quarters?

7. Which Sephirah plays a primary role in the Hexagram Ritual?

8. What does ARARITA refer to?

9. How are the letters of ARARITA assigned to the Hexagram?

10. Which Hexagram Ritual is the most complicated?

11. Which Hexagram formation is used in the Greater Ritual of the Hexagram?

12. When would you trace a confining circle around a Hexagram?

13. What is the Ritual of the Rose Cross used for?

chapter 9

THE FAR-WANDERING SOUL

In the Neophyte Ceremony, the candidate is told that a cord wrapped thrice about his or her waist is "an image of the threefold bondage of mortality" or the material inclination "that has bound into a narrow place, the once far-wandering soul." Although mortality is inherent to the human condition, the material inclination is less so. For thousands of years, humans have longed for eternal life—that is, the permanence and transcendence of the Spirit. We instinctively recognize a Divinity that exists beyond time and space. Our normal waking consciousness, like the tip of an iceberg, is but a small part of our whole being, a being that has at its fundamental core a connection with everything in the manifest Universe. We describe this connection as the immanence of God, Deity, or the Light Divine.

Yet this connection must be actively cultivated in order to remain a source of strength. The human mind is a marvel of evolution, but it can also be a double-edged sword—the dual qualities of creation and destruction come easily to us. How we choose to live and interact with fellow human beings and the natural world around us is a reflection of whether we view the world as a Sacred, magical creation and ourselves as its stewards, or not. Are we companions in the Great Chain of Being? Or are we simply users and takers of ever-dwindling resources on a blue rock? As Golden Dawn magicians, we choose the former.

Magic enables us to probe more deeply into ourselves so that we might acquire self-knowledge and thereby release ourselves from unconscious compulsions and motivations. It provides us with the means to express our inner selves, our internal spark of the Divine. By cleansing, clarifying, and strengthening our link with Divinity we can uncover gifts of psychic connection and use our reclaimed abilities to free the "once far-wandering soul," enabling us to travel and explore the various pathways leading back to the Sacred Source.

In this chapter, we examine that enigmatic human soul and how knowledge of the various parts of the self aids the magician to develop the faculty of clairvoyance, work with spiritual entities in the higher realms, invoke Deity, and assume godforms, all of which supports the ultimate goal of Divine Union.

THE QABALISTIC PARTS OF THE SOUL

According to the Hermetic tradition, the individual human soul is the "magical mirror of the Universe." The Universe we live in is not some mixture of chance factors and events, but an ordered system of correspondences and affiliations. The idea that there is a clear connection between the greater (macro) Universe and the lesser (micro) human Universe is one of the basic principles of magic. Because of this, the human soul and how it functions is important to understanding the mechanics of magic.

The soul is divided by the Qabalists into three principal parts. These are the *Neshamah*, the *Ruach,* and the *Nephesh* (Figure 88).

Neshamah

This is the first part, answering to the three Supernal Sephiroth of Kether, Chokmah, and Binah. It corresponds to the highest aspirations of the soul and what Freud called the superego. The Neshamah is further subdivided into three parts. These are the *Yechidah,* the *Chiah,* and the *Neshamah.*

The Yechidah is centered in Kether and is similar to the idea of the monad. It is our True and Immortal Divine Self. The Chiah, located in Chokmah, is our inquisitive urge to become more than human—our True Will. Both the Yechidah and the Chiah are archetypal in essence and thus they are somewhat beyond the scope of our understanding. The final subdivision, the Neshamah, is placed in Binah, although it lends its name to the other Supernals as being generally descriptive of the soul's greatest aspirations. This is our true desire or highest state of consciousness—the intuitive power that connects mankind with the Divine. According to the Qabalists, this part of the soul remains dormant in the average person until he or she gains spiritual awareness and uncovers a mystical understanding of the Universe. The descent of the Neshamah into the student's field of awareness occurs through the holy union of the King and Queen, Tiphareth and Malkuth. A dialogue between the Higher Self and the Lower Self must be opened for this descent to occur.

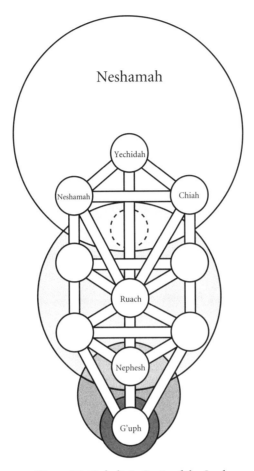

Figure 88: Qabalistic Parts of the Soul

Ruach

The middle part of the soul is located in the five Sephiroth from Chesed to Yesod, although it is centered in Tiphareth. This is the conscious part of our being also known as the ego. It is the mind and reasoning powers as well as the seat of outer consciousness, where humanity becomes aware of thought-images and is able to fashion thoughts into actions. The Ruach represents an intermediate stage between the highest and lowest portions of the soul where the ethical power to distinguish between good and evil is called into play. It is here where the individual can choose to focus either on secular, temporary desires, or on higher spiritual goals.

Nephesh

The lowest part of the human soul resides in Yesod. This is the dark side or shadow-self of the soul, answering unto the animal vitality and primal instincts. It is, however, an important part that ties humanity to the physical world of the elements and our animal ancestors. Entering the human body at birth, the Nephesh is the first part of the soul to be activated in every human being.

The Nephesh represents those basic desires that run contrary to society and to our own ideals of behavior and personality. This is the dark underside of the consciousness that dwells in the Ruach—the human mind. However, there can be no light without darkness, no day without night. Proper use of the vital, stimulating Nephesh energy is important to some aspects of magic, but it must always remain under the firm control of the Ruach. The Lower Soul or Nephesh can arouse the Middle Soul (Ruach), which in turn can stimulate the Neshamah or Divine Soul. This triggers the descent of the Neshamah down through the lower portions of the soul, bringing to the individual a conscious recognition of the Divine Self.

The G'uph

Beyond this fivefold division of the human soul is one more portion that is sometimes overlooked. This lowest part is called the *G'uph* (Figure 88). Centered in Malkuth, the G'uph is closely tied to the physical body and the total range of all psychophysical functions. It is a low level of the subconscious that communicates with the brain about the current condition of the human body.

THE SUBTLE BODIES

Similar in some ways to Qabalistic teachings on the parts of the soul is knowledge of various levels of the human Microcosm referred to as the Subtle Bodies or sometimes simply the "bodies" in Golden Dawn tradition. The five bodies constitute the knowledge of the self in the Eastern language of Theosophy, and although the Golden Dawn borrowed some of this terminology, especially in a few of the later offshoot groups, it did not rely upon it in the same way that Theosophy did, preferring the more Qabalistic approach, just as we do. Nevertheless, many Golden Dawn magicians freely use the Theosophical language to describe the inner mechanics of the Work.

The five "bodies" of the Microcosm from the lowest and densest to the highest include: the physical body, the etheric body, the astral body, the mental body, and the spiritual body (Figure 89).

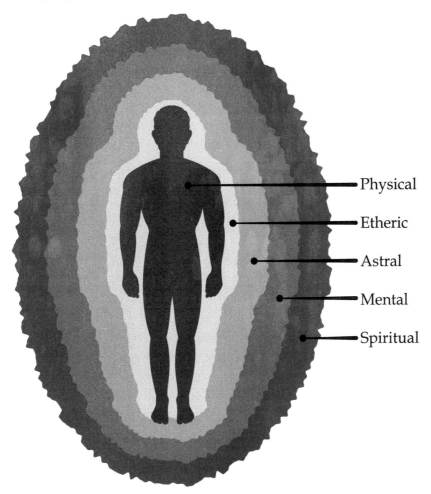

Figure 89: The Subtle Bodies

1. The Physical Body

This is the biological or material body of a human. In Qabalistic terms, it is the G'uph.

2. The Etheric Body

This body is composed of *ether* or life-force energy and is usually divided into two parts: the *etheric double* and the *aura*.

- The *etheric double* looks like the physical body and extends about an inch out from the physical body. It is composed of subtle energies that maintain the biological body and acts as a kind of energy sheath that forms the blueprint of the physical body.

- The *aura* is often called the "sphere of sensation" in the Golden Dawn manuscripts, and among the Subtle Bodies, the aura usually receives special attention. The aura is a layer of astral substance—an egg-shaped sphere of light energy that surrounds the etheric double and expands out about two or three feet from the physical body. It permeates the physical body and can be seen by clairvoyants.

As a whole, the etheric body is called the Nephesh or animal soul by Western magicians.

3. The Astral Body

Sometimes called the *emotional body*, the astral body refers to the actual human consciousness created from thoughts and feelings, which can be detached from the physical and etheric bodies under the right conditions. It is often called the *Body of Light* in spite of the fact that it resembles the idea of a mind more than a body.

The astral body is the life-body of feeling and consciousness that exists beyond the physical senses, having approximately the same size and shape as the physical body. It is this astral body of the magician that moves through and can effect changes within the Greater Universe by way of the nonphysical worlds.

Like the aura, the Body of Light is a field of energy residing in the same space as the aura. However, the astral body is constantly shaped and reshaped by thoughts and emotions. All words, images, and sensations influence the astral body and are influenced by it. It interacts freely on the astral plane of existence, and it can interact with the astral bodies of other humans and other entities. When "Traveling in the Spirit Vision," the magician directs control over the astral body in order to explore higher worlds.

The astral body includes the so-called *waking consciousness*—conscious mental functions such as reason, emotion, imagination, memory, and will. It contains the ego as well as the human personality. In Qabalistic terms, the astral body is the Ruach.

4. The Mental Body

This is the body of abstract consciousness or pure awareness that cannot be localized or visualized as occupying space in relation to the physical body. The mental body is a basic blueprint of the self, beyond all forms and images, which opens up realms of experience beyond time and space. Qabalists refer to it as the Neshamah.

5. The Spiritual Body

Finally, there is the spiritual body, the core of consciousness and the deepest, most essential part of the self. This is the divine spark or seed at the center of all the other layers of the self. It represents the point of interaction between man, the Microcosm, and God—the Macrocosmic Unity of Being. In Qabalistic terms, it is the Yechidah, the highest part of the Neshamah in Kether.

Each of these Subtle Bodies controls the one directly below it: the spiritual body controls the mental body, which in turn governs the astral body, and so on.

THE SELF

One of the primary goals of the Golden Dawn system is to prepare initiates for union with the Higher Self. Every branch of study that the magician undertakes is fundamental to laying the proper groundwork for this relationship, and every magical practice that the magician performs is essential to establishing and expanding it. Lighting the divine spark within is not a one-time event. It is an ongoing process.

In order to begin this process, it is important to know what we are dealing with. What exactly is the Higher Self? When we speak of the "self" in magic, it is not the waking self or what most people think of as their own egos. This self is the totality of the human being—it includes the body, mind, soul, and Spirit all in One. It is the entire human organism on all levels.

There are a number of confusing terms used for the Higher Self, and in order to understand them, we need to establish what they mean within a Golden Dawn context. These terms are: "Higher Genius," "Higher Self," and "Lower Self." We have come to call these the "Theurgic Triad."

It's important to remember that the terms "Higher Self," "Lower Genius," and "Higher Genius" may have different meanings in different discussions. Like alchemical terms, however, they may also take on specific meanings in specific discussions. (This is annoying but true.) Therefore, from the standpoint of the Nephesh, everything above the Ruach can be called "the Higher Self."

For our discussion, however, we mainly use the terms "Higher Genius," "Higher Self," and "Lower Self."

THE HIGHER GENIUS

First and foremost in the Theurgic Triad is the Higher Genius. In the Golden Dawn system, there are many terms used to describe this: the Divine Self, the Higher Soul, the Higher Will, and the Higher and Divine Genius. In older traditions, the Higher Genius is sometimes described as "the God of the self" because it displays the same relationship to the rest of the human Microcosm as God has to the Macrocosm as a whole.

This highest part of the self relates to Spirit, the transcendent part of the self that exists beyond the abyss. Because of this close connection with unlimited divinity, this part of the self is "shared" to some extent with all of humanity, but at a level that most people cannot directly access except through training and practice.

Today, the word "genius" is often used to refer to a person who has some unique or intellectual talent, but the original meaning of the word was that of a guardian Spirit that was often attached to a particular place or region. The plural of genius is *genii* and it is the root of the Arabic *jinn*, or "spirit." The term "Higher Genius" refers to the idea of a protective spiritual power that mediates between the highest aspirations of the magician and the Divine.

As it relates to the Qabalistic parts of the soul, the Higher Genius sits in Kether, in Yechidah, in the spiritual body. In terms of the Human Self, the Higher Genius is *our Spirit*. The magician can connect with this level of the self through spiritual discipline and magical practice.

THE HIGHER SELF

The second aspect of the Theurgic Triad is the Higher Self, also called the Lower Genius. Other terms for this include the Lower Will, the Middle Self, and "King of the Body." (Are we confused yet?) Remember that the "Higher Self" is actually the "Lower Genius" centered in Tiphareth.

The Higher Self is the hidden side of the Ruach or the conscious mind beyond the veil. Its relationship to the Higher Genius is akin to that of the soul in relation to the Spirit. It functions to *mediate* between the Higher Genius in Kether and the Lower Self in Yesod—between the divine and the mundane. Due to its reconciling function, the Higher Self is of crucial importance to the magician's work. The simple act of taking on a magical motto as one begins a ritual is meant to connect with this higher consciousness, because the magician's connection with the Higher is what lends authority—divine sanction if you will—to petition the archangels and angels to command the elementals and lesser Spirits.

THE LOWER SELF

The Lower Self is the ordinary personality, the personal consciousness that resides in Yesod. It is also the Nephesh and the etheric body and is aligned with the aura. This magical mirror is a reflection of the sphere of the Universe, wherein all the occult forces of Creation are represented; projected as on a Celestial sphere convex to the outer, but concave to the human being residing inside its frame.

Together the Theurgic Triad—Higher Genius, Higher Self, and Lower Self—can be described as divine consciousness, intermediate consciousness, and personal consciousness. In alchemical terms these relate to Spirit, Soul, and Body.

RELATED TERMS

Another term that is sometimes used for the Higher Self is the Greek word *augoeides,* meaning "shining one" or "glittering one." It is also said to mean "light vision" or "bright shape," referring to the radiant nature of the Higher Self. Third-century Greek mystic Iamblichus used the term to describe the transformed spiritual body worn by the initiate who had overcome the materialism of the physical world. This word has been a source of confusion because it is sometimes used to mean the Higher Genius in Kether, but other times to mean the Higher Self in Tiphareth.

Higher self or HGA?

Many modern authors call the Higher Self by another name—the Holy Guardian Angel or simply the HGA. The term "Holy Guardian Angel" comes from a medieval grimoire called *The Sacred Magic of Abra-Melin the Mage.* In that book, the phrase Holy Guardian Angel referred to an angel in the typical use of the word—a spiritual being completely separate from the magician who invoked it.

But language is not static; it is constantly evolving. Eventually, the term "Holy Guardian Angel" has come to denote the Higher Self and the Higher Genius, levels of the human self. Many authors including Israel Regardie have used the term this way, to the point where it may no longer be possible to separate the term "HGA" from that of the Higher Self. So for some practitioners, these two terms indicate two separate beings, while for others they are synonymous names for a single entity.

The important thing to remember is this: many Golden Dawn magicians who use the term "Holy Guardian Angel" are often referring to a higher level of the human self that lies within, and not a separate angel to be summoned from without.

SPIRITUAL ALCHEMY: THE THREE PRINCIPLES

The ancient science of alchemy is intimately concerned with the discussion of the body, soul, and Spirit. For many, the word "alchemy" conjures up an image of a crude laboratory where foolhardy pseudoscientists labor to turn lead into gold to line their pockets. Alchemy's true definition, however, encompasses the doctrine of inner transformation. Certainly many alchemists left behind a vast amount of information to prove that one version of alchemy was primarily practical and chemical in nature. This was the alchemy full of experiments and laboratory equipment: furnaces, bellows, stills, alembics, condensers, and glass beakers.

On the other hand, the principal interest of many alchemical philosophers was spiritual. These alchemists did not look merely for the substance of gold; they sought to give the quality of gold to their own being—to transmute the base metals, gross and impure parts of their own nature, to spiritual gold or wisdom. To them, gold, the metal that never tarnishes and cannot be corrupted by Fire or Water, was a symbol of illumination and salvation.

The primary goal of alchemy is to bring all things, especially humanity, to their pre-ordained state of perfection. To that end, alchemical theory states that eternal wisdom remains dormant in humanity so long as a mundane state of ignorance and superficiality exists. The objective of alchemy is the uncovering of this inner wisdom, and the removal of veils and obstacles between the mind and its intrinsically pure divine source.

Alchemy divides all matter into Three Principles of Nature, the *tria principia*, said to exist in all things: salt, sulfur, and mercury (Figure 90). These fundamental substances are not to be confused with ordinary substances of the same name.

Salt   Sulfur   Mercury

Figure 90: The Three Principles in Alchemy

Salt

Salt is the solid and stabilizing principle. It is the hardening, fixed, and crystallizing tendency. Sometimes referred to as earth, salt is the essential corpus or body.

Sulfur

Sulfur is the volatile, fiery, and energizing principle. It is the emotional, feeling, and passionate urge that motivates life. Sulfur is the essential soul.

Mercury

Mercury is the fluid and mediating principle. This is a Watery, feminine tendency that relates to the concept of consciousness. Mercury is the vital lifeforce that permeates all living matter and is symbolic of the act of transmutation. As the transforming agent of the alchemical process, Mercury is the essential Spirit.

MAGIC AND ALCHEMY

Like the Theurgic Triad, the Three Principles may be considered an undivided whole. The Great Work of alchemy is to separate, purify, and recombine these Three Principles in whatever substances the alchemist is working to transmute, cleansing them of all impurities and imbalances and exalting their essential natures.

This process is mirrored by the magical work of theurgy. A Golden Dawn magician is a spiritual alchemist who is the subject of his own alchemical experiments. While alchemists use glass beakers, furnaces, and stills, as well as prayers and invocations to perform their art, Golden Dawn magicians use symbols, meditations, invocations, willpower, visualization, vibration, and focused aspiration to achieve the same internal work of spiritual alchemy.

THE VIBRATORY FORMULA OF THE MIDDLE PILLAR

In previous chapters, readers were given various exercises in the vibration of godnames. As students advance, they are introduced to a very powerful mode of intoning divine names. Sometimes referred to simply as the Vibratory Formula, the full name of this technique is the Vibratory Formula of the Middle Pillar, because it reflects the element of Air down the Middle Pillar—focusing and maneuvering the Divine Light's energy up and down the magician's Middle Pillar with breath before projecting the current out in a forceful vibration. This formula should only be used with godnames and archangelic names. The steps are as follows:

1. Begin with your personal Pre-Ritual Meditation Practice.

2. Stand in the form of the Tau Cross, with arms extended out from the shoulders. Picture the Light of the Macrocosmic Kether above your head and breathe it into your own Kether.

3. Draw in a deep inhale of breath and *mentally* pronounce the divine name within your heart. Visualize the letters of the name (YHVH for example) in an appropriate color, resting within your Tiphareth center.

4. Exhale deeply and as you do so, picture the name empowered by the Divine Light descending to your Malkuth center at your feet, where it grounds and gathers physical force.

5. On the final inhale, draw the divine name back up the Middle Pillar to the Tiphareth center and, without pausing, vibrate the name physically and forcefully in conjunction with the Projection Sign of the Neophyte. As you do so, visualize the name shooting forth to the ends of the Universe, expelling all the Air from your lungs.

6. As the final syllable of the name is vibrated and all Air has been expelled from your lungs, give the Sign of Silence before resuming normal breathing. Remain still and contemplate the force you have invoked.

ASTRAL TEMPLE EXERCISES

The purpose of these exercises is to prepare the reader for astral workings by learning how to visualize an astral Temple. This is very important not only to the process of visualization; it is an essential part of understanding how to see and travel on the astral plane.

1. The Familiar Room Exercise

Sit in a comfortable position in your favorite room or Temple space. Close your eyes and try to recreate the room around you. Visualize the details of the room: the furniture, the pictures on the walls, the color of the carpet, the texture of the ceiling, etc. In your mind's eye, move your head and look around the room. If the room has a window, imagine walking over to it and looking out. Imagine walking around the room and picking up various familiar objects. Take a mental inventory of everything you see.

Once you have created as complete an image of the room as possible, open your eyes. What things did you miss or forget to recreate? If you have left anything out of your recreation, you can add it the next time you practice this visualization.

2. Creating an Astral Temple

Sit in a comfortable position in your favorite room or Temple space. Close your eyes and imagine that you are sitting in a different room, a bigger room with a high ceiling. The room is bare and the floor, walls, and ceiling are white. There are no windows. There is a plain white Altar in the center of the room. See the room clearly in your mind's eye before continuing.

Think of the room as a blank artists' canvas. You are going to paint the walls with color. You are going to furnish the room. You will add symbols to the Altar.

On the first day of this exercise, leave the room white. Concentrate more on the size of the room. How tall is the ceiling? How wide is it?

On the second day, add color and other symbols. Make the walls blue, and the floor white marble. Imagine two enormous marble pillars on the other side of the room; the one on the right is white and the one on the left is black. Imagine a gossamer veil hanging between the pillars. Make the central Altar orange. On top of the Altar is a silver chalice. The ceiling is still white.

Keep the astral Temple simple and uncluttered. Move around the room to observe it from different perspectives.

On the next day, change the walls to red and the Altar and pillars to emerald. Change the symbol on the Altar to a white candle. Add a door in the east, covered with a veil upon which is a symbol. On the following day, remove the door and add four windows, one in each quarter.

Practice this exercise for a number of days, changing the colors and symbolism of the astral Temple every time. Eventually, you can add more symbolism to the room. At some point, you can settle on one version of the Temple that suits you.

3. Working in the Astral Temple

When you have become proficient in creating your astral Temple, imagine yourself within the Temple dressed in ritual garb, armed with your implements. Image yourself performing various rituals within the astral Temple: the Qabalistic Cross, the Lesser Ritual of the Pentagram, or the Middle Pillar exercise.

CLAIRVOYANCE

The word "clairvoyance" comes from the French *clairvoyant*, "clear-sighted." This refers to the ability of a seer, diviner, or skryer to see things that are invisible to most people including auras, Spirits, and events that are distant in time or place, using methods other than the normal mundane senses. It is sometimes called ESP or extrasensory perception. Clairvoyance often employs the use of objects such as crystals, magic mirrors, or magical symbols as aids for enhancing one's abilities of perception.

Closely related to this topic is clairaudience or the ability to hear things that are inaudible to most people, including Spirit voices and other sounds.

Both of these abilities are topics of study and practice in our tradition. Indeed, they represent psychic faculties that magicians try to cultivate. However, the Golden Dawn teaches that there are pitfalls to be wary of. The properly trained clairvoyant has all the tools needed to explore the unseen realms: knowledge, discipline, and protection. The untrained or undisciplined clairvoyant does not have these same defenses.

Why are such defenses necessary? Because between the physical world in which we live and the highest worlds of archangels and pure Deity lies the astral world, a plane of existence that is composed of the astral light, the ever-present spiritual substance that magicians consciously mold into images and objectives in magical work. It is a world full of light and shadow, dreams and reflections, truths and deceptions. It takes a skilled magician to be able to tell the difference. Untrained clairvoyance can quickly lead a magician away from the stabilizing power of Malkuth: the magician becomes unmoored and unbalanced, subject to the ebbs and flows of the astral tides. But trained clairvoyance is a wonderful tool for opening up new worlds and raising ourselves up to scale the heights of heaven.

The Golden Dawn's method for delving into the astral world and developing the faculty of clairvoyance is through skrying, or what we like to call Spirit Vision work.

INTRODUCTION TO SPIRIT VISION WORK

The word "skry" is derived from the Old English word *descry* meaning "to see" or "to observe." Today, the word "scrying" is usually limited to the idea of perceiving psychic visions by the use of an object, such as a mirror, an image, a crystal, a bowl of Water, or other gazing device. For centuries, seers have gazed into crystals, mirrors, flames, and an array of other tools. A bowl of Water, an oil lamp, a buffed metal plate, a polished gemstone, and other reflective surfaces are among the various items that have been employed for this purpose. Such tools aid a person's concentration, train their psychic abilities, and allow spiritual visions to come through into normal waking consciousness. A skrying device helps center one's attention, which enables the skryer to focus the conscious mind, inducing a trance-state conducive to vision work.

Skrying is the conscious act of perceiving events that lie outside the reach of the normal senses through subconscious means. Skrying involves seeing, not with the physical eyes but through the mind's eye, into the astral world—the invisible blueprint that lies behind all physical manifestation. A person who skrys is referred to as a "seer" or "skryer."

The astral plane or astral world is an intermediate of reality between the physical plane and higher, more divine realms. It is part of the world of Yetzirah, the World of Formation. This nonphysical level of existence is the underlying blueprint of the physical world—the common boundary between the individual and noumenal reality. The astral plane has several layers of density and vibrational rate. The upper astral lies close to the angelic realms, while the lower astral is the domain of dreams and phantasms.

The Qabalah teaches that everything in the Universe is created or prefabricated in the astral world of Yetzirah before it manifests in the physical world. The astral plane is a level of reality that is higher than the physical world, but lower than the divine or spiritual world. It is a place that is in between—a realm of reflections, images, dreams, and visions. It is sometimes called the Treasure House of Images and is said to contain the Akashic Record or the Akashic Library. This is a part of the astral plane composed of all the memories and experiences of humanity over the course of history—embedded within the substance of the ether.

The astral plane is also an inner world of human reality. By Skrying in the Spirit Vision, the magician gazes into this invisible world for knowledge. Through astral traveling, the magician enters this world and interacts with angels, elementals, and other entities. When a magician interacts with spiritual beings, he is working with those archetypes that exist as a part of his own mind or psychic makeup. But he is also working with the elementals and Spirits as they exist in the Greater Universe around him. As above, so below. These archetypal Spirits and beings exist within the mind of the magician, just as they exist on a larger scale within the mind of the Divine Creator of the Universe. To interact with one is to interact with the other.

Some people, even some magicians, discount the value of Spirit Vision work as mere fantasy. And unfortunately, some seers abuse the art by not taking the proper precautions and safeguards. It is all too easy to become what Francis King called an "astral junky," or what Israel Regardie liked to call a "cosmic foo-foo." Lacking any real training or discipline in the methods of Spirit Vision work, these individuals can become ungrounded. They lose touch with the material world and can no longer tell the difference between astral events and physical events. They are led into the realms of illusion and self-deception.

It must be remembered that there are two halves to the astral realm. The lower astral is the home of *maya*, or illusion—full of phantoms, shadows, hallucinations, and false images created in the lower, reptilian brain of humanity. The upper astral is the abode of angelic forms and psychic awareness created in the higher, mystical mind of humanity. In legitimate schools of magic, the magician is trained in techniques that will help him avoid the pitfalls of the lower astral and seek out the true and divine visions from the upper astral. Training and discipline are essential for the magician who wants to explore the astral plane in safety.

In the Golden Dawn, Spirit Vision work is usually done by using a skrying symbol—such as a tattva or elemental symbol. But it is also performed using geomantic and planetary symbols. Tarot cards, too, make excellent skrying devices.

Exploration of the astral realm is an essential part of magical work. Through vision work, the magician learns to contact higher spiritual realms, examine their landscape, and bring back information. What we are talking about here is controlled astral visions—meaningful and intense experiences that are completely understandable. In these visions, the seer maintains complete control and all of his or her powers of choice, willpower, and judgment. Through these experiences, the magician is able to reach the deepest levels of what Carl Jung called the collective unconscious or what Hermetic philosophers called *Anima Mundi*—the Soul of the World.

Spirit Vision work in the Golden Dawn tradition can be described as a form of self-hypnosis that uses symbols in order to effect changes in consciousness. From these higher levels of awareness, the magician tries to see the underlying causes of things—to work at a problem from a higher angle or perspective—to get inside the machinery of the Universe and see just what makes it tick. The seer wishes to learn how the astral world influences the physical world, especially the world of human beings.

Astral work is also performed to call forth spiritual guardians, examine past lives, to heal or figure out the cause of an illness, or establish psychic boundaries or astral Temples. Once the seer has reached the astral destination, he or she communicates with elemental beings, Spirits, angels, and Gods. The seer carefully describes the experiences on these journeys to a group or a scribe, or writes them down in a journal. The terrain, elemental nature, plants, animals, and inhabitants seen on the journey are all recorded.

Traditionally, the Golden Dawn employs three methods of clairvoyance, although they are not always easily distinguished from one another. To some extent the differences amount to little more than a difference in perspective. In short they are:

1. Skrying in the Spirit Vision (or just skrying)

2. Traveling in the Spirit Vision (astral traveling or astral projection)

3. Rising in the Planes

These three variations can be described as seeing, traveling, and rising. The primary difference between seeing and traveling is the degree of the magician's conscious immersion into the astral plane. In seeing, the magician's consciousness is only partially immersed, while in traveling it is fully so. Rising is a form of traveling in which the magician's consciousness rises up the various Sephiroth and levels of the Qabalistic Tree of Life.

BENEFITS OF SPIRIT VISION WORK

Seeing and traveling are among the most common practices of the advanced Golden Dawn magician. It is essential to much of the work of the Inner Order. There are also numerous benefits to these practices. Spirit Vision work:

- Develops the magician's faculties of focus, willpower, and intention.

- Places the seer in alignment to accept the influx of the Higher Will.

- Creates a working relationship with divine beings through invocation.

- Improves the magician's awareness, clairvoyance, and perception.

- Provides information from the higher worlds.

- Develops links with the unseen worlds.

Skrying in the Spirit Vision is an excellent technique for exploring the unseen realms before choosing to travel in them.

SEEING: SKRYING IN THE SPIRIT VISION

The single most important aspect of all astral work is that it helps train the mind—to focus all the faculties of intellect, imagination, creativity, intuition, and intention. Consistent and disciplined practice of these methods will gradually fine-tune one's psychic awareness and increase spiritual receptiveness. The magician will be better able to see and understand any spiritual information that may be passed down from the Neshamah.

Skrying, like divination, acts as a catalyst that activates the magician's own latent precognitive abilities. But it is a more direct method than either tarot or astrology, because in skrying, the magician deals with the astral plane directly.

In skrying, the seer does *not* go forth in the astral Body of Light to the astral plane. Instead the seer remains in the physical body and clairvoyantly observes the chosen realm using a skrying device such as a mirror, or simply with the mind's eye behind closed eyelids.

Golden Dawn magicians typically use skrying symbols in their Spirit Vision work. These are images that are used as portals to gaze into or doorways to pass through in the imagination. Tarot cards may serve this purpose, but the GD also uses a series of *tattva* cards borrowed from Eastern Theosophy for this purpose. With skill and practice, the seer undergoes an intense daydream-like experience during which visions are seen and information obtained.

THE TATTVAS

The tattvas are the primordial elements of the ancient mystical system of Samkhya Hinduism, the roots of which are at least twenty-five thousand years old. The word "tattva" means "quality," and it is used to describe a characteristic, essence, truth, or element. Indian philosophy defines the entire Universe and its inhabitants as being composed of various combinations of these five qualities. Table 33 lists the five primary tattvas that conform to the five basic elements.

Table 33: The Tattvas

Tattva Name	Shape	Color	Element
Akasa	Oval/Egg	Black	Spirit
Tejas	Triangle	Red	Fire
Apas	Crescent	Silver	Water
Vayu	Circle	Blue	Air
Pritihivi	Square	Yellow	Earth

The five basic tattva symbols are shown in Figure 91. Countless magicians down through the ages have used these emblems for meditation, divination, and skrying.

In chapter 6's section on the Enochian Tablets, we explained that each of the five elements contain the other elements within them as well. No element can exist on our plane in an unmixed form; therefore, each contains within itself subtle amounts of the other elements. The result is a sub-element or a compound tattva. The sub-element known as Water of Fire would be symbolized by a silver crescent inside a red Triangle. Air of Earth would be represented by a blue circle inside a yellow square. And so on.

The five basic tattvas and the twenty compound tattva symbols are all used as doorways into the astral world.

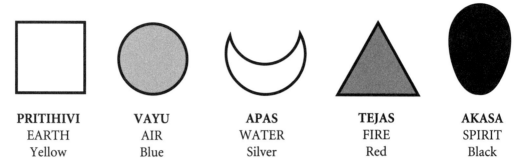

PRITIHIVI	**VAYU**	**APAS**	**TEJAS**	**AKASA**
EARTH	AIR	WATER	FIRE	SPIRIT
Yellow	Blue	Silver	Red	Black

Figure 91: Tattva Symbols

THE WESTERN ELEMENTAL SYMBOLS

The Western Esoteric Tradition has another set of symbols for the five fundamental essences—the now-familiar elemental Triangles and the circle of Spirit, symbols that alchemists and magicians have used for centuries. They date back to the time of the classical Greek philosophers such as Plato whose work *Timaeus* describes how to construct the elements from Triangles. The names of the Western elemental symbols are the same as the Hebrew names of the elements plus *Eth* ("essence") for Spirit (Figure 92).

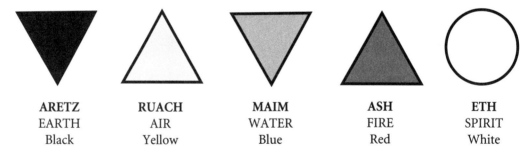

ARETZ	**RUACH**	**MAIM**	**ASH**	**ETH**
EARTH	AIR	WATER	FIRE	SPIRIT
Black	Yellow	Blue	Red	White

Figure 92: Western Elemental Symbols for Skrying

THE SUB-ELEMENTS

Just as the Eastern system has compound tattvas, the Western system has twenty-five sub-element symbols in addition to the five basic symbols. For the sake of balance, every element has a portion of every other element within its makeup.

For example, Table 34 lists the five compound Western symbols of Air.

Table 34: Compound Western Symbols of Air

Compound Name	Sub-element	Shapes and Colors
Eth of Ruach	Spirit of Air	White Spirit circle inside a yellow upright Triangle
Ash of Ruach	Fire of Air	Red upright Triangle inside a yellow upright Triangle
Mayim of Ruach	Water of Air	Blue inverted Triangle inside a yellow upright Triangle
Ruach of Ruach	Air of Air	Violet upright Triangle inside a yellow upright Triangle (when the sub-element is the same as the primary element, the sub-element is in the Flashing Color)
Aretz of Ruach	Earth of Air	Black inverted Triangle inside a yellow upright Triangle

Whether you use the Eastern tattvas or the Western elemental symbols, a full set of these symbols (twenty-five tattvas or thirty Western symbols) should be painted and wrapped in a clean white cloth until they are used for Spirit Vision work.

---

why we prefer the western elemental symbols

Both as symbols of the elemental essences and as images for meditation and Spirit Vision work, the Eastern tattvas and the Western symbols are equally valid. But we prefer to use the Western forms. Here's why:

Color: The Western alchemical symbols are shown in colors that fit our traditional view of the elements. The Triangles use the three primary colors (red, yellow, and blue) and achromatic black, which are all complemented by their natural Flashing Colors in the Golden Dawn tradition.

Shape: The Western symbols use four Triangles to represent the basic elements. When the Fire and Water Triangles are superimposed one over the other, they create the Triangles of Air and Earth and also the balanced form of the Hexagram. When placed next to each other apex to apex, the four Triangles make a square divided into four colors. This calls to mind the symbol of Malkuth, the tenth Sephirah, which symbolizes the manifested Universe composed of the four elements. The symbol for Spirit is a circle, which sets it apart from the other four. The union of the circle and square (Spirit and matter) is constantly referred to in mysticism and represents one of the great mysteries of the Western Esoteric Tradition.

Enochian Tablet Correspondences: The Western system allows for more sub-elements than the traditional tattva system, which only has twenty sub-elements. The Enochian system calls for more than twenty—it requires the additional sub-elements of Fire of Fire, Water of Water, Air of Air, Earth of Earth, and Spirit of Spirit, which the traditional tattva system lacks.

In our opinion, calling on the energies of the Sanskrit tattvas using Hebrew godnames and archangels is a bit like calling the Sephiroth "chakras." We prefer not to mix the two. Nevertheless, the tattvas are a part of our tradition and many practitioners use them with great effect in their Spirit Vision work. So choose whichever set of symbols you prefer and use them to create a deck of skrying cards (out of paper, cardstock, poster board, or canvas board) in color against a neutral achromatic background of white, gray, or black. You will have a set of either twenty-five tattva cards or thirty Western elemental symbol cards.

CHOOSING A SKRYING SYMBOL

The only true skrying tool ever needed is a receptive human psyche. However, the human mind communicates with the various levels of the soul through symbols. A symbol has been defined as "a sign by which one knows a thing." Magical symbols have been used for centuries to define the parameters of the magical Universe. In this respect they are truly signposts along the road of our Divine Cosmos. Centuries of magical work have caused these symbols to become pregnant with mystical significance that speaks to the human psyche at a deep, primal level. "By names and *images* are all powers awakened and reawakened." Symbols are a powerful aid to the intuitive facilities of the human psyche. Therefore, magical emblems, such as the Western alchemical symbols, are transformative. Just gazing at the yellow Air Triangle of Ruach will immediately conjure up a host of ideas associated with the element of Air in the mind. And it is far easier to navigate the shifting currents of the astral plane when one is equipped with a familiar signpost or symbol that clearly points the way to the desired destination. Tattvas and Triangles can be used as symbol-doorways to gain knowledge of the unseen worlds. They may also be used as portals for astral traveling.

When choosing a symbol to meditate on, you may wish to consider the various qualities associated with the elemental realms. These symbols may be used as touchstones for invoking or exploring the qualities attributed to them:

- *Spirit:* spiritualism, divinity, purity, enlightenment, bliss

- *Fire:* Strength, courage, ambition, energy, passion

- *Water:* Emotions, attitude, love, relationships, pleasure, creativity

- *Air:* Intellect, communications, health, travel, planning, magic

- *Earth:* Possessions, business, responsibility, employment, physical manifestation

By its nature Spirit Vision work requires invoking Hebrew godnames and seeking archangels and angels as protective guides in the astral plane. Therefore, the seer should have some familiarity with Hebrew names and entities associated with the elemental skrying symbols. Table 35 provides basic Qabalistic information that the seer should know.

Table 35: Elemental Names Used in Skrying

Element	Inner Divine Name	Outer Divine Name	Archangel	Angel	Direction	Ruler	Elementals	Elemental King
Aretz	Adonai	Adonai ha-Aretz	Uriel	Phorlakh	North	Kerub	Gnomes	Ghob
Ruach	YHVH	Shaddai El-Chai	Raphael	Chassan	East	Erel	Sylphs	Paralda
Mayim	El	Elohim Tzabaoth	Gabriel	Taliahad	West	Tharsis	Undines	Nichsa
Ash	Elohim	YHVH Tzabaoth	Michael	Ariel	South	Seraph	Salamanders	Djin
Eth	Eheieh Agla		—	—	—		—	—

NEGATIVE AFTER-IMAGES

The Golden Dawn devised a method for using skrying symbols in conjunction with a common optical effect known as negative after-images, a phenomena that dovetails perfectly with the Order's teachings on Flashing Colors. Negative after-images are the patches of complementary color formed in the retina of the eye by prolonged exposure of the eye to colors of high saturation. The after-image continues to appear in one's vision after exposure to the color ceases. Readers have likely experienced this effect several times by simply staring at a fixed object and then suddenly shifting one's gaze elsewhere. The resulting after-image of the original object can be either positive (retaining the object's original colors) or negative (reversing the original colors).

Negative after-images are particularly useful for shifting the magician's focus into higher planes of existence. For example, if you stare without blinking at a red Triangle for a few moments, then either close your eyes or stare at a white piece of paper; you will "see" the after-image of the Triangle in flashing green. In Spirit Vision work, the transition between the symbol and its after-image is used as a trigger for the opening of a portal into the astral world.

TESTING AND PROTECTIONS

Spirit Vision work is an excellent method for communing with spiritual entities in the Great Chain of Being leading to the Divine Source. Yet it is vitally important to maintain proper safeguards within your practice. Delusion, obsession, and ego-inflation are ever-present hazards for seers who do not test their visions, learn to banish on the astral plane, or skry too often without maintaining a firm connection with Malkuth. For this reason, it is recommended that Spirit Vision work be performed no more than once a week.

There should be no blending of the astral plane into normal consciousness. To avoid this, it is best to always follow definite techniques when coming and going from astral journeys.

If you have any doubts about an entity that you encounter in your journey, test it with the following symbols and words of protection:

- Divine names that relate to the realm you are exploring

- Magical gestures (grade signs) that relate to the realm you are exploring

- Pentagrams

- Hexagrams

- The Banner of the West

- The Hiereus Lamen

- The Banner of the East

- The Rose Cross

Use a banishing Pentagram or Hexagram to dismiss a scene or an entity that does not seem right. If you ever feel threatened by an astral being, mentally create an image of the Banner of the West—a symbol used to bar evil and keep it at bay. The Lamen of the Hiereus can be similarly used. A hostile entity will disappear immediately at the sight of the Banner, while a helpful being will not mind being tested. No balanced force will ever resent being tested with the Banner or any other holy symbol.

The Golden Dawn's Banner of the East, a potent symbol of the Divine Light, may be used for protection and strength. You can visualize the Banner wrapped around you like a cloak. A visualized Rose Cross Lamen can be similarly employed.

As the saying goes, "Don't believe everything you see." Never trust things on face value alone. There are certain symbols that can be traced to help clarify an astral vision or test for errors, since the magician does not want the vision to be influenced by tricks of memory or fantasy. The Hebrew letters of the seven planets can be used as important test symbols for the following errors in vision:

1. **Vestiges of a memory:** If you suspect that some image from your memory or a preconception is influencing your vision, trace the symbol of the letter Tau ת in white Light. (Tau is the letter of Saturn, the planet that governs memory.)

2. **Your mind has created and is controlling an image:** If you think that you have constructed or exaggerated the scene in your imagination, rather than receiving a true astral image, trace the letter Kaph כ. (Kaph is the letter of Jupiter, the planet of construction.)

3. **Vestiges of emotion:** To vanquish feelings of revenge, hatred, fear, anger, or impatience, use Peh פ, the letter of Mars.

4. **Your mind or an astral being is merely flattering you:** To rid yourself of delusions of grandeur, arrogance, insecurity, or inflated ego, use Resh ר, the letter of the Sun.

5. **Wish-fulfillment fantasy:** If your vision lapses into a pleasure-seeking fantasy, selfish indulgence, or frivolity, use Daleth ד, the letter of Venus.

6. **Complete distortions and lies:** If you suspect that what you are looking at is a complete deception, a falsehood, or overrationalization, use Beth ב, the letter of Mercury.

7. **Lack of concentration:** For wandering thoughts, lack of focus, sentimentality, or gullibility, use Gimel ג, the letter of the Moon.

If the scene disappears or changes after tracing any of these symbols, then banish with a Pentagram and start over with the vision. See if a different scene appears.

At times, it is possible to spend too much of your energy tracing test symbols. In such a case, you can bring some energy back into yourself by performing the Neophyte Signs: the Projection Sign followed by the Sign of Silence.

Over time and with practice, your visions can grow from faint pictures to dynamic and powerful experiences. But even when these powerful experiences occur, you should never take them at face value, or fail to test them.

SKRYING IN THE SPIRIT VISION: PROCEDURE

Spirit Vision workings can be performed with any number of different skrying symbols. We choose the basic Western symbol of Air or Ruach, the yellow upright Triangle, to exemplify the procedure.

You should always keep a record of your Spirit Vision workings, even for those times when you may consider the session to be a flop. This is the best way to gauge your own progress and improve your skryings. You will also need to work out the details of the session ahead of time. What godnames and angels will you call upon? What Pentagram or Hexagram rituals will you use? And so on. Students may find the worksheet in Table 36 helpful.

Table 36: Sample Spirit Vision Worksheet

Spirit Vision Worksheet	
Element: Air (Ruach) *Symbol:* Yellow Air Triangle *Divine Name:* YHVH *Quarter:* East *Archangel:* Raphael *Angel:* Chassan *Ruler:* Erel *Elemental King:* Paralda *Elementals:* Sylphs	*Seer:* Frater Veritas *Date:* 2/9/18 *Start Time:* 12:00 p.m. *Place:* Atlanta, GA *Sun in:* Aquarius *Moon in:* Sagittarius *End Time:* 12:30 p.m.
Ritual Format *Preliminary Meditation:* Focused on breathing *Opening:* LBRP. Purification and Consecration *Invocation Ritual Used:* SIRP of Air	
Summary of the Work Record the details of your vision here.	

On the center of the Altar should be the Cross and Triangle surrounded by the Elemental Weapons (Air Dagger-east, Fire Wand-south, Water Cup-west, Earth Pentacle-north). The magician should be relaxed and robed in full ceremonial regalia.

Place a chair next to the Altar, facing the direction of the force to be skryed. If the working involves a planet or a zodiacal sign, find the direction of the force and place your chair to face it. Place the skrying symbol in an elevated position in front of the direction where you have determined the force to be.

There are five basic parts to a Spirit Vision working:

1. Opening

2. Invocation

3. Opening the Symbol

4. The Vision or working

5. Closing

Opening

1. Begin with your Pre-Ritual Meditation Practice.

2. Perform the LBRP to cleanse the area and set up Sacred Space.

3. Purify and consecrate the Temple with Water and Fire (as described in "Purification and Consecration" in chapter 6).

Invocation

4. Take up the implement that corresponds to the skrying symbol. (In our example, we chose Air, so our implement is the Air Dagger. If one is not available, a rose or a fan could be used.)

5. Perform the Supreme Invoking Ritual of the element (in this case, Air) in all four quarters.

6. Perform the Circumambulation followed by the Adoration (as described in chapter 7, Opening by Watchtower steps 26 and 27).

Opening the Symbol

7. Trace a circle over the skrying symbol (in this case the yellow Triangle of Air) followed by the appropriate Pentagram(s) and vibrate the relevant godname, **"YHVH"** (for Air), as many times as you feel is necessary.

8. Use the Vibratory Formula to invoke the force of the godname "YHVH" and send a ray of thought empowered by your Higher Will though your physical Tiphareth (Air) center into the Tiphareth of your aura and into the skrying symbol before you. Imagine the force of the name passing through the symbol and into the realm beyond.

9. Sit back in a chair facing the quarter of the desired element and relax. Gaze passively at the skrying card for some time, and assume a rhythmic breath. When you feel you are ready, stare at the symbol without blinking for at least thirty seconds.

10. When your mind is fully focused upon the image, relax, close your eyes, and continue the meditation. At this point, the image of the symbol is seen in reverse or Flashing Color (in this case an upright violet Triangle). Let the image remain in your mind as if your eyes were still open. The physical vision slides into astral vision—the reality of a dream image in a conscious state. It becomes a kind of thought-vision that remains after the eyes are closed. You should receive images and scenery pertaining to the skrying symbol reflected back to your consciousness from the Macrocosm.

11. The appropriate divine names should be physically vibrated several times.

The Vision or Working

12. In skrying, the image of the symbol appears like a window into another world. The symbol keeps its shape but its color becomes transparent, as though you were looking through glass. You should observe some landscape or scene that is reflected into the image of the symbol. Objects may seem reversed as they would be if reflected into a mirror. The images seen are alive but may seem flat and two-dimensional, like watching a movie. Concentrate on the landscape until it becomes clearer.

13. Observe any figures and beings that relate to the element. It is important to constantly test the scene and any spiritual beings with the appropriate divine names, magical gestures, and elemental symbols. Physically vibrate divine names as needed.

14. When you are finished with the vision, thank any spiritual beings you may have encountered. Then dissolve the mental image and return slowly to normal consciousness.

Closing

15. Give the appropriate banishing figures over the skrying symbol.

16. Perform the Reverse Circumambulation (counterclockwise) followed by the Adoration.

17. Perform the Supreme Banishing Ritual of the Element (in this case Air) in all four quarters.

18. Declare the Temple closed.

At this point, you should be able to adapt what you have learned in previous chapters to your Spirit Vision work. We have provided only one example here for skrying procedures, so you will need to alter these steps depending upon the nature of your working as follows:

- If you are exploring a planetary or Sephirotic realm, follow the LBRP with a LBRH. You will use the Greater Ritual of the Hexagram in the direction of the planetary force and over the skrying symbol, which could be a planet emblem or appropriate tarot card.

- To explore a sub-elemental realm such as Earth of Water, you need to determine the divine names and angelic beings for both the primary element (Water) and the secondary element (Earth). The invocation will be an SIRP of Water and you will use the Water Cup as your implement for the entire working. Over the sub-elemental skrying symbol, you will trace the Pentagrams of Water first, then the Pentagrams of Earth second, since the primary element is always invoked first.

- To explore a zodiacal force such as Aries, you can use the symbol of Aries or the tarot card of The Emperor. Use an implement that is aligned with the sign's elemental triplicity (a Fire Wand or candle). The invocation will be an SIRP of Aries.

TRAVELING IN THE SPIRIT VISION: PROCEDURE

Astral projection or astral traveling is closely related to skrying, and many of the steps for both are similar if not the same. In skrying, the magician is primarily a spectator who observes an astral vision but does not project himself or herself into it. Skrying is two-dimensional whereas astral projection is three-dimensional. Skrying is somewhat flat and observant while astral traveling is more interactive: it involves sending a Body of Light along a ray of thought into the astral realm that is the destination of the working. In astral projection, the magician travels along this ray of thought in a duplicated or reflected astral body projected into the astral world through a symbol that acts as a portal. Astral traveling can be compared to a state that is between sleeping and waking. It is a kind of deeply felt waking dream-vision, where the traveler has a limited degree of freedom from the physical body, can pass through objects, and explore new places.

People often make the mistake of thinking that in astral projection the magician's entire consciousness takes off and goes elsewhere—leaving the body in an unconscious sleep-like state. In fact, a certain portion of consciousness must remain behind in the body to protect the ray of thought beyond the aura. Therefore, the consciousness as it exists in an astral projection is not as strong as the consciousness of everyday waking life centered in the physical body.

In setting up your Temple for traveling, follow the same rules as in skrying. For this example, we choose the basic Western symbol of Water or Mayim (the blue inverted Triangle). For an alternative symbol, you can use the tarot card of The Hanged Man.

Opening

1. Begin with your Pre-Ritual Meditation Practice.

2. Perform the LBRP to cleanse the area and set up Sacred Space.

3. Purify and consecrate the Temple with Water and Fire.

Invocation

4. Take up the implement that corresponds to the skrying symbol. (In our example, we chose Water, so our implement is the Water Cup.)

5. Perform the Supreme Invoking Ritual of the Element (in this case Water) in all four quarters.

6. Perform the Circumambulation followed by the Adoration.

Opening the Symbol

7. Trace a circle over the symbol followed by the appropriate Pentagram(s) and vibrate the relevant godname, **"Aleph-Lamed, AL"** or simply **"AL"** (for Water), as many times as you feel is necessary.

8. Use the Vibratory Formula to invoke the force of the godname "AL," to send a thought-ray empowered by your Higher Will though your physical Tiphareth center into the Chesed (Water) center of your aura and into the skrying symbol before you. Imagine the force of the name passing through the symbol and into the realm beyond.

9. Sit back in a chair facing the quarter of the desired element and relax. Gaze passively at the skrying card for some time, and assume a rhythmic breath. When you feel you are ready, stare at the symbol without blinking for at least thirty seconds.

10. When your mind is focused fully upon the image, relax, close your eyes, and continue the meditation. At this point, the image of the symbol is seen in reverse or Flashing Color (in this case an inverted orange Triangle).

11. The appropriate divine names should be physically vibrated several times.

The Working

12. As soon as this reverse image is seen, imagine it becoming very large, like a huge door or gateway that is large enough to walk through.

13. Empowered by the Higher Will, send a ray of thought from the Chesed center of your aura, drawing from it a refined Body of Light to send directly through the portal.

14. Enter this portal with the Projection Sign performed astrally. At the point of destination on the other side of the portal, a sphere of astral light is formed. Your astral image or Body of Light is reflected into this sphere of astral light on the ray of thought, making an astral duplicate of your aura in the other realm, which unites your consciousness in one ray of thought.

15. Visualize the symbol behind you. Then begin looking for objects, beings, or a landscape.

16. At this point, vibrate the divine and angelic names appropriate to the path. The names should be physically vibrated several times.

17. The landscape may change as the names are vibrated. It may become more clearly defined. A being may appear, whose clothing and appearance corresponds to the desired path. You should wait until one of these guides appears, or until you feel that a guide is present. (Sometimes there is no clear vision of these guides, but only a powerful intuition that a guide has manifested.)

18. Test the being to make sure that it is a true guide and not just an astral deception. Assume the grade sign of the element attributed to the path (in this case Water) astrally. A true guide should be able to answer this sign. If it is a false guide, it will show distress or disappear altogether.

19. Clearly ask the being if he or she comes to act as your guide in the name of the appropriate divine name. If all is answered to your satisfaction, you may proceed to follow the guide, taking note of where he or she goes and asking questions about what you see.

20. If at any time you become unsure of the truth of the vision, test it. The elemental grade signs, the vibration of divine names, and the tracing of appropriate Pentagrams or Hexagrams are symbols that have a powerful effect on the native of the astral. These will uncover any deceptions or illusions. However, it is generally unnecessary to trace a Pentagram. The vibration of the divine Hebrew names is usually enough.

Ritual Note: If you use a compound element (or a sub-element) such as Water of Air, you may find yourself being brought from one guide to another, and from one plane to another. The same tests should be applied to the new guide. The divine names of the secondary element should be vibrated and the appropriate grade sign given. If satisfied, you may then proceed.

Always treat astral beings with respect in accordance with their rank, especially the higher forms: Gods, archangels, angels, and rulers. Elementals should be treated with polite firmness.

---

21. When finished, thank your guide or guides.

22. To end the astral journey, simply reverse the process. Retrace your path and find the astral door or skrying symbol. Pass through the door with the Projection Sign. Withdraw the ray of thought.

23. Take a few moments to adjust to normal consciousness. Finally, stand up and give the Sign of Silence. A banishing ritual should be performed.

Traveling in the Spirit Vision allows the magician to participate in archetypal events in the higher worlds. Done correctly, traveling can result in powerful initiatory experiences.

PRAYER AND INVOCATION

Someone once asked us if it is possible for an atheist to become a Golden Dawn magician. We had to tell him no—it is not possible for a person to be both an atheist and a theurgist. One of the primary goals of a Golden Dawn magician is to complete the Great Work and to achieve union with the Divine.

Magical change works through the Unmanifest, through subtle manipulations of the invisible, spiritual realms. The magician is part of an uninterrupted Chain of Being between the lowest portions of the Divine Universe and the Ineffable One, the Ultimate Source of Divinity—God. Thus the practice of magic involves working with, praying to, and invoking spiritual beings—deities, archangels, angels, and other entities.

The Universal Unity expresses its many aspects in various godnames and attributes as well as in the multitude of deities that are beloved by many cultures and faiths. After archangels and angels, human beings are ranked in the middle of this divine hierarchy, connected to it by virtue of the human soul and the Higher Self—one's personal angelic contact with the higher realms. Next in line after humans come the lower Spirits and elementals.

Golden Dawn magicians adhere to this chain of command whenever they perform ritual magic, first invoking the highest divine names of God followed by archangels and angels who are asked to "look with favor upon this ceremony" and give their aid and support in carrying out the magician's objective. Prayers and invocations are among the basic tools that every ritual magician employs in his or her work. They are the primary means by which the magician opens a channel of communication with the higher powers, the essential first step toward developing an intimate relationship—a two-way conversation—with an aspect of God, a Deity, or an angel. Partnering with a divine being makes the goal of any ritual or magical working much more attainable. Not only this, it also helps orient the Higher Self of the magician toward union with the Divine.

Strictly speaking, a prayer is a communication to a divine being, usually to ask or petition for something. A prayer can also be a form of adoration that sings a Deity's praises. An invocation is the process by which a magician calls a Deity forth to begin an intimate communication or obtain the authority of a portion of the Deity's power. But in magic these distinctions often disappear: there are a good many invocation-prayers.

The pages that follow contain some of the best-known prayers and invocations from our tradition. They are not intended to be merely read in a droning voice: they are meant to be felt, to move, and to raise energy. Many of them are employed in the practice of godform assumption, discussed later in this chapter. They are used in conjunction with visualization, vibration, and energy movement to summon the blessings of Deity, and to align oneself with Divinity in order to enact magical change with the power and approval of the Sacred.

Magicians often use these prayers, in whole or in part, to create their own magical invocations. It is fully expected that theurgists will devise their own versions for their personal magical work.

THE PRAYER OF OSIRIS

This beautiful invocation-prayer to the Egyptian God is recited before the Mystic Repast in the Neophyte Ceremony. It is often used in godform assumption work involving Osiris.

For Osiris Onnophris who is found perfect before the Gods, hath said:
These are the Elements of my Body,
Perfected through Suffering, Glorified through Trial.
For the scent of the Dying Rose is as the repressed Sigh of my suffering:
And the flame red Fire as the Energy of mine Undaunted Will:
And the Cup of Wine is the pouring out of the Blood of my Heart:
Sacrificed unto Regeneration, unto the Newer Life:
And the Bread and Salt are as the Foundations of my Body,
Which I destroy in order that they may be renewed.
For I am Osiris Triumphant, even Osiris Onnophris, the Justified.
I am He who is clothed with the Body of Flesh,
Yet in whom is the Spirit of the Great Gods.
I am the Lord of Life, triumphant over Death.
Those who partaketh with me shall arise with me.
I am the Manifester in matter of Those Whose Abode is in the Invisible.
I am purified. I stand upon the Universe.
I am its Reconciler with the Eternal Gods.
I am the Perfector of Matter,
And without me, the Universe is not.

A Mystic Repast of the Four Elements

The Mystic Repast is an important element of the Neophyte Ceremony. As in the following version, it can be easily adapted for use at the end of many advanced ceremonies to express fellowship with one's companion magicians as well as with spiritual entities summoned in magical work.

Surrounding the symbols of the Cross and Triangle upon the Altar should be the following:

- *East:* A rose

- *South:* A red candle

- *West:* A cup of wine

- *North:* A platter of bread and salt

1. Stand west of the Altar and face east. Perform the Qabalistic Cross.

2. Raise your hands in the Air and say: **"I invite all you Beings of Elemental Air, Archangels, Angels, Kings, Rulers, and Elementals to partake with me of the Mystic Repast of the Four Elements."**

3. Pick up the rose and say: **"I invite you to inhale with me the perfume of this Rose as a symbol of Air."** Smell the rose.

4. Pick up the candle and say: **"To feel with me the warmth of this candle flame, as a symbol of Fire."** Hold your hand over the flame.

5. Pick up the platter and say: **"To eat with me this bread and salt, as types of Earth."** Dip a piece of bread into the salt and eat it.

6. Pick up the cup and say: **"And finally, to drink with me this wine, the consecrated emblem of Elemental Water."** Drink the wine. Place the empty cup between the cross and the Triangle.

7. Then say: **"It is finished."**

THE EXORDIUMS OF THOTH

The two parts of this invocation are often used in godform assumptions involving the Egyptian God of Wisdom.

The General Exordium

> *The Speech in the Silence:*
> *The Words against the Son of Night:*
> *The Voice of Thoth before the Universe*
> *in the presence of the eternal Gods:*
> *The Formulas of Knowledge:*
> *The Wisdom of Breath:*
> *The Radix of Vibration:*
> *The Shaking of the Invisible:*
> *The Rolling Asunder of the Darkness:*
> *The Becoming Visible of Matter:*
> *The Piercing of the Coils of the Stooping Dragon:*
> *The Breaking forth of the Light:*
> *All these are in the Knowledge of Tho-oth.*

The Particular Exordium

> *At the Ending at the Night: At the Limits of the Light:*
> *Tho-oth stood before the Unborn Ones of Time!*
> *Then was formulated the Universe:*
> *Then came forth the Gods thereof:*
> *The Aeons of the Bornless Beyond:*
> *Then was the Voice vibrated:*
> *Then was the Name declared.*
> *At the Threshold of the Entrance,*
> *Between the Universe and the Infinite,*
> *In the Sign of the Enterer, stood Tho-oth,*
> *As before him were the Aeons proclaimed.*
> *In Breath did he vibrate them:*
> *In Symbols did he record them:*
> *For betwixt the Light and Darkness did he stand.*

TO THE ANGELS OF THE CELESTIAL SPHERES

This prayer for strength and protection of the Temple is adapted from the Adeptus Minor Ritual.

> *I invoke ye, ye Angels of the Celestial spheres, whose dwelling is in the invisible. Ye are the guardians of the gates of the Universe, be ye also the guardians of this mystic sphere. Keep far removed the evil and the unbalanced. Strengthen and inspire me so that I may preserve unsullied this abode of the mysteries of the eternal Gods. Let my sphere be pure and holy so that I may enter in and become a partaker of the secrets of the Light Divine.*

INVOCATION OF THE RECONCILER

This invocation is found in the Adeptus Minor Ritual. Based in part on Scripture, it invokes aspects of Christ, Amoun, and Osiris, who are blended here into one transcendent Deity.

> *I am the Resurrection and the Life. He that believeth in Me, though he were dead, yet shall he live. And whosoever liveth and believeth in Me, shall never die. I am the First and I am the Last. I am He that liveth and was dead, and behold, I am alive for evermore, and hold the Keys of Death and of Hell.*
>
> *For I know that my Redeemer liveth and that he shall stand at the latter day upon the earth. I am the Way, the Truth, and the Life, No man cometh unto the Father but by Me. I am the Purified. I have passed through the Gates of Darkness unto the Light. I have fought upon Earth for Good. I have finished my work. I have entered into the invisible.*
>
> *I am the Sun in his rising. I have passed though the hour of cloud and night. I am Amoun, the Concealed One, the Opener of the Day. I am Osiris Onnophris, the Justified One. I am the Lord of Life triumphant over Death. There is no part of me that is not of the Gods. I am the Preparer of the Pathway, the Rescuer unto the Light. Out of the Darkness, let that Light arise. Before was blind, but now I see.*
>
> *I am the Reconciler with the Ineffable. I am the Dweller in the Invisible. Let the White Brilliance of the Spirit Divine descend!*

Introduction to the Bornless Ritual

The Bornless Ritual is a forceful invocation adapted from a series of magical papyri from Greco-Roman Egypt. The original invocation contained a section in which the ancient magician took on the identity and powers of a powerful Deity known as the Bornless One or "the Headless One," possibly referring to "the One without Beginning." It appears to be a straightforward invocation and godform assumption of a Hebrew High God, probably Yahweh. For most of the invocation, the magician invokes and then assumes the godform of the Creator of the Universe. Once the magician has assumed the form of the God, then all Spirits everywhere will obey the magician.

One of the features of the Bornless Invocation was the use of the so-called barbarous names that were often "Greek-i-fied" or corrupted Hebrew, Gnostic, Latin, and unknown godnames, thought by virtue of their cryptic nature to be very powerful.

Variations of the Bornless Invocation are numerous. In the 1930s, Israel Regardie created his own elaborate version, called "The Bornless Ritual for the Invocation of the Higher Genius," published in his seminal work *The Golden Dawn.*

The earliest version used by the Order was short and uncomplicated; it was simply known as "An Extremely Powerful Invocation for Daily Use and Work." Besides the normal Temple arrangement, the only tools required were the Elemental Weapons and a stick of incense. No Pentagrams are traced, only the Kerubic symbols and the Spirit Wheel.

The Bornless Ritual

In addition to the standard Temple setup, you will need the four Elemental Weapons and a stick of incense.

1. Stand west of the Altar facing east. Recite the Bornless Invocation:
      Thee I invoke, the Bornless One!
      Thee that didst create the earth and the Heavens,
      Thee that didst create the Night and the Day,
      Thee that didst create the Darkness and the Light.
      Thou art Osorronophris, whom no man hath seen at any time.
      Thou art Iabas; thou art Iapos.
      Thou hast distinguished between the Just and the Unjust.
      Thou didst make the Female and the Male.

Thou didst produce the Seed and the Fruit.
Thou didst form Men to love one another,
and to hate one another.
Hear thou me, for I am Mosheh thy servant,
unto whom Thou hast committed thy Mysteries,
the ceremonies of Israel.
Thou hast produced the moist and the dry,
and that which nourisheth all created life.
Hear me, for I am the Angel of Paphro Osorronophris:
this is Thy true name, handed down to the prophets of Israel.

2. Trace the Aquarius symbol toward the east with the Air Dagger. Then say:

Hear me: Ar, Thiao, Rheibet, Atheleberseth, A, Blatha, Abeu, Ebeu,
Phi, Chitasoe, Ib, Thiao.

Hear me and make all Spirits subject unto me: so that every Spirit
of the firmament and of the ether; upon the earth and under the earth;
on dry land or in the Water; of whirling Air or of rushing Fire; and every
spell and scourge of God may be obedient unto me.

3. Trace the Leo symbol toward the south with the Fire Wand. Then say:

I invoke Thee, the terrible and invisible God who dwellest in the void
place of Spirit: Arogogorobrao, Sothou, Modorio, Phalarchao, Ooo, Ape,
The Bornless One.

Hear me and make all Spirits subject unto me: so that every Spirit
of the firmament and of the ether; upon the earth and under the earth;
on dry land or in the Water; of whirling Air or of rushing Fire; and every
spell and scourge of God may be obedient unto me.

4. Trace the symbol of the eagle's head toward the west with the Water Cup. Then say:

Hear me: Roubriao, Mariodam, Balbnabaoth, Assalonai, Aphniao, I,
Thoteth, Abrasax, Aeoou, Ischara, Mighty and Bornless One.

Hear me and make all Spirits subject unto me: so that every Spirit
of the firmament and of the ether; upon the earth and under the earth;
on dry land or in the Water; of whirling Air or of rushing Fire; and every
spell and scourge of God may be obedient unto me.

5. Trace the Taurus symbol toward the north with the Pentacle. Then say:

I invoke Thee: Ma, Barraio, Ioel, Kotha, Athorebalo, Abraoth.

Hear me and make all Spirits subject unto me: so that every Spirit of the firmament and of the ether; upon the earth and under the earth; on dry land or in the Water; of whirling Air or of rushing Fire; and every spell and scourge of God may be obedient unto me.

6. Trace the Spirit Wheel toward the floor below at the base of the Altar with the incense. Then say:

Hear me: Aoth, Abaoth, Basum, Isak, Sabaoth, IAO.
This is the Lord of the Gods;
This is the Lord of the Universe;
This is He Whom the winds fear;
This is He Who, having made Voice by His commandment,
is Lord of all things—King, ruler and helper.

Hear me and make all Spirits subject unto me: so that every Spirit of the firmament and of the ether; upon the earth and under the earth; on dry land or in the Water; of whirling Air or of rushing Fire; and every spell and scourge of God may be obedient unto me.

7. Trace the Spirit Wheel toward the ceiling above the Altar with the incense. Then say:

Hear me: Ieou, Pur, Iou, Pur, Iaot, Iaeo, Ioou, Abrasax, Sabriam, Oo, Uu, Adonaie, Ede, Edu, Angelos Ton Theon, Anlala Lai, Gaia, Apa, Diachanna Chorun.
I am He, the Bornless Spirit!
Having sight in the feet—strong, and the Immortal Fire!
I am He, the Truth!
I am He, who hate that evil should be wrought in the world.
I am He who lighteneth and thundereth.
I am He from whom is the shower of the life on Earth.
I am He whose mouth ever flameth.
I am He, the Begetter and Manifester unto the Light.
I am He, the Grace of the World.
"The Heart Girt with a Serpent" is My name.

*Come thou forth and follow me, and make all Spirits subject unto
me, so that every Spirit of the firmament and of the ether, upon the earth
and under the earth, on dry land and in the Water, of whirling Air and of
rushing Fire, and every spell and scourge of God, may be obedient unto me.
IAO. Sabao. Such are the words!*

GODFORM ASSUMPTION

A godform is an archetypal image of a God or Goddess that is constructed by visualization on the astral plane. It is the outer expression of a Deity created by the magician.

Godform assumption is a magical technique for working with the energies, powers, and qualities of a particular Deity by assuming its form. This involves controlled manipulation of the aura and the astral body. A clairvoyant should be able to see or become aware of this shift in the magician's astral body.

The archetypal image of the Deity is created on the astral plane by intense visualization, vibration of the Deity's name, tracing its sigil, etc. The magician then steps into this astral image and wears it like a garment or mask, continuing to strengthen the image with focused concentration. This is performed in order to create a vehicle for that particular aspect of the Divine that the theurgist is working with. The magician respectfully imitates but does not "channel," get possessed by, or lose him- or herself in the Deity, although the practitioner may receive communication from the Deity during this process. It is more a matter of creating a godform to serve as a reflected emissary of the powers of the God or Goddess.

There are four basic steps for creating and assuming a godform:

1. Preparation

2. Building the Astral Form

3. Assuming the Godform

4. Taking Off and Dissolving the Godform

Note: Always maintain self-control and do not completely identify yourself with a particular Deity. Remember that a godform is a created astral vessel used to facilitate connection, not submersion, with a Deity. Those who forget this warning risk becoming deluded through egotism.

Preparation

1. Find a drawing or description of the Deity you wish to base the godform on.

2. Determine the Hebrew or Coptic form of the Deity's name (many of these can be found in our books on *Self-Initiation into the Golden Dawn Tradition* and *Tarot Talismans*). Create a sigil of this name from the Rose Cross Lamen's Rose of Twenty-Two Petals shown in chapter 10, Figure 99. Memorize the form of the sigil.

3. Commit the colors and details of the godform drawing to memory.

4. Begin your work with your preferred techniques of rhythmic breathing and meditation.

5. Perform the LBRP.

6. Perform the exercise of the Middle Pillar.

Building the Astral Form

7. Softly vibrate the name of the Deity a number of times. Trace the sigil in your mind's eye as you vibrate the name. (Once you become more skilled at this, you can vibrate the name mentally.)

8. Project a white ray of light from your Tiphareth center to the place where you want to build up the image of the godform. Trace the Deity's sigil toward the area. (This might simply be the area where you are already standing or sitting.)

9. Strongly visualize the image forming where you have projected it. Do not rush the process.

Assuming the Godform

10. Step into the tzelem, or astral form, of the Deity that you have created. You may step into the image from behind, back into the image, or simply visualize the image forming around you. Whichever way you choose, you will be wearing the astral image like a garment. Always maintain the divine white light of the Middle Pillar within you.

11. Link your reasoning mind to the tzelem of the godform by concentration, mentally seeing the image over yourself. Quiet vibration of the godname will strength the tzelem.

Once fully formulated, the main working or meditation can begin.

Taking Off and Dissolving the Godform

12. After the main working or meditation is complete, unlink your reasoning mind from the tzelem of the godform by ceasing your concentration on it. Mentally disconnect yourself from the form.

13. Step out of the astral form. If you stepped into the image from behind, you may back out of it. If you backed into the figure, step forward and out of it. If you simply visualized the godform around you, begin to dissolve it. See the image once again outside yourself.

14. Withdraw the white ray of light, which empowered the godform, back into your Tiphareth center.

15. Visualize the figure dissolving before you, until it is completely gone.

USES AND BENEFITS OF GODFORM ASSUMPTION

Assuming a godform is a powerful method for strengthening and controlling the aura. It is also a wonderful technique for aligning yourself with Deity. If your connection to the Higher Self is strongly maintained and safeguards are observed during the process, it is possible to obtain valuable insights.

Golden Dawn magicians often employ the technique of godform assumption in more complex rituals such as the consecration of talismans, spiritual development rituals, and other advanced ceremonies that fall under the classification of the Magic of Light. For example, assuming the godform of Thoth in a ritual consecration of a Mercury Talisman links the auric sphere of the magician to the powers of the Deity that correspond to the energies desired. On the astral plane, it would appear that the reflected godform of Thoth is charging the talisman.

Godforms can also be created in different areas of your Temple to be used as vessels of magical energy during a ceremony.

An Exercise in Godform Assumption

This is a ritual exercise to take on the godform of Ma'at, the Egyptian Goddess of justice, truth, and balance. In the order setting, Ma'at is the godform associated with the Hegemon, seated between the pillars facing west. It utilizes the Coptic form of the Goddess's name, Thmê.

If you have black and white pillars, they should be placed between the central Altar and the eastern wall of the Temple. Place a chair between the pillars.

1. Begin with your personal Pre-Ritual Meditation Practice.

2. Perform the LBRP to cleanse the Temple space.

3. Give five knocks on the Altar with your wand. Then go to the northeast and say, **"Hekas, Hekas, Este, Bebeloi! Far, far from this Sacred place be the profane!"**

4. Circumambulate the Temple thrice, giving the Neophyte Signs when passing the east. Then go to the west of the Altar and perform the Adoration to the Lord of the Universe. (See chapter 7, the Opening by Watchtower Ritual, step 27.)

5. Perform the exercise of the Middle Pillar.

6. Once the Middle Pillar is completely formulated within your sphere of sensation, trace the Coptic letters of the name Thmê in pure white within your heart (Figure 93). Then trace the letters and sigil of the name between the pillars.

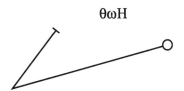

θωH

Figure 93: Sigil and Coptic for Thmê

7. Bring the Divine Light down from your Kether center to your Tiphareth center, and as you do so give the Projection Sign, at the same time vibrating the name **"THMÊ"** (Tah-may) for as long as your exhalation of breath will last. At the end of the vibration, give the Sign of Silence. Repeat this a total

of three times, once for every transliterated letter of the name of the Thmê in Hebrew (תממא)

8. After the third vibration of the name, project a white ray of light from your Tiphareth center toward the seat between the pillars and formulate the god-form of Thmê or Ma'at standing there between the pillars (Figure 94).

Figure 94: The Goddess Thmê

Her serene face is golden yellow, and her calm expression seems as though it could soothe even the hardest of hearts. Her nemyss is striped yellow and violet and is sur-mounted by a white Shu feather. Her linen gown is yellow, and her collar is banded with red, yellow, and blue. Her right wristband is yellow and blue, while her left wristband is yellow and red. She holds a Phoenix Wand, and her throne is yellow trimmed with violet upon a black and white pavement.

9. Continue projecting the white ray until the astral figure is well formulated. Step into the godform of Thmê that you have built up between the pillars, facing west. Feel your mind and reasoning faculties (Ruach) empowering the shell of the astral godform, breathing life into it. When you have felt this happen, proclaim, **"Nuk nes! Netert en Mêet!"** ("I am She! The Goddess of Truth!")

10. Be seated between the pillars but remain in this godform, contemplating its attributes and spiritual qualities, identifying these qualities as your own. At times you may imagine two enormous wings attached to your arms that reach out to touch the pillars beside you. After a pause, read the following invocation:

I am the daughter of Rê and the Lady of all the Gods and Goddesses. I stand with the God Thoth in the boat of Rê, the ship of the Sun. The scales and the feather belong to me. My feather is that which is weighed against the heart of the initiate in the Hall of Judgment. My name is Justice and my word is Truth. I am the Goddess of all that is upright, genuine and steadfast. I am the eye of the storm and center of the wheel. Upon me resteth the balance of the Hall of the Mysteries. Upon me dependeth the equilibrium of the Universe. None can pass between the Pillars whose heart is not Ma'at. When I cast my glance upon the Crown, I am Thma-Ae-st, Before the Face of the Gods in the Place of the Threshold. When I cast my glance to the right, I am Thma-ash, the Fiery One of Severity. When I cast my glance to the left. I am Thma-ett, the Fluid One of Mercy. For I am the Ma'ati, the dual Goddesses of North and South.

Pause and contemplate. Then read the following:

For the Soul of the Initiate cried out in anguish and in joy toward the Hidden Light. The Soul stepped forward through blinding darkness in aspiration toward the Light. The Light glittered in the darkness, but was not comprehended thereby. Then the voice of the Guardian of the Threshold spoke and said, "I am the Preparer of the Way between Light and Darkness. I am the Purity of the Light. I am the atonement of error. I am the self-sacrifice offered to another in a time of need. Take my hand and let thy heart, thy soul, and thy word be Ma'at."

Continue to meditate upon the godform.

11. When you are ready, step out of the godform, which once again becomes inanimate. Withdraw the white ray from the godform back into your Tiphareth center. Imagine the figure of the Goddess slowly beginning to fade until it vanishes entirely.

12. Perform the Reverse Circumambulation followed by the Adoration.

13. Perform the LBRP.

14. Give five knocks (4+1) and declare the Temple duly closed.

PATHWORKING

A pathworking is a guided visualization on one of the Qabalah's Thirty-Two Paths of Wisdom or a similar magical landscape. They are meant to be read aloud (or recorded and played back) to listeners who are taken on a recited journey. Pathworkings can be derived from Spirit Vision workings and developed into narratives designed to give listeners a type of static skrying exercise that might be similar in imagery to an actual skrying, but is purely passive in nature. A true skrying experience would be entirely active, dynamic, personal, and unique to the one performing it in "real time."

Several pathworkings can be found in our annotated edition of Israel Regardie's book *A Garden of Pomegranates: Skrying on the Tree of Life.*

REVIEW QUESTIONS

1. Name the various Qabalistic parts of the soul.

2. What are the three parts of the Neshamah?

3. Name the two parts of the etheric body.

4. What is another name for the aura?

5. What is another name for the astral body?

6. What is the Theurgic Triad?

7. How does the Theurgic Triad relate to the Qabalistic parts of the soul?

8. What are the Three Principles of Nature?

9. What is the Great Work of alchemy?

10. Where does the term "clairvoyance" come from?

11. What is the astral plane?

12. What is the difference between Skrying in the Spirit Vision and Traveling in the Spirit Vision?

13. What are the tattvas?

14. What are the Western Elemental Symbols?

15. What are negative after-images?

16. In Spirit Vision work, what symbol would you trace to guard against wandering thoughts?

17. What symbol would you trace to guard against an inflated ego?

18. What is the difference between a prayer and an invocation?

19. What is one of the first magical prayers that a Golden Dawn student learns?

20. What does the term "Bornless One" indicate?

21. What is a godform?

22. What does it mean to assume a godform?

chapter 10

THE MAGIC OF LIGHT

This chapter sets out to accomplish two things. First, it describes five basic categories of practical magic in the Golden Dawn tradition. Second, it shows how all of the information in the preceding chapters has been presented as building blocks for aspiring magicians to use in creating their own effective magical rites. Students who understand this material can select whatever energies and correspondences they find herein and utilize them for more complex workings such as the talisman consecration given in the pages that follow.

There is a particular set of teachings within the Golden Dawn system of magic collectively known as the "Z Documents," the "Z Docs," or simply the "Zeds," which can be found in Israel Regardie's *The Golden Dawn*, 7th edition, page 479. These manuscripts explain how the various aspects of the order's Neophyte Ceremony can be used as ritual formulae for endless varieties of practical procedures. One of these documents is known as "Z.2: The Formulae of the Magic of Light."

The Magic of Light refers to the Golden Dawn's formula of practical magic, the various forms of which are hidden under many layers of symbolism within the Neophyte Ceremony. There are five divisions of the Magic of Light, representing five different areas of magical work. These are grouped under the five letters of Yeheshuah, the Pentagrammaton. They are classified as follows:

Yod: The works of ceremonial magic, including evocations and invocations, falls under the letter Yod and the element of Fire.

 Heh: The consecration of talismans and the production of natural phenomena (rains, storms, earthquakes) fall under the letter Heh and the element of Water.

 Shin: All works of spiritual development and transformation fall under the letter Shin and the element of Spirit—the quintessence. This category is further divided into three types of magic that correspond to the three Yods or flames of the Shin. These three flames are further assigned to the three Mother Letters:

> א Aleph—Invisibility
>
> מ Mem—Transformations
>
> ש Shin—spiritual development

 Vav: Divination and astrology fall under the letter Vav and the element of Air.

 Heh Final: All works of alchemy fall under the letter Heh Final and the element of Earth.

It is within these five divisions of practical magic that the magician begins to bring all aspects of the Golden Dawn system together. Everything that the student has learned up to this point is utilized: the study and memorization of the Hebrew alphabet, Qabalistic principles, astrological correspondences, meditation, visualization, dramatic invocation, vibration, projection of energized willpower, assumption of godforms, and various Rituals of the Pentagram and Hexagram. All of this knowledge becomes part and parcel of the ritual tool kit of the practicing Golden Dawn magician.

Adepts study the outlines of magical rites provided in the Z.2 document and create their own unique versions of the same in fully expanded rituals. Israel Regardie supplied readers with rituals that he had created based on the Z.2 outlines as examples, but he also admonished students not to slavishly copy or simply cut and paste his versions.

Skilled students are fully expected to fashion their own rituals using their own ingenuity and inspiration. Having the ability to create one's own *effective* rituals in this manner is one of the marks of the advanced magician.

Our tradition recognizes that each magician is unique: each brings individual skills and personal experience to base upon the process of spiritual growth. Building upon the teachings and efforts of previous adepts while crafting new avenues for magical work helps ensure that the GD tradition is kept vital, balanced, and productive on many levels.

The Z.2 document supplies the aspirant instructive outlines for creating rituals of evocation, talisman consecration, invisibility, transformation, spiritual development, divination, and alchemy. For the practical work exemplified later in this chapter, we will focus on the consecration of a talisman, as this is a good representation of the type of ritual provided for in the Magic of Light. For the other Z.2 outlines and rituals based on them, readers should consult Regardie's *The Golden Dawn*.

' YOD: EVOCATION

Evocation is derived from the Latin term *evocatio,* meaning "calling forth." This refers to the act of summoning a spiritual entity into physical or visible manifestation. During an evocation, the magician stays within a magical circle of protection while the Spirit is evoked inside the Triangle of manifestation (Figure 95). One of the primary differences between invocation and evocation is that the former summons a Deity or angelic being into the magician's sphere of sensation, while the later summons a spiritual entity into some form of containment external to the magician.

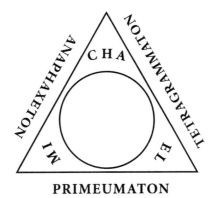

PRIMEUMATON

Figure 95: The Triangle of Manifestation

While the smoke of incense and the substance of herbs can aid in a visible manifestation, the evoked Spirit often takes its shape and visible form from the etheric substance of the magician. Thus evocation is not a suitable practice for beginners. Describing the mechanics of it lies beyond the purview of this book.

The magic circle is an area that has been purified and consecrated to serve as Sacred Space. It is a sanctified area of protection in which the magician can perform his or her art. The magic circle as depicted in the grimoires was often drawn on the floor with chalk, or paint, or sometimes salt. Figure 96 shows a magic circle from *The Key of Solomon the King*. Around the circumference were written various divine and angelic names as well as Pentagrams and other sigils of power.

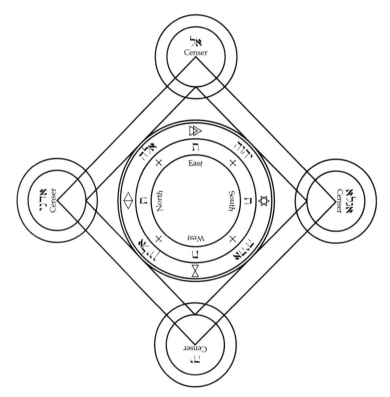

Figure 96: Magic Circle from the Key of Solomon

Many of the old grimoires were penned by medieval Christian clerics who had access to books of exorcism and were expected to command and banish demons if need be. It is no surprise then that the grimoires often reflect a dualistic perspective in which humans and Spirits have an adversarial relationship. Some of these texts deal with goetic Spirits and fallen angels who were assumed to be hostile witnesses and unwilling participants—present only because they are ordered to be so through the commandment of God. This reflects a medieval worldview that holds that part of the punishment for fallen Spirits is that they are bound to serve human magicians who know the right rituals and the proper divine names.

For modern magicians, the subject of evil Spirits is complicated and usually breaks down between those who work magic according to a Jungian psychological model, and those who ascribe to the older grimoiric traditions. Some hold that all spiritual beings, whether angel or demon, are entirely within the human psyche: that evil Spirits are simply personifications of buried, harmful subconscious impulses. Others believe that all such beings exist entirely outside the human realm—they are completely separate entities. The Golden Dawn teaches that both views can and do exist simultaneously, for *As Above, so Below*. Every man or woman is a Microcosmic reflection of the Macrocosm— we are all magic mirrors of the Universe and contain the same "star stuff." While personifications of angels and demons exist within us, they are also linked to the unseen by very real spiritual forces that abide outside of us.

One problem with goetic Spirits, qlippoth, and other historically "fallen" Spirits is that they were often based on Pagan Gods and Goddesses. Many others were derived from Persian, Arabic, and Jewish sources. However, all were seen and developed through the biased lens of the medieval Christian exorcist-cleric who thought that *all* Pagan Gods were evil Spirits.

Since Golden Dawn magicians do not believe that Pagan Gods and Goddesses are fallen Spirits, we have no need to call upon corrupted forms and their associated baggage. We work with deities from various pantheons as well as angels, archangels, and planetary Spirits in their pure original forms and even their chthonic forms with respect, without the need to force, threaten, or torture a hostile or unwilling entity to do our bidding. The medieval worldview of antagonistic human-spirit interaction is not one we share.

can ı phone a friend?

One person we know of wanted to perform a Solomonic evocation, complete with a magic circle and Triangle of art. He wasn't at all confident about his own ritual abilities but still wanted to evoke a "sketchy"

Spirit. So he did what he thought was the common sense thing to do—he brought a telephone into the circle of protection. That way if things got out of hand he could call a more experienced magician for assistance. (This was before the age of the cell phone, when phones were tethered to the wall.) Of course, things DID get out of hand and he was faced with a very nasty Spirit that refused to leave the Triangle when he tried to banish it. So the phone within the circle apparently came in handy—and a frantic call for help went out to the more experienced magician. The moral of the story: If you think your magic is going to fail, it probably will. And don't perform advanced rituals just to "see what happens next." You might just get what you wish for, and you might not like it at all.

The fact of the matter is that evocation can be a dangerous proposition. It requires a great deal of skill, balance, and know-how. Within the order system, any work whatsoever with hostile Spirits is strictly off limits to all but the most skilled magicians who have attained the grade of Adeptus Major. Even then, the work of evocation in our tradition has an entirely different spiritual focus from that portrayed in the medieval grimoires.

There are a multitude of beneficial spiritual entities that can be evoked to visible appearance, including Qabalistic and Enochian archangels and angels, zodiacal angels, planetary intelligences and Spirits, and elemental rulers and Spirits. This is exactly how Israel Regardie demonstrated the practice in his example of a Z.2 evocation ritual summoning the Enochian servient angel AXIR from the Elemental Tablet of Earth.

The highest forms, archangels and angels, are "of God," and therefore the human magician cannot command them to do anything. Instead, the adept must approach these beings with humility and in friendship, through prayer and invocation, respectfully requesting their presence and aid. These powerful beings can be petitioned to send those angels and Spirits under their command to render assistance to the magician in whatever capacity is sought. If the magician's will and intent is in harmony with that of the Divine, the goal of the ritual can be fulfilled.

The heavy emphasis on physical circles and Triangles for protection developed out of the old grimoiric traditions that dealt with adversarial, hostile Spirits. Today, it is presumed that the Golden Dawn adept who wishes to evoke an entity is already skilled at invoking, banishing, consecrating, visualization, etc. Therefore, there is really no need to construct a physical magical circle on the floor. Instead, the magic circle is created on the astral plane by the performance of the appropriate banishing rituals, invoking rituals, and consecrations, with great effect. A trained magician who is working only with archangels, angels, and similar holy beings may view the Triangle of art not as a prison for an unruly Spirit, but more like a landing pad or a portal between the worlds—an area that helps to facilitate manifestation. As the polygon associated with Binah, the Sephirah of form-building, the Triangle is the perfect figure for realizing an entity's visible appearance.

Some entities, such as planetary Spirits, though not considered evil or hostile, are seen as blind, potent, raw forces that must be controlled by their immediate angelic superiors in their respective spiritual hierarchies. If evoking a planetary Spirit such as the Mercurial Spirit Taphthartharath, having a physical circle on the floor can be protective and insulating. There is certainly no harm in constructing a full-blown magical circle, which is a useful tool like any other. It can add focus to the magician's visualization, mental poise, and concentration. But such tools are not meant to be crutches for practitioners who are unsure of themselves. A fearful or unskilled magician is one who should stay away from evocations of any kind.

Today it is far more common for Golden Dawn magicians to perform Spirit Vision work rather than evocations. The reason is that in Spirit Vision work the magician ascends in consciousness to the spiritual realm where the entity dwells, rather than bringing the entity down to the magician's level on the physical plane as in an evocation. As one of our esteemed companions put it, evocation is like hiring a tutor to come to your house and teach you French, while Spirit Vision work is like going to Paris to study French at a university.

Nevertheless, a carefully rehearsed evocation of an angelic being is an excellent method for exploring nearly every tool in the magician's tool kit of knowledge and ceremonial practice.

ה Heh: Talismans and Flashing Tablets

Magic classified under Heh, the letter corresponding to the element of Water and the Creative World of Briah, is attributed to the production of natural phenomena such as rains, storms, and earthquakes. However, these goals (especially earthquakes!) are rarely if ever the focus of Golden Dawn magic. The primary objective of magic in this category is the consecration of talismans and flashing Tablets.

Talisman is a term that comes from the Arabic *tilsam*, which in turn comes from the Greek words *telein*, "to consecrate," and *tetelesmenon* or "that which has been consecrated." A talisman is an object that has been charged or consecrated with magical energies toward the achievement of a given purpose. It is considered a lifeless object before the magician brings it to life, ritually charging it with specific energies that are usually astrological or Qabalistic in nature. Charged with a powerful divine force, a talisman radiates magical energy that has been customized to create the specific change desired by the magician.

At every stage in their magical development within the order setting, Golden Dawn magicians swear to "never debase their mystical knowledge in the pursuit of evil magic at any time tried or under any temptation." Therefore, it should go without saying that ethical magicians only make talismans for positive, beneficial purposes.

There may be instances where the magician might *think* that his or her reasons for creating a talisman or performing some other magical working are benign, but are actually harmful, such as trying to change another person's karma, or making a talisman to secure the love of another person—essentially trying to exercise control over the will of another. Use great discernment in creating talismans for mundane purposes.

Talismans can be created out of virtually anything: metal, stone, leather, jewelry, a tarot deck, paper, etc. Some talismans have a material basis that is sympathetic to the work that the magician wishes to bring about. For an elemental working, this could be a vial of Water, Air, or Earth; a candle flame; or a stone. Keep in mind that all talismans work best when the material that has gone into their creation has not been used for any other purpose.

Golden Dawn–style talismans are usually created on paper or parchment because they require the magician to inscribe Hebrew names, sigils, and other figures, and paper is an easy medium to work with. They are often two-sided, allowing for various inscriptions including the magician's magical motto. (Regardie suggested making two circles connected with a tab, creating a four-sided talisman.) Sigils drawn from the magic squares or the Rose of Twenty-Two Petals play an important part in the construction of talismans.

Planetary and Sephirotic talismans can be circular or they can be cut into the shape of the polygon that corresponds to their planetary number. A Saturn talisman having the assigned number three could be in the shape of a Triangle. That of Jupiter, whose number is four, could be cut into a square. A talisman of Mars, corresponding to the number five, could be in the shape of a pentagon. And so on.

A *flashing Tablet* is a type of talisman that is specifically used in Spirit Vision work. It consists of a square inscribed with the symbols of an element, a planet, a planetary seal, a zodiacal sign, Sephirah, etc. All are painted in Flashing Colors, consecrated like a talisman to accomplish some particular goal, and wrapped in linen. From each day of the working until the end of the process, the magician unwraps the Tablet and sets it upright upon the Altar. He or she then astrally travels though the Tablet into the realm of the force bound to the Tablet through ritual consecration. Once inside that realm, the magician performs an invoking ritual of the same energy, calling in additional power for the fulfillment of the Tablet's purpose. This process charges the Tablet from within, making it far more potent than the average talisman.

Care should be taken to make talismans and flashing Tablets as beautiful and accurate as possible. Remember that a talisman is to be consecrated with divine forces, so the more exact the symbolism, the easier it is to attract the force.

As with the creation of magical wands and other implements, the time and effort that it takes for a magician to make a talisman is more than just a preoccupation with minute details. The labor and energy put into it engages the mind on many different levels—spiritual, intellectual, and creative. It is ultimately a determined act of will that focuses the mind of the magician upon the energies that he or she wishes to work with, making the success of the endeavor much more likely. And the careful crafting of a talisman is a form of consecration in and of itself.

How Talismans Work

Once the talisman is constructed, it is energized through a ritualized process that mimics the creation of the Universe by activating the appropriate divine forces in accordance with the Four Qabalistic Worlds. The first part of this process commences when the magician inscribes the talisman with divine names and sigils relevant to the working as they exist within the four realms.

For example, if you wanted to create a Sephirothic talisman for Chesed, you would inscribe it with the names of the powers and their sigils found in Table 37.

Table 37: Divine Names for a Chesed Talisman

Qabalistic World	Power	Chesed Talisman
Atziluth (Divine)	Deity, Godname	El
Briah (Creation)	Archangel	Tzadqiel
Yetzirah (Formation)	Angelic Host	Chashmalim
Assiah (Matter)	Material Manifestation	Tzedek (Jupiter)

If you wanted to create a planetary talisman for Mercury, you would inscribe it with the names and sigils found in Table 38.

Table 38: Divine Names for a Mercury Talisman

Qabalistic World	Power	Mercury Talisman
Atziluth (Divine)	Deity, Godname	Elohim Tzabaoth
Briah (Creation)	Archangelic	Raphael
Yetzirah (Formation)	Angel (Intelligence)	Tiriel
Assiah (Matter)	Spirit, Material Manifestation	Taphthartharath, Kokab (Mercury)

If you wanted to create a zodiacal talisman for Libra, you would inscribe it with the names and sigils found in Table 39.

Table 39: Divine Names for a Libra Talisman

Qabalistic World	Power	Libra Talisman
Atziluth (Divine)	Deity, Godname	YHVH (for Air)
Briah (Creation)	Archangel	Zuriel
Yetzirah (Formation)	Angel	Chadaqiel
Assiah (Matter)	Material Manifestation	Moznaim (Libra)

Chapter 2 provides additional information. You can find godnames and archangels for all the Sephiroth in Tables 6 and 7. Divine and angelic names for the planets can be found in Tables 9 and 10. Magic squares and planetary seals are shown in Figures 14 and 15. Godnames and angelic names for the four elements and the twelve zodiacal signs are found in Tables 19 and 20.

Talisman Colors

Various color scales, particularly the King and Queen Scales, are used in the creation of Golden Dawn talismans. Following the model of the Minutum Mundum diagram, talismans for each of the ten Sephiroth are usually painted in their assigned Queen Scale colors while those of the elements, planets, and zodiacal signs are painted in their respective King Scale colors. All Hebrew names, sigils, and magical figures would be added in the appropriate Flashing Colors.

Creating Your Own Talisman

1. Decide which sphere of influence rules over your intended goal, whether elemental, zodiacal, planetary, or Sephirotic.

2. Formulate and record (in writing) the exact nature of your goal in a single sentence. Be specific and concise. Ambiguity is a cause for failure.

3. Determine the divine powers and angelic names that need to be invoked, along with their Hebrew spellings and sigils. (Hebrew spellings for all of these can be found in our books, *Self-Initiation into the Golden Dawn Tradition* as well as *Tarot Talismans: Invoke the Angels of the Tarot*.)

4. Choose which symbol or set of symbols embodies the essence of your objective. These will be inscribed on your talisman. Such symbols may include the following:

For a Planetary Talisman

- This can be circular or polygon-shaped as appropriate to the planet

- A qamea or magical square

- A planetary seal formed from the qamea (chapter 2, Figure 14)

- The planet's symbol

- The planet's polygram

- The godname (in Hebrew and in English) of the divine force that rules over the planet, along with its sigil

- The names (in Hebrew and in English) of the planetary archangel (intelligence), angel, and Spirit, along with their sigils

- The geomantic tetragrams assigned to the planet (optional)

- Painted mainly in the appropriate King Scale colors with symbols painted in Flashing Colors

Note: While any sigil can be created using the Rose of Twenty-Two letters, planetary sigils are traditionally created from the appropriate qamea.

For a Sephirotic Talisman

- This can be circular or polygon-shaped as appropriate to the Sephirah

- The Sephirotic symbol (the polygram associated with the sphere)

- The name of the Sephirah (in Hebrew and in English)

- The godname (in Hebrew and in English) that rules over the Sephirah, along with its sigil

- The names (in Hebrew and in English) of the Sephirotic archangel, angelic host, and angel, along with their sigils

- It is to be painted mainly in the appropriate Queen Scale colors with symbols painted in Flashing Colors

For a Zodiacal Talisman

- This can be circular or triangular (for the elemental triplicity)

- The astrological symbol of the zodiacal sign

- The godname (in Hebrew and in English) that rules over the elemental triplicity of the sign, along with its sigil

- The names (in Hebrew and in English) of the archangel and angel of the sign, along with their sigils

- The geomantic tetragram assigned to the sign (optional)

- It is to be painted mainly in the appropriate King Scale colors with symbols painted in Flashing Colors

For an Elemental Talisman

- This can be circular, tattva-shaped, or triangular (for the elemental triplicity)

- The elemental symbol: tattva or Triangle (circle of wheel for Spirit)

- The godname (in Hebrew and in English) that rules over the elemental, along with its sigil

- The names (in Hebrew and in English) of the archangel, angel, element, and sigil

- The Enochian Names (in English) of the Three Holy Secret Names of God and the Enochian King of the element

- The names of the Elemental King and the Ruler

- The geomantic tetragram assigned to the element (optional)

- Painted mainly in the appropriate King Scale colors with symbols painted in Flashing Colors

A sample talisman consecration ritual based on the Z.2 outline is given later in this chapter.

SIGILS

We already talked quite a bit about sigils. So what exactly are they? A sigil or seal is an abstract symbol that represents a Spirit or magical force. The word is derived from the Latin word *sigillum,* which means "sign" or "signature." Several examples of sigils can be found in medieval magical texts or grimoires. Drawing a sigil enables the magician to focus the mind on a specific Spirit or Deity he or she wishes to invoke. The sigil of an entity's name can be created from a variety of different methods, but in Golden Dawn magic it is usually obtained by a process of numerical conversion using a planetary qamea or similar device. The Aiq Beker diagram shown in chapter 2, Figure 7, is often used for drawing sigils on a qamea.

For example, if one wanted to trace the sigil of Agiel, the intelligence of Saturn on the Saturn square, the numerical value of each Hebrew letter of the name would have to be reduced to 9 or less than 9, since 9 is the highest number on the Saturn square. The letters in the name Agiel are: Aleph—1, Gimel—3, Yod—10, Aleph—1, and Lamed—30.

The only letters that need to be reduced in this case are Yod and Aleph, which can be reduced to 1 and 3, respectively, using the Aiq Beker chart. The resulting numbers of the name are 1, 3, 1, 1, 3 which can be used to trace the sigil on the qamea (Figure 97).

Intelligence of Saturn
Agiel
אגיאל

Figure 97: Agiel Sigil on the Saturn Square

Creating a sigil: When tracing a sigil on a qamea, the first number of the name is marked with a small circle. From there a line is drawn following the progression of the numbers. When the final number of the name is reached, a short line is drawn to indicate the completion of the sigil.

Variations in tracing sigils: If two letters of the same kind, such as two Beths or two Gimels, are side by side within a name, this is represented in the sigil by a wave or crook in the line at that point. If there is a letter in the name through which the line of the sigil passes straight through to meet another letter, a loop or noose is formed at that point to indicate that the letter is indeed a part of the name (examples in Figure 98).

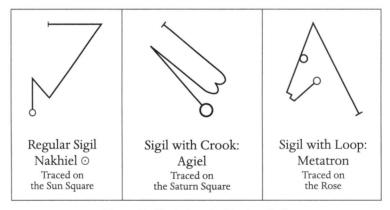

| Regular Sigil
Nakhiel ☉
Traced on
the Sun Square | Sigil with Crook:
Agiel
Traced on
the Saturn Square | Sigil with Loop:
Metatron
Traced on
the Rose |

Figure 98: Variations in Tracing Sigils

THE ROSE OF TWENTY-TWO PETALS

The Golden Dawn developed a method for creating sigils from the Rose of Twenty-Two Petals on the Rose Cross Lamen (Figure 99). Using this technique, a name is transliterated into its Hebrew letters and a continuous line is drawn from one Hebrew letter to the next to form the sigil. Sigils drawn from the rose are often more practical to use than those drawn from traditional qameas since there is no need to reduce the number value of letters.

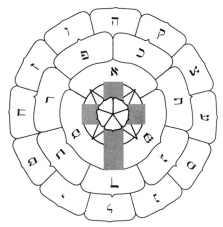

Figure 99: The Rose of Twenty-Two Petals

TELESMATIC IMAGES

All of the work that goes into the planning of a talisman consecration ritual is a crucial part of the ritual. Preparation helps the magician focus on the goal of the ceremony rather than worrying about ad-lib speeches or unrehearsed movements. Telesmatic magic, a system developed by the Golden Dawn, is all about correspondences, preparation, and visualization.

The word *telesmata* is a Greek term meaning "talismans." A Telesmatic image is an image of a Deity or angel that a magician consciously constructs. The energy that is put into the Telesmatic image is known as *telesma*. This is the force used to activate and charge the image.

A Telesmatic image is an illustration constructed according to a predetermined set of correspondences. The image is then consecrated and charged to achieve a specific purpose. This vitalized image becomes a Sacred icon—a powerful living symbol of the force it represents. The image of the angel may be drawn or painted to serve as a physical talisman in its own right, or it may be simply envisioned on the astral to give power and energy to a talisman consecration ritual.

General Telesmatic Images

A general Telesmatic image is a coherent, logically constructed image of a Deity or angel that is formulated in accordance with a standard set of colors, symbols, and other correspondences employed by Western magicians. These include but are not limited to the Flashing Colors of the elements and the Four Color Scales. Table 40 gives a breakdown of the color correspondences for the Thirty-Two Paths of Wisdom, used to create these magical images.

Table 40: Flashing Colors of the Thirty-Two Paths of Wisdom

Force	Hebrew Letter	Main Color	Complementary Color
1. Kether	—	White	Black
2. Chokmah	—	Gray	White
3. Binah	—	Black	White
4. Chesed	—	Blue	Orange
5. Geburah	—	Red	Green
6. Tiphareth	—	Yellow	Violet
7. Netzach	—	Green	Red
8. Hod	—	Orange	Blue
9. Yesod	—	Violet	Yellow
10. Malkuth	—	Citrine, Olive, Russet, Black	White
11. Air △	Aleph א	Yellow	Violet
12. Mercury ☿	Beth ב	Yellow	Violet
13. Luna ☽	Gimel ג	Blue	Orange
14. Venus ♀	Daleth ד	Green	Red
15. Aries ♈	Heh ה	Red	Green
16. Taurus ♉	Vav ו	Red-orange	Blue-green
17. Gemini ♊	Zayin ז	Orange	Blue
18. Cancer ♋	Cheth ח	Yellow-orange	Blue-violet

Force	Hebrew Letter	Main Color	Complementary Color
19. Leo ♌	Teth ט	Yellow	Violet
20. Virgo ♍	Yod י	Yellow-green	Red-violet
21. Jupiter ♃	Kaph כ	Violet	Yellow
22. Libra ♎	Lamed ל	Green	Red
23. Water ▽	Mem מ	Blue	Orange
24. Scorpio ♏	Nun נ	Blue-green	Red-orange
25. Sagittarius ♐	Samekh ס	Blue	Orange
26. Capricorn ♑	Ayin ע	Blue-violet	Yellow-orange
27. Mars ♂	Peh פ	Red	Green
28. Aquarius ♒	Tzaddi צ	Violet	Yellow
29. Pisces ♓	Qoph ק	Red-violet	Yellow-green
30. Sol ☉	Resh ר	Orange	Blue
31. Fire △ Spirit ✸	Shin ש	Red White	Green Black
32. Saturn ♄ Earth ▽	Tau ת	Blue-violet Citrine, Olive, Russet, Black	Yellow-orange White

The main color is sometimes referred to as the field or ground color. This is the principal color of a magical image. The complementary color is sometimes called the charge color. This is a secondary color that is often used to ornament the main color in a magical image. By utilizing these basic color attributions as well as other symbolism, anyone can create a general Telesmatic image of a given angel.

For example, the archangel of Saturn and the Universe card of the tarot is Kassiel. This entity could be pictured as a mighty winged angel dressed in a hooded robe of indigo (blue-violet) ornamented with yellow-orange. He might appear to be surrounded by a halo of rings like the planet Saturn. The symbol of Saturn or the Hebrew letter Tau could be emblazoned on the front of Kassiel's robe. He might carry the symbol of an hourglass, a scythe, or an astrolabe—all symbols associated with the planet Saturn.

Literal Telesmatic Images

A literal Telesmatic image is an image of a Deity or angel that is constructed from its own name, letter by letter. The Hebrew name of a spiritual entity is first analyzed, and the various correspondences of each Hebrew letter are then used to build the image of the being.

To create a literal Telesmatic image of an angel, you must first have its name transliterated into Hebrew letters. Next, construct the image of the angel so that the first letter of the name represents its head and the last letter represents its feet. All the remaining letters would represent the rest of the body in order from head to feet. There will be as many body parts as there are letters in the name.

Example: Suppose you were working with the tarot trump of the Hierophant (attributed to Taurus) and wanted to make a literal Telesmatic image of the archangel Asmodel. The Hebrew letters of this angel's name are: Aleph, Samekh, Mem, Vav, Daleth, Aleph, and Lamed. The first letter, Aleph, will represent the head and the last letter, Lamed, will represent the feet, with all the middle letters comprising the body parts in between:

א Aleph = crown of head

ס Samekh = face and neck

מ Mem = shoulders and arms

ו Vav = chest and stomach

ד Daleth = hips and thighs

א Aleph = legs

ל Lamed = feet

Once you have determined the letters of the angel's name, refer to Table 41.

Table 41: Telesmatic Attributions of the Hebrew Alphabet

Letter	Meaning	Attribution	Traditional (GD) Telesmatic Attribution
א Aleph	ox	△ Air	Generally hermaphroditic but leaning more toward masculine. Spiritual. Winged. Slender.
ב Beth	house	☿ Mercury	Masculine. Active. Slender.
ג Gimel	camel	☽ Luna	Feminine. Gray. Beautiful, yet changeable. Full face and body.
ד Daleth	door	♀ Venus	Feminine. Beautiful. Attractive. Full face and body.
ה Heh	window	♈ Aries	Feminine. Fiery. Strong. Fierce.
ו Vav	nail, hook, pin	♉ Taurus	Masculine. Steady. Strong. Heavy. Clumsy.
ז Zayin	sword	♊ Gemini	Masculine. Thin. Intelligent.
ח Cheth	fence, enclosure	♋ Cancer	Feminine. Full face without expression.
ט Teth	serpent	♌ Leo	Feminine. Strong and fiery.
י Yod	hand	♍ Virgo	Feminine. White. Delicate.
כ Kaph	fist, palm of hand	♃ Jupiter	Masculine. Big and strong.
ל Lamed	oxgoad	♎ Libra	Feminine. Well-proportioned.
מ Mem	Water	▽ Water	Generally hermaphroditic but leaning more toward feminine. Reflective. Dreamlike.
נ Nun	fish	♏ Scorpio	Masculine. Square, determined face. Full. Dark. Sinewy.
ס Samekh	prop	♐ Sagittarius	Masculine. Thin. Expressive face. Active.
ע Ayin	eye	♑ Capricorn	Masculine. Mechanical.
פ Peh	mouth	♂ Mars	Feminine. Fierce. Strong, full, and resolute.
צ Tzaddi	fishhook	♒ Aquarius	Feminine. Thoughtful and intellectual.
ק Qoph	back of head	♓ Pisces	Masculine. Full face.
ר Resh	head	☉ Sol	Masculine. Proud and dominant.
ש Shin	tooth	△ Fire ✴ Spirit	Generally hermaphroditic but leaning more toward masculine. Fierce and active.
ת Tau	cross	♄ Saturn ▽ Earth	Generally hermaphroditic but leaning more toward feminine. Dark and gray.

From Table 42, you can determine the telesmatic attributions of each letter of the name Asmodel and build up the figure of the angel.

Table 42: Telesmatic Attributions of Asmodel

א Aleph	crown of head	yellow	Generally hermaphroditic but leaning more toward masculine. Spiritual. Winged. Slender.
ס Samekh	face and neck	blue	Masculine. Thin. Expressive face. Active.
מ Mem	shoulders and arms	blue	Generally hermaphroditic but leaning more toward feminine. Reflective. Dreamlike.
ו Vav	chest and stomach	red-orange	Masculine. Steady. Strong. Heavy. Clumsy.
ד Daleth	hips and thighs	green	Feminine. Beautiful. Attractive. Full face and body.
א Aleph	legs	yellow	Generally hermaphroditic but leaning more toward masculine. Spiritual. Winged. Slender.
ל Lamed	feet	green	Feminine. Well-proportioned.

These colors can be blended together to get the overall color of the image. They may be used on the figure's clothing or as an aura of light that surrounds the being.

The gender of the figure is determined by the predominance of the gender of the letters. In higher divine beings, gender can be described more in terms of movement and stability. So when we talk about the sex of a Telesmatic image or a Hebrew letter, we are really talking about its gender in terms of energy forces. However, these classifications are merely for our convenience.

ש SHIN: SPIRITUAL DEVELOPMENT

א *Aleph: Invisibility*

The practice of invisibility falls under the Mother Letter Aleph, which is assigned to Air. This brings to mind the idea of clouds and mist obscuring one's vision.

Of all the ritual categories outlined in the Z.2 document, the one least used is probably the Shin-Aleph working on invisibility. This is because the idea of turning oneself invisible seems ludicrous to most of us, bringing with it images of Harry Potter covering himself with a cloak that instantly causes him to disappear. It does not help that tales of Aleister Crowley's adventures with invisibility make for good storytelling and endless chuckles among one's fellow magicians. One story tells of Crowley parading around the Cafe Royal in full regalia, not drawing any attention, until a visitor or tourist asked a waiter who he was. The waiter would reply, "Don't worry, that's just Mr. Crowley being invisible."

Even if such stories were true, it is hard to imagine that Crowley would have thought he was completely invisible to those around him. But it goes to show how misunderstood the magical concept of invisibility is. And the notion of a magician being able to render him- or herself invisible has been around for quite some time—it is frequently mentioned in various grimoires.

The problem is that we often equate invisibility with physical transparency. To comprehend the true meaning of invisibility as indicated in the Z.2 document, we must return to the original concept of invisibility as "the inability to be seen." As was the case with "seeing" a Spirit in magical evocation, we cannot read the language of the Z.2 document with absolute literalism. Understood in a figurative sense, invisibility can be a very practical magical tool. To become invisible means to become unnoticeable, inconspicuous, and forgettable. It entails a kind of astral camouflage or the ability to pass by others without drawing attention, being noticed, or being remembered.

Why would someone need the ability to become invisible? The reasons may vary. Temporary protection against some perceived threat may be one reason. Also, the Z.2 document tells us that the performance of the Invisibility Ritual can result in "… a certain Divine Exstasis (ecstasy) and an exaltation desirable, for herein is a sensation of an exalted strength."

Invisibility is an inherently protective practice. For centuries, magicians have had to shield their activities from the prying eyes of those who would persecute them for it. According to the story of the so-called "Invisible Rosicrucians," initiates were not to wear any distinctive form of dress but rather blend into society. This impulse for remaining hidden in plain sight is one of the legendary four powers of the Sphinx: to Know, to Will, to Dare, and to *Keep Silent*. It also lies at the heart of the Hiereus's statement to the Neophyte, "the seed of wisdom is sown in silence and grows in darkness and mystery."

The practice of invisibility given in the Z.2 document instructs the magician to create what is called the Shroud of Concealment, an astral shield around the physical body. The shroud is charged to distract the consciousness of anyone in the magician's vicinity: while they may see the magician, they will fail to take any notice. After ritually creating the Shroud, the magician leaves the Temple and conducts whatever activity necessitated the making of it.

The Shroud of Concealment is described as "a shroud of darkness and mystery." It is understandable why some find the language and verbiage of "darkness" uncomfortable. But it must be remembered that darkness in this sense does not indicate something evil or contrary to the Divine Light, but rather the manifestation of Spirit into form as processed through the dark sphere of Binah. Additionally, darkness is a metaphor for the subconscious mind, which is also represented by the concept of the Underworld. Thus the darkness invoked in this ritual is the Holy Darkness of Binah and is merely another facet of the Holy Dyad of day and night, male and female, Fire and Water, etc.

After the Shroud of Concealment has fulfilled its intended purpose, it must be dissolved completely so as not to attract unwanted energies.

ꦩ Mem: Transformations

Magical transformation falls under the letter Mem, assigned to Water. Fluidity and changeability mark the practice of transformation, or what some may call shape-shifting. Similar to the Golden Dawn's instruction on invisibility, transformation does not mean physical shape-shifting, but involves creating an astral form that is worn over the physical body like a mask or garment. Godform assumption, which we explored in chapter 9, falls into this category. The Z.2 ritual outline for transformation goes further, however: the magician can transform the appearance of his or her astral body into any animal. Performed correctly, clairvoyants, as well as onlookers caught up in the energy of the transformation ritual, should be able to see the astral form worn by the magician.

Transformation rituals are performed to obtain spiritual insight and wisdom and for seeking further Light of hidden knowledge. They can provide new perspectives into magical powers such as healing and precognition. Interaction with others while in animal form can also provide fresh perspectives into human behavior and psychology.

After ritually creating the animal form, the magician leaves the Temple and conducts activity in the outer world wearing the animal form. When the work is complete, the animal form is taken off and dissolved.

ש Shin: spiritual Development

Although the topic of spiritual development broadly describes this entire section, the Z.2 rubrics for creating a ritual that focuses on spiritual development fall under the subdivision of Shin, the letter that corresponds to the element of Spirit.

The Z.2 ritual outline provides instructions for invoking and forging a link with the magician's Higher Self. In this ritual, the magician casts him- or herself in the dual role of candidate and Hierophant in an astral reenactment of the Neophyte initiation ceremony. Combined with potent visualizations, meditation, astral projections, and prayers for divine guidance, the magician enfolds him- or herself with a radiant glory that takes on the form of the theurgist's augoeides.

After making the connection with the Higher Self, the magician can request it to render guidance, understanding, and instruction in all spiritual matters.

ו Vav: Divination

Divination is assigned to Vav, the letter of Air in the Pentagrammaton. Air is the element of consciousness, thought, and communication; therefore, all forms of communication with the divine, including astrological interpretation of a chart, tarot reading, geomancy reading, or any other form of divination, fall into this category.

We touched upon the subject of divination in chapter 5. The word "divination" is based upon the Latin *divinatio,* which means "the faculty of foreseeing." The root word is itself based upon a Latin word for "divine power" or "of the Gods," and thus exposes a more subtle meaning that is *to make divine.* This sheds an entirely different light on the subject. Far from being a superstitious practice, the art of divination reveals itself as a spiritual science that seeks to discover the divine significance behind "chance" events. And like the other magical arts, divination has existed as a tool for psychic development and spiritual health long before the development of modern psychology, which has often borrowed heavily from the techniques of ceremonial magic—putting new names on old magical ideas. In short, divination is the act of listening in order to hear what the Divine has to say through the symbol set chosen by the diviner.

Divination can open your mind to the mechanics of the spiritual realm behind the visible Universe. The various methods of divination are good exercises for developing your psychic faculties of intuition and insight. Divined intuition is a message sent from the unconscious to the conscious: it is a flash of insight from the Lower Genius or Higher Self that answers a question or solves a problem.

The many methods of divination are as varied as the inventive minds from which they sprang. It does not seem to matter what form the divination takes; it is more important that the *diviner* be able to quiet the mind enough to attune with the higher forces and perceive certain signs or symbols by means of an inner vision that can interpret their implications.

The various forms of divination provide us with different symbol-systems for defining the Universe of magic into a pattern or blueprint. For example, astrology divides the Universe into twelve zodiacal houses or fields of activity wherein the planetary energies perform their cosmic dance. In the Qabalah, the Universe is defined within ten aspects of Deity that influence each other through the twenty-two paths that connect them. A standard tarot deck defines the Universe into seventy-eight distinct sections of activity, and the divinatory method known as geomancy sections the Universe into sixteen abodes defined by the sixteen tetragams.

Is one symbol-system better than the others? No. In each of the systems mentioned, the Universe is completely defined within the context of that system. All aspects of the Universe are divided among the various sections of the divinatory system, regardless of how many sections there are. However, a greater number of divisions can provide for more detailed and fine-tuned interpretations. In this regard, the tarot remains a perennial favorite among Golden Dawn magicians.

The Z.2 document provides an outline for a complete ritualized divination invoking the forces required for a potent reading. Divinations performed in this manner should always reflect the Sacred work of the divine Magic of Light, and not indicate simple curiosity or any low purpose.

In the higher grades, students are taught a unique method of tarot divination known as the *Opening of the Key*, a long and detailed technique that requires five separate card spreads. The first spread in the series, the YHVH Spread, was introduced in chapter 5. The fifth spread in the series, the Tree of Life Spread, is given below. The complete Opening of the Key method for tarot divination can be found in our *Golden Dawn Magical Tarot Kit*.

THE TREE OF LIFE SPREAD

The Tree of Life Spread is the fifth and final part of the tarot method known as the Opening of the Key mentioned earlier. Not only is this spread an excellent method for divination in and of itself, performed with a divination ritual outlined in the order's Z.2 manuscript, it can help the magician gain an additional understanding of the divine forces of the Sephiroth.

The enquirer shuffles the cards while concentrating on the matter at hand. The cards are not cut.

1. **The Significator.** Before you begin, choose a card to be the Significator.

2. **Formulate the Question.** Shuffle the entire deck of seventy-eight cards while thinking about the matter at hand.

3. **Build the Tree.** Deal all of the cards into the pattern of the Tree of Life (Figure 100). (The eleventh card is placed on top of the first, etc.)

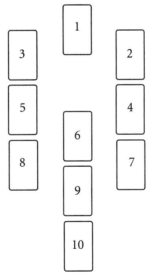

Figure 100: Tree of Life Spread

4. **Find the Significator.** Find which pile has the Significator in it. This is a general indication of the matter and the character of its operation. This does not mean that the reading is solely concerned with the sphere of influence associated with the Sephirah assigned to the pile, but rather what energy is prevalent concerning the matter at hand.

Interpret the pile by using the following Qabalistic knowledge:

- **Card 1 = Kether** (Crown), Primal Will. Spirit. The overall spiritual aspect.

- **Card 2 = Chokmah** (Wisdom), Archetypal Father. The force behind the matter.

- **Card 3 = Binah** (Understanding), Archetypal Mother. The form that the matter takes.

- **Card 4 = Chesed** (Mercy), Beneficence. Expansion. A helpful influence.

- **Card 5 = Geburah** (Severity), Karmic Law. Contraction. An oppressive influence.

- **Card 6 = Tiphareth** (Beauty), the Reconciler or Mediator. Divine aid and advice. What connects everything. The heart of the matter.

- **Card 7 = Netzach** (Victory), Emotion. Feelings.

- **Card 8 = Hod** (Splendor), Intellect. Thoughts. Rationale.

- **Card 9 = Yesod** (Foundation), the Astral Realm.

- **Card 10 = Malkuth** (Kingdom), Physical Universe, the world, the Body. Physical manifestations, possessions.

5. Horseshoe. Work with the pile containing the Significator. Put the other piles aside. Without altering the cards' order at all, spread them out to form a horseshoe.

6. Similar cards. First check to see if there is a majority of several similar cards and interpret your findings.

7. Card counting. Beginning with the Significator, move in the direction it is looking, and use the counting method described in chapter 5 to interpret the cards.

8. Card pairing. Starting with the opposite ends of the horseshoe, pair and read the cards as per previous instructions given in the YHVH Spread.

9. The tarot journal. Record your findings in the tarot journal.

A SIMPLE TREE OF LIFE CARD SPREAD

For an easy card spread that does not involve horseshoeing or card counting, simply shuffle the entire deck and, when ready, lay out ten cards in the Tree of Life formation. Put the rest of the deck aside. Consider card 1 the Significator and interpret the cards in relation to their Sephirotic placement as in step 4 above.

If desired, you can lay an additional card between cards 1 and 6 to represent Da'ath. This card indicates hidden knowledge or insight, or something that is unknown.

ה HEH FINAL: ALCHEMY

In the Z.2 document, all works of practical alchemy fall under the letter Heh Final and the element of Earth. As with all the other categories in the Golden Dawn's Magic of Light, Z.2 provides a ritual outline for magicians to use in crafting their own alchemical rituals. The outline on alchemy shows that the Golden Dawn's method was a mixture of practical (laboratory) alchemy and ritual invocation. But it is also hard to follow, especially for students who do not practice laboratory alchemy.

Some of the best examples of Golden Dawn alchemical rituals are found in Book Four of our edited and annotated edition of Israel Regardie's *The Philosopher's Stone: spiritual Alchemy, Psychology and Ritual Magic*, so we refer interested readers to it.

RITUAL FRAMEWORK: CREATING A GOLDEN DAWN–STYLE RITUAL

In keeping with the Spirit of the Z.2 document, we shall provide students with a basic outline for creating their own rituals. Such workings can be as simple or as complicated as you like, but they should contain these essential steps.

Before beginning a ritual, take some time to shift consciousness away from the daily grind of the mundane world to a more elevated frame of mind. The methods of meditation described earlier will go a long way in transferring your focus to spiritual pursuits.

Generally, there are three fundamental segments in any given Golden Dawn ceremony: the opening, the middle point, and the closing. These three segments can be further divided into fourteen steps that we have outlined below.

The Opening

    1. Declaration of the Commencement

    2. A Banishing Ritual

3. Initial Purification and Consecration

4. The Mystic Circumambulation

5. The Adoration

The Middle Point

6. Preliminary Invocation Ritual

7. An Invocation to the Highest

8. The Main working

The Closing

9. Final Purification and Consecration

10. The Reverse Circumambulation

11. The Adoration

12. License to Depart

13. A Banishing Ritual

14. Declare the Temple Closed

These steps are further explained below.

1. DECLARATION OF THE COMMENCEMENT

Go to the northeast corner of the Temple and say: **"Hekas! Hekas! Este Bebeloi!"** ("Far, far from this place be the profane!") Originally uttered at the Eleusinian Mysteries, this phrase is used to open a Golden Dawn ritual. It gives any unwelcome entities present the opportunity to leave on their own before they are banished.

2. A BANISHING RITUAL

The most common form is the LBRP. This cleanses the area of all unwanted energies and astral remnants of previous activities. It sets up a magic circle of protection.

3. INITIAL PURIFICATION AND CONSECRATION

(See chapter 6, Purification and Consecration.)

4. THE MYSTIC CIRCUMAMBULATION

(See chapter 7, the Opening by Watchtower Ritual, step 26.)

5. THE ADORATION

(See chapter 7, the Opening by Watchtower Ritual, step 27.)

6. PRELIMINARY INVOCATION RITUAL

Everything leading up to this point amounts to a cleansing of the ritual space, sweeping out the "astral cobwebs," if you will. The preliminary invocation begins the creation of the magic circle. Students may employ the traditional LIRP to this end. Alternatively, you could bring in those specific forces that would be beneficial to the nature of the working, such as the SIRP, the SIRP of a single element or zodiacal sign, or the LIRH for a planet or Sephirah.

7. AN INVOCATION TO THE HIGHEST

Golden Dawn magicians always invoke the highest aspect of Divinity before commencing any important magical working. Here, the beginner may use a prayer or invocation of his or her own choosing, so long as the Deity invoked represents the magician's highest ideal of the Eternal Source of the Universe. The prayer that follows is one that Israel Regardie adapted from the Adeptus Minor Ritual:

> *Unto Thee, Sole Wise, Sole Eternal, and Sole Merciful One,*
> *Be the praise and glory forever.*
> *Who hath permitted me, who now standeth humbly before Thee,*
> *to enter thus far into the sanctuary of Thy mysteries.*
> *Not unto me, Adonai, but unto Thy name be the Glory.*
> *Let the influence of Thy Divine Ones descend upon my head,*
> *and teach me the value of self-sacrifice*
> *So that I shrink not in the hour of trial.*
> *But that thus my name may be written on high,*
> *And my Genius stand in the presence of the Holy One.*
> *In that hour when the Son of Man is invoked before the Lord of Spirits*
> *And His Name before the Ancient of Days.*

8. THE MAIN WORKING

This is the point in the ceremony that is the primary reason for performing the ritual in the first place. The main working may be a divination, such as a tarot reading, to find a solution to a difficult problem; to bring peace, balance, or healing to a chaotic environment or strenuous situation; to increase one's personal energy or health; a meditation; a pathworking; a consecration; a reading from a Sacred text; the performance of an exercise such as the Middle Pillar; a Mystic Repast of the Four Elements; or simply a contemplation of further spiritual growth. The magician should clearly state his or her reason for performing the rite, and should always address it to the Highest Divine Power.

For example, **"Lord of the Universe, I invoke Thee! I,** (*state your magical motto*)**, open this Temple to perform a working in the Magic of Light. I seek** (*Example: a Spirit Vision into the tarot card of the High Priestess*)**. Look with favor upon this ceremony. Grant me what I seek, so that through this rite I may obtain Greater Understanding and thereby advance in the Great Work."**

9. FINAL PURIFICATION AND CONSECRATION

After the main working of the ceremony has been completed, purify and consecrate the Temple again, exactly as in step 3. This helps to re-equilibrate the energies of the Temple, particularly after any fluctuations in energy.

10. THE REVERSE CIRCUMAMBULATION

(See chapter 7, Closing by Watchtower: Version 1, step 1.)

11. THE ADORATION

This is performed exactly as in step 5.

12. LICENSE TO DEPART

(See chapter 7, Closing by Watchtower: Version 1, step 10.) Other Qabalistic godnames could be substituted for *Yeheshuah, Yehovashah,* depending on the nature of the working.

13. A BANISHING RITUAL

Perform the LBRP exactly as in the beginning.

14. Declare the Temple Closed

Say: **"I now declare this Temple duly closed. So mote it be."**

Talisman Consecration Ritual Outline

The blueprint for talisman consecrations outlined in the Z.2 document is the perfect example of how various formulae of practical magic are hidden within the Neophyte initiation ceremony. Like the candidate undergoing initiation, the talisman is "blindfolded" with a veil and bound with a cord. It is then moved around the Temple, periodically barred (stopped from entering an area of the Temple prematurely), then purified and consecrated in the same manner as a Neophyte. Both talisman and Neophyte are exposed to subtle manipulations of the astral light, which attract the appropriate divine energies.

The following outline is a simplified version of the rubric found in the Z.2 manuscript.

Ideally, the magician should perform the ritual on the day and hour assigned to the planet that rules the talisman. (See chapter 2, Tables 13, 14 and 15.)

What Is Needed

- Furnished Temple space plus: Magic Sword, Lotus Wand, a lamp in the southwest.

- The magician, readied by Pre-Ritual Meditation Practice.

- A list (or ritual script) of the relevant divine forces and their sigils.

- The talisman or material basis, covered with a black bag or veil and tied thrice with a black cord (see Figure 101 for an example). (Have a white veil or bag ready for afterward.)

Steps Involved

Opening

1. **The Magic Circle.** First cleanse the area with a banishing ritual (LBRP, LBRH, or both). Then create the magic circle with an invoking ritual (LIRP or LIRH).

2. **Invocation of the Highest Divine Powers.** Formulate a clear statement of your intention and purpose for the creation of the talisman.

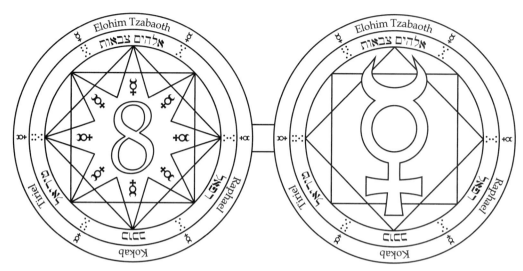

Figure 101: A Mercury Talisman

3. **First Purification and Consecration.** Place the talisman in the west of the Temple. Purify and consecrate the talisman.

4. **Statement of Intention.** Place the talisman at the foot of the Altar. Firmly repeat your intention and goal. Assert that your goal will be attained and that all is in readiness.

5. **The Triangle.** Place the talisman on the white Triangle on the Altar.

Initial Invocations, Purifications, and Consecrations

6. **First Invocation.** Recite a prepared invocation and summon the force(s) you want to attract into the talisman, vibrating the relevant divine and angelic names, while tracing their figures and sigils above the talisman.

   • Tap the talisman thrice with the flat of the sword blade.

   • Stamp the ground thrice with your foot.

7. **First Speech.** Place the talisman in the north and recite the "Magician's Oration in the North." (See below, Ritual Consecration of a Mercury Talisman, step 24.)

8. **First Barring.** Go to the SW and take up the lamp. Make a full Circumambulation around the Temple. Take up the talisman and place it in the south.

- Bar it with the sword.

- Purify and consecrate the talisman again.

- Hold it up and say: **"Creature of Talismans, twice purified and twice consecrated, thou mayest approach the gate of the west."**

9. **Second Speech.** Take the talisman to the west, partly unveil it, tap it with the sword once and recite the "Magician's Oration in the West." (See below, Ritual Consecration of a Mercury Talisman, step 28.) Reveil the talisman.

10. **Second Barring.** Make a full Circumambulation around the Temple. Stop in the north.

- Bar it with the sword.

- Purify and consecrate the talisman again.

- Hold it up and say: **"Creature of Talismans, thrice purified and thrice consecrated, thou mayest approach the gate of the east."**

11. **Third Speech.** Hold the talisman in the left hand, the Lotus Wand in the right.

- Partly unveil the talisman.

- Tap it with the sword once and recite the "Magician's Oration in the East." (See below, Ritual Consecration of a Mercury Talisman, step 31.)

- Reveil the talisman.

Potent Conjurations and Projections

12. **Second Invocation.** Return to the west of the Altar and place the talisman on the white Triangle.

- Pass to the east of the Altar and hold your left hand over the talisman and with your right hand hold the sword over the talisman.

- Recite a powerful invocation of the force(s) you want to attract into the talisman, vibrating the divine and angelic names and tracing all the relevant symbols and sigils.

13. **The Unveiling.** Hold the talisman on high. Remove the veil but keep the cord in place.

   - Say, **"Creature of Talismans, long hast though dwelt in darkness. Quit the night and seek the day!"**

   - Place the talisman back on the Triangle and hold the pommel of the sword over it.

   - Then say: **"By all the names, powers, and rites already rehearsed, I conjure upon thee power and might irresistible." Khabs Om Pekht, Konx Am Pax, Light In Extension!"**

14. **Projection, Invocation, and Flashing.** State: **"As the light hidden in the darkness can manifest therefrom, so shalt thou become irresistible."**

   - Take the talisman to the east facing west.

   - Address a potent invocation to the powers and archangels who rule over the assigned Spirit to command it to fulfill the talisman's objective, requesting them to make the talisman powerful.

   - Then place the talisman between the pillars.

   - Standing east of the pillars facing west, use the projection sign to impel the force of your willpower upon the talisman. Keep projecting until you feel your willpower start to weaken. Then give the Sign of Silence.

   - Observe the talisman. Look clairvoyantly for signs of flashing light or a halo effect around the talisman. If this is not seen, repeat the invocation and projection (this may be repeated twice).

   - If after the third time the talisman still does not flash, take it back to the white Triangle on the Altar, stand west of the Altar facing east, sword in hand, and address a humble prayer to the Divine to grant the force necessary to complete your work. Then place the talisman between the pillars and repeat the invocation and projection.

   - As soon as the talisman is seen to flash, purify and consecrate it again.

Circumambulation and Final Invocations

15. **Unbinding and Circumambulation**. Remove the cord and tap the talisman with the flat of the sword, and proclaim: **"By and in the Names of** *(relevant divine names)* **I invoke upon thee the power of** *(relevant force)."* Then circumambulate thrice with the talisman in the right hand.

16. **The Great Invocation**. Stand in the east facing west and recite a powerful invocation consonant with the Working. The talisman should flash clairvoyantly.

17. **Angelic Invocation**. Address an invocation to the angelic ruler(s) of the assigned Spirit to command it to fulfill the talisman's objective.

18. **Command of Purpose**. Carefully formulate your demands, stating clearly what the talisman is intended to do.

Conclusion

19. **Closing**. Command that the Spirit do no harm in carrying out the objective of the talisman.

    • Wrap the consecrated talisman in a white veil or bag, especially before any final banishings.

    • Then give all beings the License to Depart.

    • Once the goal of the talisman has been fulfilled, the energies invoked into it should be discharged by firmly banishing them with the appropriate Pentagrams or Hexagrams. Finally, destroy the talisman. (If the material basis is Earth, then grind it to powder and shatter it; if Water, pour it out; if a vial of Air, release it; if a flame, extinguish it.)

Although it is not necessary, consecrated talismans can be tested psychically. Place the consecrated talisman and five unconsecrated talismans each in a plain envelope. A clairvoyant should be able to determine which talisman has been charged.

Ritual Consecration of a Mercury Talisman

The following is a ritual based on the outline above for the Consecration of a Mercury Talisman. As with all rituals based on the Z.2 rubrics, advanced magicians are encouraged to add their own ingenuity and not follow the guidelines to the letter. For the sample ritual that follows, the stated intention will be an increase in knowledge of the Qabalah.

This ceremony would be best performed during the day and hour of Mercury. Have the talisman wrapped in a black piece of cloth and bound three times with a black cord. Upon the Altar should be the Cross and Triangle, Tablet of Union, a chalice of Water, and incense. A Lotus Wand and a sword for banishing should be close at hand. The position of Mercury should be determined for the time of the ritual, and a symbol of the planet should be placed on the floor, ceiling, or hung on the wall corresponding to the direction noted. A white cloth used to wrap the talisman after consecration is also required. (For this ritual it would be helpful to place a small pedestal between the pillars.)

Initial Banishings and Cleansings

1. Commence the ritual with five knocks (4+1). Go to the northeast and say in a loud voice, **"Hekas, Hekas Este Bebeloi!"**

2. Go to the east (or center) and perform the LBRP.

3. Perform the LBRH.

4. Purification and Consecration. (See chapter 6, Purification and Consecration.)

Casting the Circle of Mercury

5. Perform the Lesser Invoking Hexagram Ritual of Mercury, commencing with the Qabalistic Cross (Figure 102).

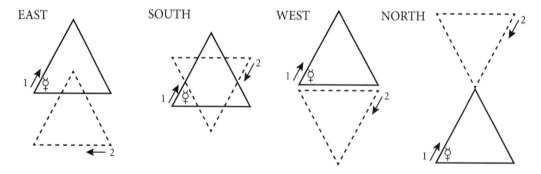

Figure 102: Lesser Invoking Hexagrams of Mercury

Ritual Note: Hold the Lotus Wand by the white band for the QC. Then trace the four Lesser Hexagrams of Mercury in their respective quarters, holding the Lotus Wand by the orange band of Gemini (the Day House of Mercury) or by the yellow-green band of Virgo (the Night House of Mercury), or by the band that represents the zodiacal sign that Mercury is in at the time of the working.

Invocation and Intention

6. Go clockwise to the northeast and say: **"The visible Sun is the dispenser of Light to the earth. Let me therefore form a vortex in this chamber that the Invisible Sun of the Spirit may shine therein from above."**

7. Grasping the Lotus Wand by the white portion, circumambulate the Temple three times clockwise, saluting with the Neophyte Signs when passing the east.

8. Then stand west of the Altar facing east and perform the Adoration to the Lord of the Universe:

   Holy art Thou Lord of the Universe! (Projection Sign)
   Holy art Thou Whom Nature hath not formed! (Projection Sign)
   Holy art Thou the Vast and the Mighty One! (Projection Sign)
   Lord of the Light and of the Darkness. (Sign of Silence)

9. Say: **"I invoke ye, ye Angels of the Celestial spheres, whose dwelling is in the invisible. Ye are the guardians of the gates of the Universe, be ye also the guardians of this mystic sphere. Keep far removed the evil and the unbalanced. Strengthen and inspire me so that I may preserve unsullied this abode of the mysteries of the eternal Gods. Let my sphere be pure and holy so that I may enter in and become a partaker of the secrets of the Light Divine."**

10. Perform the Qabalistic Cross, strongly visualizing the divine image of the cross within you. Then visualize a large Banner of the East. After the image is firmly within your mind, see it enveloping you like a brilliant cloak.

11. Put the wand aside and take up the sword.

12. Place the wrapped talisman at the edge of the circle to the west. Push it into the circle with the tip of the sword. Then say: **"Creature of Talismans, enter thou within this Sacred circle, that thou mayest become a worthy dwelling place for the Forces of Kokab."**

13. Consecrate the talisman with Water and Fire. Dip your fingers into the Water and mark the talisman with a cross. Sprinkle thrice in the form of the Invoking Water Triangle. Wave the incense in the form of a cross and give an additional three waves in the form of the Invoking Fire Triangle.

14. Place the talisman at the foot of the Altar, and say: **"Lord of the Universe, I invoke Thee! I,** (*magical motto*), **do solemnly pledge to consecrate this talisman in due ceremonial form. I further promise and swear to use it to obtain true knowledge and insight into the teachings of the Qabalah. May the powers of Hod, the sphere of Splendor, witness my pledge."**

15. Then say: **"The Holy Guardian Angel of** (*magical motto*) **under the authority of the Concealed One is in command of those beings who have been summoned to this ceremony. I charge all ye Archangels, Angels, Rulers, Kings, and Elementals called to this place to witness and aid in this Rite. I call upon the Crown, EHEIEH, the One Source Most High, to look with favor upon me as I perform this ceremony. Grant me success in this, my search for the Hidden Wisdom and my aspiration toward the Light Divine. To the glory and completion of the Great Work. So mote it be!"**

    In the Divine Name of ELOHIM TZABAOTH, I, (*magical motto*), **command ye, O ye dwellers in the Invisible realms, that ye fashion for me a magical base in the Astral Light wherein I may invoke the Divine Forces to charge this talisman of Mercury for the purpose of expanding my knowledge of Qabalah.**

16. Place the veiled talisman on the white Triangle on the Altar.

Initial Invocations, Purifications, and Consecrations

17. Turn to face the direction where you have determined Mercury to be at the time of the working. Grasping the Lotus Wand by the same band used to invoke the Lesser Mercury Hexagrams, trace a large yellow Greater Invok-

ing Hexagram of Mercury (Figure 103). Vibrate the name **"ARARITA"** while drawing the Hexagram. Intone "**ELOHIM TZABAOTH**" when tracing the Mercury sigil in violet at the center. Trace the Hebrew letter Tau in violet and intone the name of the letter. Give the LVX Signs. Imagine the divine energies ruling over Mercury entering the portal you have just drawn.

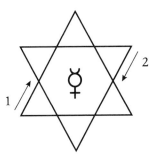

Figure 103: Greater Invoking Hexagram of Mercury

18. Trace the sigil and Hebrew letters of Elohim Tzabaoth (אלהים צבאות) in the air with the wand. Then trace the sigil and the letters over your heart. Vibrate the name "**ELOHIM TZABAOTH**" ten times, once for every Hebrew letter, using the Vibratory Formula of the Middle Pillar. Strongly endeavor to feel the divine presence.

19. Say: "**In the Name of ELOHIM TZABAOTH, I,** (*magical motto*), **proclaim that I have invoked ye in order to form a true and potent link between my human soul and the Light Divine. To this end I have brought into this circle a talisman covered with a black veil and bound thrice with a cord, so that this creature of talismans shall not see the light nor move until it be duly consecrated unto me. I proclaim that this talisman shall be charged by the archangel RAPHAEL KOKABIEL, so that through its use, I may gain spiritual wisdom and occult knowledge in the** (*teachings of the Qabalah*), **so that I may be better enabled to perform the Great Work.**

20. Say: "**In the Divine Name of ELOHIM TZABAOTH, I command ye, O ye dwellers in the Invisible realms, that ye fashion for me a magical base in the astral light wherein I may invoke the Divine Forces to charge this**

talisman. Grant unto me the presence of RAPHAEL, the great archangel of the star of Kokab!"

21. Trace the Greater Invoking Hexagram of Mercury over the talisman and in it the sigil of the godname Elohim Tzabaoth, and the angels Raphael and Tiriel. Vibrate these names strongly. Trace the sigil of the Spirit Taphtharth-arath (Figure 104).

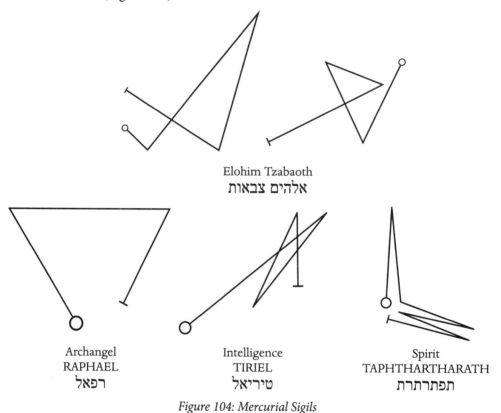

Elohim Tzabaoth
אלהים צבאות

Archangel
RAPHAEL
רפאל

Intelligence
TIRIEL
טיריאל

Spirit
TAPHTHARTHARATH
תפתרתרת

Figure 104: Mercurial Sigils

22. Then say: **"O ye angels and archangels of Mercury, I conjure ye by the name of the Almighty One, the Lord God of Hosts! And by the name of Raphael, whose throne and seat ye are. Be present at this ceremony and fill this Temple with your magic power! Command unto me the presence of Raphael, the angel of KOKAB, the Star, and his intelligence TIRIEL that they may consecrate this most powerful symbol. I conjure ye potently to make manifest your presence within my soul that this**

Mercury talisman may be charged. Guide and command the Mercurial Spirit Taphthartharath to make it so. Come forth, all ye powers and forces of the Mercurial realm. Come forth and obey in the Holy Name of ELOHIM TZABAOTH, the divine ruler of your kingdom, RAPHAEL, your archangel, and the mighty angel TIRIEL!"

23. Lift the talisman in your left hand. Tap it thrice with the flat of the sword blade. Stamp the ground thrice with your foot.

24. Take the talisman to the north and recite the Magician's Oration in the north: "The voice of the Exorcism said unto me, 'Let me shroud myself in darkness, peradventure thus shall I manifest myself in Light. I am the only being in an abyss of Darkness. From the Darkness came I forth ere my birth, from the silence of a primal sleep.' And the Voice of Ages answered unto my soul, Creature of Talismans, the Light shineth in the Darkness, but the Darkness comprehendeth it not. Let the Mystic Circumambulation take place in the path of Darkness with the symbolic light of Occult Science to lead the way."

25. Visualize the light of a lantern held by an angelic hand before you. Circumambulate the Temple once with the talisman and the sword, following the visualized light.

26. After one complete Circumambulation, stop in the south and lay the talisman on the ground. Bar it with the sword, saying: "Unpurified and unconsecrated, thou canst not enter the Gate of the West."

27. Purify the talisman with Water and consecrate with Fire as before. Then lift it with the left hand, face the west, and say: "Creature of Talismans, twice purified and twice consecrated, thou mayest approach the Gateway of the West."

28. Pass to the west with the talisman in the left hand. Partly unveil it, tap it once with the sword, and recite the Magician's Oration in the west: "Thou canst not pass from concealment unto manifestation, save by the virtue of the name 'ELOHIM.' Before all things are the Chaos and the Darkness, and the gates of the Land of Night. I am He whose Name is Darkness. I am the Great One of the Paths of the Shades. I am the Exorcist in

the midst of the Exorcism. Take on therefore manifestation without fear before me, for I am he in whom fear is not."

29. Replace the veil over the talisman and carry it once more around the circle. Then stop in the north, place the talisman on the floor, and say: **"Unpurified and unconsecrated, thou canst not enter the Gate of the East."**

30. Purify and consecrate the talisman with Water and Fire as before. Lift it in the left hand and say: **"Creature of Talismans, thrice purified and thrice consecrated, thou mayest approach the Gateway of the East."**

31. Go to the east and partly unveil the talisman. Tap it once with the sword and recite the Magician's Oration in the east: **"Thou canst not pass from concealment unto manifestation save by the virtue of the name YHVH. After the formless and the Void and the Darkness, then cometh the knowledge of the Light. I am that Light which riseth in darkness. I am the Exorcist in the midst of the Exorcism. Take on therefore manifestation before me, for I am the wielder of the forces of the Balance."**

Potent Conjurations and Projections

32. Replace the veil over the talisman. Take it to the west of the Altar. Place it again on the white Triangle. Go to the east of the Altar, facing west. Hold your left hand over the talisman and in your right the sword with its pommel directly over the talisman.

33. Recite the following invocation, vibrating the divine and angelic names and tracing all the relevant symbols and sigils: **"ELOHIM TZABAOTH! Thou Throne of the Powers of Splendor! Thou who art known as the God of Hosts and the Absolute or Perfect Intelligence! Thou art the mean of the Primordial, which has no root by which it can cleave or rest, save in the hidden places of Gedulah, from which emanates Thy proper essence. Thou who art the Glory and the Vision of Splendor. Eighth in number! Lord of the Powers of Intellect and Thought! The Keys to the mysteries are in Thy grasp! The Divine Mind is Thy abode! ELOHIM TZABAOTH! Let a ray of Thy perfection descend upon me, to awaken within my being that which shall prove a channel for the working of Thine abundant power.**

"May this Mercury talisman which I am about to consecrate be a focus of Thy light so that through it I may receive an influx of Qabalistic knowledge which will better enable me to understand the hidden mechanism of the Universe! Thus will I be enabled to rightly vibrate the Holy Names of Power! Thus may I more perfectly manifest the Rise of the Light Divine!

"Command unto me the presence of RAPHAEL, the angel of KOK-AB, the Star, and his intelligence TIRIEL that they may consecrate this most powerful symbol. I conjure ye potently to make manifest your presence within my soul that this Mercury talisman may be charged. Guide and command the Mercurial Spirit Taphthartharath to make it so. Come forth, all ye powers and forces of the realm of Hod. Come forth and obey in the Holy Name of ELOHIM TZABAOTH, the divine ruler of your kingdom!"

34. Hold the talisman on high. Remove the veil but keep the cord in place. Say: **"Creature of Talismans, long hast though dwelt in darkness. Quit the night and seek the day!"**

35. Place the talisman back on the Triangle and hold the pommel of the sword over it. Then say: **"By all the names, powers, and rites already rehearsed, I conjure upon thee power and might irresistible. KHABS AM PEKHT. KONX ON PAX. LIGHT IN EXTENSION. As the Light hidden in darkness can manifest therefrom, so shalt thou become irresistible."**

36. Take the talisman to the east, facing west. Recite the following invocation: **"Lord God of Hosts, Mighty Elohim Tzabaoth! Divine Power of Thought! The Divine is not to be transcended—it is unbounded and endless; unto Itself without Beginning. The Incorporeal cannot be expressed by the imperfect; nor the Eternal by the transient. God is not a Mind but the causality of Mind; God is not a Spirit, but the Causality of Spirit; God is not a Light, but the Causality of Light. God the Divine is Unmanifest, and yet is the One Most Manifest. The Image of God is Eternity; the Image of Eternity is the Cosmos. Hence this God is called by the Gods silent, and is said to consent with mind, and to be known by souls through mind alone.**

"Invincible Elohim of Hosts! Command unto me the presence of Raphael, the great archangel of KOKAB, the Star of Mercury. Mighty RAPHAEL, lay Thy hands invisibly on this talisman and give it life! Oh Tiriel, intelligence of Mercury, sanctify and consecrate this most powerful symbol! Give it Light!

"I conjure ye potently to make manifest your presence within my soul that this Mercury talisman may be charged. Guide and command the Mercurial Spirit Taphthartharath to make it so. Come forth, all ye Divine powers and forces of the star of Kokab! Come forth and obey in the Holy Name of ELOHIM TZABAOTH, the divine ruler of your kingdom!"

37. Put the talisman on the floor (or on a small pedestal) between the pillars east of the Altar. Stand just east of the talisman and face west.

38. Use the projection sign to impel the force of your willpower upon the talisman. Visualize the Divine Light energy streaming from your Kether into Tiphareth, your heart center, down your arms, out your fingertips and into the talisman. Keep projecting until you feel your willpower start to weaken. Then give the Sign of Silence and stamp your left foot to cut off the current of force, sealing it into the talisman.

39. Clairvoyantly, you should be able to see a light flickering about the talisman. Return it to the white Triangle upon the Altar. Purify and consecrate it again.

40. Remove the black cord from the talisman. Tap the talisman three times again with the sword and proclaim: "By and in the Name of ELOHIM TZABAOTH, I invoke upon thee the Powers and Forces of KOKAB!"

Circumambulation and Final Invocations

41. Then circumambulate thrice with the talisman in the right hand.

42. Return to the east facing west (or return to the west of the Altar) and recite the following Great Invocation: "ELOHIM TZABAOTH! Lord of the Radiant Staff about which the two serpents are entwined! Exalted Herald of the Gods! Thee I invoke! Divine Messenger and Bringer of Dreams! Protector and Guide of Humanity! Thee I invoke! Swift Lord of Oracles! Giver of light to the mind! Patron of arts and sciences! Thee I invoke!

Divine Scribe and Lord of the Sacred Texts! Thou who art known as THOTH as HERMES, as MERCURY! Lord of Magic! I invoke thee to enter this Sacred place and grant unto me your Wisdom and Intellectual Powers. Thus may I at length comprehend the Hidden Forces which move through the Universe, so that I may be better enabled to complete the Great Work. ELOHIM TZABAOTH!

"I INVOKE THEE! Administer your divine guidance over these proceedings to insure that this Mercury talisman be properly charged. Grant unto me that through its use, my spiritual wisdom may be increased. May it aid me in all areas of Qabalistic knowledge. ELOHIM TZABAOTH! I also ask that you instill within this talisman the power of transformation and truth!

"Grant that this Mercury talisman provide me with grace, knowledge and understanding emanating from the Highest. I invoke thee, exalt my soul to the feet of thy glory. Hear me and manifest in splendor to one who aspires to the Light of the Hidden Wisdom.

"I invoke into this talisman the Forces and Powers of KOKAB, the bright star of Mercury. Oh Thou Master of Speech Divine! The God enthroned upon the Seat of Wisdom! Thou who measures and numbers the stars! You are the giver of numbers and of medicine. You are the creator of astronomy and astrology. You are the father of all the sciences. You established the worship of the Gods. You composed the hymns and prayers which men addressed to them. You are the author of every book. You art the creator of alphabets and hieroglyphs. You invented the laws and taught the priests and priestesses. You are known by the names DJE-HOTI, THOTH. HERMES. MERCURY. I invoke thee! Bestow upon this talisman your powers of knowledge and understanding. May the perfume of thy essence anoint this Mercury talisman so that through its use my magical abilities may be increased. May it become a living telesma consecrated to my spiritual growth. Thus may I be better able to comprehend the Hidden Nature of the Universe.

"Thy Word is Knowledge. Thy Word is Vibration. Thy Word is Movement. Thy Word is Transformation! Thy Word opens the Gate of Ecstasy! Mighty is Thy Word! Hear now the Word of Djehoti! Hear now the Speech of Thooth!

"The Speech in the Silence. The Words against the Son of Night. The voice of Thoth before the Universe in the presence of the eternal Gods. The Formulas of Knowledge. The Wisdom of Breath. The Radix of Vibration. The Shaking of the Invisible. The Rolling Asunder of the Darkness. The Becoming Visible of Matter. The Piercing of the Coils of the Stooping Dragon. The Breaking Forth of the Light. All these are in the Knowledge of Thooth.

"At the Ending of the Night; At the Limits of the Light: Thoth stood before the Unborn Ones of Time! Then was formulated the Universe. Then came forth the Gods thereof. The Aeons of the Bornless Beyond. Then was the Voice vibrated. Then was the Name declared. At the Threshold of the Entrance, between the Universe and the Infinite, in the Sign of the Enterer, stood Thooth, as before him were the Aeons proclaimed. In Breath did he vibrate them. In Symbols did he record them. For betwixt the Light and the Darkness did he stand!

43. Address an invocation to the angels: "I invoke the great archangel RA-PHAEL KOKABAEL! Angel of knowledge and medicine! Mighty RA-PHAEL! Lay Thy hands invisibly on this talisman and give it life. Anoint it, so that through its use I may receive an increase in Wisdom and Understanding of the Qabalah, Thus may I tread the path of a learned Magician, to the glory of Thine ineffable name. Assist me, your companion in the Work, in this my invocation of the Mercurial Powers! Send hither the intelligence of Mercury, TIRIEL that he concentrate and bind into this talisman life and power undeniable."

44. Address the Spirit who will carry out the talisman's purpose: "I command you Mercurial Spirit Taphthartharath, hear and obey! Harm none in the fulfillment of the talisman's goal! Consecrate this talisman with the power to assist me in gaining true knowledge, perfect wisdom, and correct understanding of the Qabalah. Make it a powerful tool to aid my spiritual attainment! Charge this talisman aright, that it may become a powerful tool consecrated to the work of the Magic of Light!"

Closing

45. Wrap the newly consecrated talisman in a white veil or bag.

46. Give all spiritual beings the License to Depart.

47. Perform the Lesser Banishing Ritual of Mercury (Figure 105).

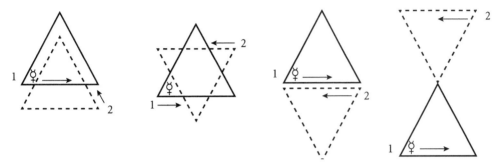

Figure 105: Lesser Banishing Hexagrams of Mercury

48. Knock five times as in the beginning.

49. Then say: **"I now declare this Temple duly closed. So Mote it Be!"**

Middle Pillar Method of Consecration

Israel Regardie taught us a method for charging talismans using the exercise of the Middle Pillar. Properly vibrating a specific godname causes the aura of the magician to become charged with energy. Once the divine names of the Middle Pillar are activated, the magician can use visualization to manipulate the color of his or her aura so it is identical to that of the element, planet, or Sephirah that is being invoked. When the aura is fully charged with the necessary color, the divine names inscribed on the talisman itself are vibrated. If you hold the talisman over your Tiphareth center throughout this procedure, it becomes highly charged by a strong current of energy linked to your Higher and Divine Genius, transmitted through the four parts of the soul.

REVIEW QUESTIONS

1. What is the Magic of Light?

2. What Hebrew letter is assigned to the practice of divination?

3. What Hebrew letter is assigned to the practice of invisibility?

4. What is a flashing Tablet?

5. What does a wave or crook in a sigil signify?

6. What does a loop or noose in a sigil signify?

7. What is a Telesmatic image?

8. What is the difference between a general and a literal Telesmatic image?

9. In the Magic of Light, what practices do the three Mother Letters represent?

10. What practice can be likened to shape-shifting?

11. What are the sixteen figures of geomancy called?

12. What is the Opening of the Key?

13. What is the Reverse Circumambulation?

14. What is meant by the License to Depart?

15. How is the Z.2 outline on talisman consecration similar to the Neophyte ceremony?

EPILOGUE

In writing this book, we have tried to provide a comprehensive introduction to the many facets of Golden Dawn magic. It was never our intention to furnish this material in the same manner that an initiate would receive within an order setting. Instead, our focus has been on beginners who are drawn to this path as well as probationers who wish to understand the principles and mechanics of the system before committing to study it further. Nevertheless, any magician already working within the order system, whether Neophyte or adept, can profit from exploring or reviewing the material covered here. From learning the language of magic, to practicing the meditations and exercises, to performing the final talisman consecration ritual, readers have been given a steady, graduated course for undertaking Golden Dawn ceremonial magic.

We have supplied the framework for the path ahead. The rest, O aspirant, is up to you. Israel Regardie liked to encourage students with a favorite quotation about persistence and determination, two qualities that he felt were essential to the Great Work. In a similar vein, we would like to close with kindred words of wisdom.

Great works are performed not by strength but by perseverance.

———————

Patience and perseverance have a magical effect
before which difficulties disappear and obstacles vanish.

FURTHER READING

Cicero, Chic, and Sandra Tabatha Cicero. *The Essential Golden Dawn: An Introduction to High Magic.* Woodbury, MN: Llewellyn, 2003. An introductory text.

———. *Golden Dawn Magical Tarot.* Woodbury, MN: Llewellyn, 2010. A complete tarot kit with card deck and the accompanying book: *The New Golden Dawn Ritual Tarot: Keys to the Rituals, Symbolism, Magic and Divination.*

———. *Secrets of a Golden Dawn Temple: Book 1: Creating Magical Tools.* Loughborough, UK: Thoth, 2004. A manual for creating all kinds of Golden Dawn implements.

———. *Self-Initiation into the Golden Dawn Tradition.* St. Paul, MN: Llewellyn, 1998. A rigorous text with knowledge lectures and initiation rites for the solo practitioner and the working magical group.

———. *Tarot Talismans: Invoke the Angels of the Tarot.* Woodbury, MN: Llewellyn, 2006. Examines the various divine forces, archangels, and angels of Western magic and develops new techniques for ritual work employing tarot cards.

DuQuette, Lon Milo. *The Chicken Qabalah.* Newburyport, MA: Weiser, 2001. One of the best and funniest books on Qabalah ever written.

Dykes, Dr. Benjamin N., and Jayne B. Gibson. *Astrological Magic: Basic Rituals & Meditations.* Minneapolis, MN: The Cazimi Press, 2012. A complete manual filled with Golden Dawn style rites and exercises.

Golden Dawn Community. *Commentaries on the Flying Rolls.* Dublin: Kerubim, 2013. Contains all the "Flying Roll" essays written by original Golden Dawn members and provides commentaries on each one by contemporary magicians.

Greer, John Michael, Clare Vaughn, and Earl King, Jr. *Learning Ritual Magic: Fundamental Theory and Practice for the Solitary Apprentice.* Newburyport, MA: Weiser, 2004. Overflowing with exercises designed to aid the magician's practice and knowledge.

Regardie, Israel. *A Garden of Pomegranates: Skrying on the Tree of Life.* 3rd ed. Annotated. St. Paul, MN: Llewellyn, 1999. Regardie's classic text on the Qabalah combined with pathworkings for each of the Thirty-Two Paths of Wisdom.

———. *The Golden Dawn: An Account of the Teachings, Rites and Ceremonies of the Order of the Golden Dawn.* 7th ed. Woodbury, MN: Llewellyn, 2003. The twentieth century's most influential magical text.

———. *The Middle Pillar: The Balance Between Mind and Magic.* 3rd ed. Annotated. St. Paul, MN: Llewellyn, 1998. An in-depth examination of the Middle Pillar exercise and the Lesser Ritual of the Pentagram.

———. *The Philosopher's Stone: Spiritual Alchemy, Psychology, and Ritual Magic.* Annotated. Woodbury, MN: Llewellyn, 2013. A comprehensive exploration of spiritual alchemy.

Wildoak, Peregrin. *By Names and Images: Bringing the Golden Dawn to Life.* Gloucestershire, UK: Skylight Press, 2012. A valuable introduction to Golden Dawn magic and the mechanics behind the system.

INDEX

To Write to the Authors

If you wish to contact the authors or would like more information about this book, please write to the authors in care of Llewellyn Worldwide Ltd. and we will forward your request. Both the authors and the publisher appreciate hearing from you and learning of your enjoyment of this book and how it has helped you. Llewellyn Worldwide Ltd. cannot guarantee that every letter written to the authors can be answered, but all will be forwarded. Please write to:

Chic Cicero & Sandra Tabatha Cicero
℅ Llewellyn Worldwide
2143 Wooddale Drive
Woodbury, MN 55125-2989

Please enclose a self-addressed stamped envelope for reply,
or $1.00 to cover costs. If outside the U.S.A., enclose
an international postal reply coupon.

Many of Llewellyn's authors have websites with additional information and resources. For more information, please visit our website at http://www.llewellyn.com.